Dear Mark Twain

JUMPING FROGS

UNDISCOVERED, REDISCOVERED, AND CELEBRATED WRITINGS
OF MARK TWAIN

Named after one of Mark Twain's best-known and beloved short stories, the Jumping Frogs series of books brings neglected treasures from Mark Twain's pen to readers.

1. *Is He Dead? A Comedy in Three Acts,* by Mark Twain. Edited with foreword, afterword, and notes by Shelley Fisher Fishkin. Text established by the Mark Twain Project, The Bancroft Library. Illustrated by Barry Moser.

2. *Mark Twain's Helpful Hints for Good Living: A Handbook for the Damned Human Race,* by Mark Twain. Edited by Lin Salamo, Victor Fischer, and Michael B. Frank of the Mark Twain Project, The Bancroft Library. Illustrated by Barry Moser.

3. *Mark Twain's Book of Animals,* by Mark Twain. Edited with introduction and afterword by Shelley Fisher Fishkin.

4. *Dear Mark Twain: Letters from His Readers.* Edited with introduction and notes by R. Kent Rasmussen.

Dear Mark Twain

Letters from His Readers

Edited by

R. Kent Rasmussen

UNIVERSITY OF CALIFORNIA PRESS

Berkeley   Los Angeles   London

University of California Press, one of the most distinguished university presses in the United States, enriches lives around the world by advancing scholarship in the humanities, social sciences, and natural sciences. Its activities are supported by the UC Press Foundation and by philanthropic contributions from individuals and institutions. For more information, visit www.ucpress.edu.

University of California Press
Berkeley and Los Angeles, California

University of California Press, Ltd.
London, England

Library of Congress Cataloging-in-Publication Data

Dear Mark Twain : letters from his readers / edited by R. Kent Rasmussen.
   p. cm. — (Jumping frogs ; 4)
   Includes index.
   ISBN 978-0-520-26134-1 (cloth : alk. paper)
   1. Twain, Mark, 1835–1910—Correspondence. 2. Authors, American—19th century—Correspondence. 3. Authors and readers—United States. 4. Humorists, American—19th century—Correspondence. I. Rasmussen, R. Kent. II. Twain, Mark, 1835–1910.
   PS1331.A435 2013
   818'.409—dc23

                           2012033968

Manufactured in the United States of America

21 20 19 18 17 16 15 14 13 12
10 9 8 7 6 5 4 3 2 1

In keeping with a commitment to support environmentally responsible and sustainable printing practices, UC Press has printed this book on Rolland Enviro100, a 100% post-consumer fiber paper that is FSC certified, deinked, processed chlorine-free, and manufactured with renewable biogas energy. It is acid-free and EcoLogo certified.

*To the
memory of
Mary Keily,
faithful friend of
John Wilkes Booth
and John the Baptist*

The publisher gratefully acknowledges the generous support of the Humanities Endowment Fund of the University of California Press Foundation.

CONTENTS

ILLUSTRATIONS

Reading this book gave me the fantods. The good fantods, if Huck will permit me such a distinction, not the bad ones. In fact it made me feel transported.

Transported back up the river of time, like some Connecticut Yankee, and deposited among a few of the ordinary Americans, along with a sprinkling of Europeans, who read the works of Mark Twain while he was still alive. Able to listen to them as they formed their thoughts about how his books affected them; their reckonings as to what sort of fellow he might be; their frequently nursed fantasies of him stepping from the ether and directly into their own lives. (And of hitting him up for a sawbuck or two—another frequently nursed fantasy.)

R. Kent Rasmussen is not a time traveler, but he is the next best thing. In *Dear Mark Twain* he has achieved a triumph of warmhearted and bravura scholarship unique, as far as I can determine, in the plentiful annals of literary correspondence.

Granted, our library bookshelves are well stocked with collections of letters going back and forth between authors and those who knew them: family members, friends, enemies, editors, other eminences of their time. Mark Twain himself is well represented in this genre. Beginning with his first biographer, Albert Bigelow Paine, editors have issued volumes of his epistolary conversations with his great friend William Dean Howells and with the financier Henry Huttleston Rogers, and of his tender courtship and married-love letters to Olivia Langdon. The splendidly annotated six-volume series *Mark Twain's Letters,* edited by the Mark Twain Project at Berkeley, published by the University of California Press, and now available online, amounts virtually to a work of historical literature in itself. What we have not had before Mr. Rasmussen's fine endeavor is an assemblage of letters to an author from common readers. Perhaps this is because few great writers have considered such messages to be worth keeping. Perhaps it is because their executors lacked the curiosity to riffle through any stacks of mail from obscure or anonymous sources. My own hunch is that the author of *Life on the Mississippi* and *Adventures of Huckleberry Finn* struck a chord among his fellow proletarian citizens that the prevailing priests of prose writing—the Emersons and Longfellows and Holmeses and Hawthornes, bless them all—were unable to reach. I will explore below the reasons why this is likely to be truth.

Whatever the reasons, *Dear Mark Twain* gives us an extremely rare, and thus exhilarating, glimpse into the sensibilities of nineteenth-century people. Of course one might point as well to documents such as letters from Civil War soldiers and the slave narratives gathered in the 1930s by WPA interviewers. Yet those chronicles, though often brilliant in style and sentiment, tend to be self-limiting: their concerns distill to their estranged families, their personal struggles, and their strategies for survival. The correspondence collected (and tirelessly annotated) here by Mr. Rasmussen is from everyday folks writing from the security of their everyday habitats, and thus more disposed to reveal themselves on a wide range of topics. They were people of both genders and all ages. They were farmers, schoolteachers and schoolchildren, businessmen, preachers, customs agents, inmates of mental institutions, con artists, dreamers of various sorts, and at least one former president.

Among the desires they held in common was one expressed in the oft-repeated postscript: "Please write soon."

They could be cheekily artful ("Gracious Sir:—You are rich. To lose $10.00 would not make you miserable. I am poor. To gain $10.00 would not make me miserable. Please send me $10.00 [ten dollars]") and achingly artless ("What I want to know is by what rule a fellow can infallibly judge when you are lying and when you are telling the truth. I write this in case you intend to afflict an innocent and unoffending public with any more such works"). A fair amount were naive ("Dear Huck—I like your book and you and Tom Sawyer and Jim. . . . I wish you would write another book and tell us if Aunt Sally 'civilized' you. How old are you? I am thirteen"); a few were dyspeptic ("Dear Sir: For Gods sake give a suffering public a rest on your labored wit.—Shoot your trash & quit it.—You are only an *imitator of* Artemas Ward & a sickening one at that & we are *all sick of you*, For Gods sake take a tumble & give U.S. a rest.—").

Many of the letters—a good deal too many, for Mark Twain's taste—were bids for his signature. ("A *few lines* with your Name would be *very acceptable*"; "I am taking a great deal of interest in your collection of long German words. I send you hereby [a] 'noble' specimen, at the condition that you will send me your autograph, an autograph written by *you* not by your secretary"). Clearly, the commodity value of this ancient fetish was rising in the Gilded Age. Even more infuriating to the author were the brazen assumptions that his literary talents were available to any stranger on demand:

> I am on the ragged edge of sending a book of nonsense to the nonsense reading public. . . . I want the people to see that I am known to the literary world, and my object in writing to you is simply to give me a few words . . . with your name (Mark Twain) attached. Thus, a few scratches of your pen will cost you nothing and will help me a great deal. For instance, you might say "It ought to sell" or something similar. You see my object.

Message received. And then there were the jackleg entrepreneurs—plenty of those, too.

> We are two sin twisters (we meant to write twin sisters) of Cape Cod, have lived here all our lives with a few interruptions; we never went to a big city, never saw a publisher, are afraid of big cities and publishers. But something happened in this locality a while ago that we have written into a book and want dreadfully to publish. So we want to know if you will let us send you the M.S.S. and read it and approve it and send it to that unknown animal the publisher and tell him to put it in print. . . . Don't forget to answer.

He didn't answer, but filed the epistle away under the scrawl: "Villains."

Mark Twain, voracious pack rat that he was for any scrap of Americana—see his wildly eclectic notebooks, also compiled and published by the Mark Twain Project—hoarded his readers' letters as did few if any of his contemporaries. As with the "sin twisters" ploy, they seem to have given him only sporadic cause for satisfaction. ("From an ass" was another favorite verdict.) His compassion was triggered in unpredictable ways. A woman named Ellen Keily, who signed herself "Mary," wrote him more than a dozen long, semicoherent letters from incarceration at an insane asylum in Pennsylvania in the 1880s. "From my lunatic" was his identifying annotation on this bundle, and he answered only one. But the tone of his reply was distinctly gentler than his responses to those he considered mountebanks and fools. To Keily's request for "five dollars to buy a turkey and other eatables to make up a Plain dinner that I would cook myself" and invite several ministers including the Rev. Henry Ward Beecher to share it, he was consummately tactful, even playful. "I think your idea of getting those clergymen together at a dinner table is a very good one," he told her. "They will have to put up with each other's society a good long time in heaven, so they may as well begin to get used to it here." He demurred on the opportunity to show up and carve the turkey, explaining, "Always when I carve a turkey I swear a little. . . . I think a person ought not to swear where clergymen are, unless they provoke him."

One might think that Mr. Rasmussen's task here was almost embarrassingly simple—"pie," as Tom Sawyer would have put it: just show up at Robert Hirst's overflowing archive, put in a request for photocopies of letters written to Mark Twain, arrange them chronologically, think up a title, and send them off to that unknown animal the publisher. Had he been content with that approach, the book in front of you would have remained an entertaining curiosity. But Rasmussen had a more challenging goal in mind. Like a good novelist who understands the importance of touching every character in a story with the human spark, Rasmussen desired to make as many of those letter writers as possible come alive on the page, if only for a few moments.

Thus commenced the "time travel." Burrowing into census records in scores of municipalities, scrolling through microfiche reels of century-old newspapers for obituaries, checking out city directories, consulting history volumes of towns, businesses, and civic organizations, and even (horrors!) keying into online sources, Rasmussen has reconstructed a small cross section of American people as they lived, breathed, thought, and behaved in their time.

The writer of one admiring but unremarkable letter, for example, Henry Gauthier-Villars, emerges as the first husband of the French novelist Colette (1873–1954) and as the first person to publish a book about Mark Twain. A woman named Vashti D. Garwood, who wrote a rather elegant request for money to help buy a house, offering to make Mark Twain a beneficiary of her life insurance policy as collateral, is revealed to have outlived him by eight years. We further find that Garwood was an ambitious graduate of Boston University's homeopathic medical school; that she bore four children and then in the 1880s separated from her presumably more complacent husband and became an assistant to two professors at the University of Michigan; that she had been involved in the women's temperance movement in Kansas and later, with a daughter, helped found the Ann Arbor Equal Suffrage Club. And for good measure, Rasmussen tosses in the fact that her first name "was an icon of the women's rights movement: in the Bible, Vashti was a Persian queen who defied her husband and was replaced by Esther." These details add complexity and poignance to a figure who otherwise would have seemed pathetic.

Dear Mark Twain, in short, leaves the reader with little doubt as to the singular and powerful chord that this author struck in the hearts of the American public. But what were the psychic integuments of that chord? What created this subtext of yearning that courses through so many of these letters? Why did so many of the writers not simply reach out to Mark Twain, but yearn to close the distance and touch him? To possess him, in some cases, as his works had taken possession of them. The answer may lie in the fact that he had touched them first—if not as individuals, then as representatives of typic American individuals. An entire book could be written that simply lists and illuminates the astounding number of intersections he made, first as Samuel Clemens and later as Mark Twain, with the people and the seminal developments and events that defined nineteenth-century America. No other important American author could come close to matching his perambulations across the continent and, later, the globe.

His arrival in the world in 1835 coincided with the dawn of mass communications, mass transportation, and mass education. Steam presses now propelled the rise of the great urban dailies in the East. Steam engines chugged along the newly laid railroad lines eating westward through the wilderness, turning remote outposts into towns and small cities. The trains' cargoes included the recently perfected lightweight, hand-operated Ramage presses that were to enable every hamlet to boast its own *Gazette* or *Courier.* By 1835 such presses had reached the Mississippi River. Hard on the presses' trail, Samuel Morse's telegraph began unspooling its cables. By the 1840s, telegraph lines were flashing news of great events that found its way into the smallest of weekly papers.

Newspapers, railroads, and the telegraph began reshaping the American West just in time for Sammy Clemens to form his consciousness of it. Among his first jobs was as a paper boy for the Hannibal *Gazette;* not long afterward, he was setting type for his older brother Orion's *Journal.*

Sam made his first journey of discovery involving other people when he was four. He scampered through an orchard and a stand of hickory trees to a few rough cabins on the far side of his uncle John Quarles's farm in Florida, Missouri, where his family lived for a while before moving to Hannibal. Pushing through a doorway, the pale red-haired child would enter a subcivilization that had endured in the New World for 210 years, and whose existence would mercifully vanish in another twenty-six. These were slave quarters, repositories of suffering and stunted human lives, yet also repositories of a rich, encoded oral tradition that Sammy absorbed and intuitively understood. His immersion in the currents of Negro voices—singing voices, praying voices, storytelling voices—opened his mimetic mind and his heart to this jazzlike bounty of rhythmic speech, and he heard the vernacular poetry inside the speech and eventually enshrined that poetry in his literature.

While still in his teens, Sam Clemens rocketed out of Hannibal one spring evening and improvised an eastward itinerary that took him eventually to Washington and the visitors' gallery of the U.S. Senate, where he watched as Stephen A. Douglas and William H. Seward debated whether to repeal the Missouri Compromise. He would return to the capital after the Civil War as a reporter. There, he would gather character sketches and insights into corrupt power for his contributions to *The Gilded Age* (1873), America's first novel of Washington politics, which he would coauthor with Charles Dudley Warner.

Then it was back west to the "Interior," where in 1857 he boarded a packet on the Cincinnati docks, talked his way into a pilot apprenticeship, and floated into America's first mythic age, the age of steamboating. He became its greatest chronicler, and again immersed himself in the voices and behavior of its denizens. Then came a brief toe-dipping in the Civil War as an irregular Confederate "Marion Ranger" in Missouri—three weeks that would later inspire him to write a short story that would become one of the war's enduring works, "The Private History of a Campaign That Failed."

Sam excused himself from the war and headed out to Nevada with his older brother, Orion, who had secured a political secretary position in the new territory. Here Sam found himself present at another creation of Americana. Drawn to mining for gold and silver on the Comstock Lode, he rubbed shoulders with speculators, gamblers, gunslingers, showgirls, prostitutes, and other denizens of what came to be known as the Wild West.

A failure at mining, Sam in desperation turned to newspapering as a reporter for the Virginia City *Territorial Enterprise*. Here, at this freewheeling ancestor of the "alternative" newspaper, he was free to develop these rough new acquaintances and their pared-down speaking styles into fodder for his newspaper dispatches and sketches: the first drafts of the great writing to come. It was in this period that he took his pen name Mark Twain.

His next stop was the city, and the demimonde, that incubated the American counterculture. "Absquatulating" to San Francisco ahead of a furious rival editor who had taken him seriously in his giddy challenge to a duel, Sam alighted, as if guided by radar, in the midst of that city's bohemian artist community, and he soaked up its attitudes and styles. The actors, dancers, poets, and tale tellers who welcomed him (Bret Harte and the wild protofeminist Adah Isaacs Menken among them) further legitimized Sam's appetite for the revisive view, the satirical take, and the stance of unterrified, biting honesty. "Tell all the truth but tell it slant," his contemporary Emily Dickinson wrote at some point in her cloistered life. Mark Twain may never have read those lines, but he put them into practice.

He brought those vernacular voices with him when he returned East in 1867. They joined the vast inventory of other voices stored in his remarkable mimetic memory: the slave voices from his toddler years; the voices of Mississippi steamboatmen and their passengers; the Kentucky-seasoned voice of his mother, Jane; the homespun voices of the preachers and teachers and his fellow typesetters in Hannibal; the voices of Washington politicians and poltroons; the voices of pursed-lipped matrons and naïve pretty girls and the children who conspired and frolicked everywhere. He rammed them into the nation's emerging nativist literature, which he largely legitimized, sending the once-dominant Anglophilic voice of polite learned discourse sprawling like the Dandy dunked by the Squatter.

The Americans who bought his books and read his magazine pieces recognized themselves in him. They rejoiced in this writer who thought and framed his thoughts as they did (only better), who "writes English as if it were a primitive and not a derivative language," as Howells put it, "without Gothic or Latin or Greek behind it, or German and French beside it." They welcomed an author and essayist of substance who was self-assured enough to reject the European-derived pieties and flourishes favored by the Boston Brahmins who still unconsciously accepted Europe's condescending verdict on American culture: that it remained an oxymoron.

Their gratitude was summed up by a letter from a self-confessed "old man, farmer and invalid of two years standing" from Georgia who wrote in 1870

> to thank you for filling a void in the Galaxy. . . . [I]t is hard labour to read continuously the stilted sentiment of the time and of the hundreds of books & papers I have read during several years back, excepting Mr Dickens works, I do not remember to have seen humour enough in any one to excite a laugh, until yr appearance in the Galaxy.

Rejecting "the stilted sentiment of the time": therein lay the core affinity between Mark Twain and his readers, the quality that distinguished him from his more learned, and often equally profound, literary peers.

What enabled him to achieve this rejection and employ his nonpareil ear for vernacular, un-Latinate speech and sentiments? Yet another of those "intersections" between Mark Twain and his times, perhaps the most important intersection of all.

Samuel Clemens came of age with the first generation of mass readers in the nation's history—the world's history. The Promethean spark that tore through his countrymen's social, economic, and rural–urban classes (all save its enslaved classes) in the 1850s ignited Sammy Clemens of the western backwater village Hannibal, Missouri.

The spark had a quite specific origin. "By the time of the Civil War (1861–65), America had seen the first mass-educated and mass-literate generation in the modern world come of age, largely through schools adopting en masse William H. McGuffey's *Eclectic Readers*." So writes the Ulster scholar of popular culture John Springhall. By the 1870s this generation had swelled to span the republic's cities and towns and far-flung farms and villages and frontiers.

Mark Twain makes no specific mention of the famous McGuffey's Reader, which replaced the difficult *New England Primer* (an early "whole-language" model) with phonics. But the Reader was sold door-to-door across the hinterlands during Sam Clemens's boyhood, and Dixon Wecter, one of his most observant scholars, cites it as a learning tool for him.

Sam and his generation were not much interested in the "high and fine" literature, endorsed by the Brahmins, that he slyly lampooned in an 1887 letter to his friend Howells. They were interested in information: about their republic-inchrysalis; about their fellow citizens beyond the curve of the earth; about them-selves. They wanted this information delivered with the inflections of someone like *themselves* and who told the truth. Mainly.

While the "high and fine" works of the eastern literati decorated the shelves of the eastern urban bookstores, Mark Twain's books were sold door-to-door, by subscription, just like the Reader itself. And the "water" in them coursed through the American consciousness and that of the world like the Mississippi.

Nor did that water run dry with his death in 1910. The yearning, affinity-seeking correspondents in the present volume have their counterparts in readers today, including readers from around the globe who open *Dear Mark Twain* and find themselves staring back from the mirror of history. It was an admirer from Denmark, one Carl Jensen, who may have most strikingly summed it all up:

> Please to excuse that I fall with the door in the house, without first to begin with the usual long ribble-row. I want to become the autograph of the over alle the world well known Mark Twain, whose narratives so apt have procured me a laughter.

Perhaps Mr. Jensen had not completed his mastery of English syntax. I prefer to think that he was awash in the fantods. The good fantods.

Ron Powers
Castleton, Vermont
January 27, 2012

Introduction

More than one hundred years after his death, Mark Twain ranks as one of the most thoroughly documented and studied writers of his time. In addition to countless reprints of his books, the past century has seen publication of scores of editions of his previously unpublished works, plus collections of his journalism, speeches, letters, notebooks, autobiographical dictations, and interviews. Books about Mark Twain now number in the hundreds, articles in the thousands, with no letup in sight. Can anything truly fresh still be added to our understanding of him? One answer may be found in this volume.

Dear Mark Twain presents a selection of previously unpublished letters Samuel L. Clemens received from readers between 1863, the year he adopted the pen name "Mark Twain," and 1910, the year he died. Most are from ordinary people he never met. Though long known to scholars, these letters constitute an important documentary resource that has been little tapped. More than any other type of documents, they reveal what *average* readers thought of Clemens, "Mark Twain," and his works. Writing with no thought that their letters would ever be seen by other eyes,[1] many readers expressed an incredible warmth of feeling and closeness to Clemens, often bursting with eagerness to declare how he touched their lives. Although many letters exhibit considerable passion, the warmth they exude is not always positive. Numerous letters are highly negative. Others are self-serving bids for personal help, attention, or publicity.

This volume is not a collection of "fan mail," but rather a broadly representative cross section of the wide range of opinions, feelings, and subjects expressed in all the letters Clemens received from readers. Each letter offers a fascinating glimpse into what people outside the worlds of professional criticism and scholarly study thought of Clemens during his lifetime. Many are deeply moving, more than a few are hilarious, some may be shocking, few are dull.

THE COLLECTION

Dear Mark Twain may lay claim to two notable firsts. It is the first published collection of letters to Clemens from readers. As early as a century ago, Albert Bigelow Paine, Clemens's literary executor and the first editor of the Mark Twain Papers, inserted extracts from reader letters in his monumental study, *Mark Twain: A Biography—The Personal and Literary Life of Samuel Langhorne Clemens* (New York, 1912).[2] Since Paine's death in 1935, Clemens's correspondence files have been open to other researchers, many of whom have discussed and quoted reader letters in their own books.[3] Until now, however, no one troubled to gather a selection of these letters into a book.[4] This long delay may have had something to do with the fact that no collection of similar letters to *any* nineteenth-century author had ever been published. Had other such collections already existed, a book like *Dear Mark Twain* probably would have appeared well before now.[5] The present volume therefore is also very likely the first published collection of authentic reader letters to any nineteenth-century author and, at the least, one of the few such collections for an author of any era.[6]

The absence of similar collections of letters to other authors in itself says much about Clemens, who was not the only writer known to receive large volumes of mail from readers. Some writers, in fact, may have received even more mail than he did. The English novelist Charles Dickens is one possible example. Although he received an immense volume of mail from readers; however, virtually none of it has survived. Alarmed by the prospect that his intimate correspondence might one day be published, Dickens put his accumulated letters and papers to the torch in 1860. He continued to burn his mail throughout the rest of his life. More than fourteen thousand of his own letters have survived, but almost none written to him escaped the flames.[7]

The French novelist Jules Verne, a closer contemporary of Clemens, provides another interesting case. In 1890, a magazine reported that Verne had "filed away over two thousand letters" from his American readers alone.[8] Claims that Verne received more fan mail than any other author cannot be confirmed, however, because virtually all his reader letters have apparently disappeared.[9]

Clemens differed from most authors in his attitude toward saving manuscripts and correspondence. He seemingly tried to keep almost everything. Equally remarkable is the fact that so much of his manuscript material survived the dislocations not only of his shifting residences and extensive travels but also vicissitudes in their later stewardship. Some correspondence has certainly been lost, but thanks to Clemens's pack-rat habits and the meticulous preservation of documents by the Mark Twain Papers of the University of California's Bancroft Library, a substantial trove of letters from readers has survived to make possible the present book.[10] One wonders *why* Clemens saved these letters. Did he simply hate to discard manuscript material? Was he conscious of its possible value to his future literary reputation? Or did he think he might later find uses for some of the letters?[11]

CONTENT OF THE LETTERS

Considered purely on their intrinsic interest, these letters make for fascinating and often entertaining reading. Many strain to be humorous, but the funniest are often those that are unintentionally amusing, such as a Dane's autograph request written in English so badly fractured that Clemens specially marked it for preservation.[12] Especially common are letters with presumably serious but outlandish requests and propositions. What makes them comical is their authors' presumption in thinking that Clemens would respond with anything other than angry expletives. A curious example is a struggling writer who wanted to test the literary judgment of editors by having Clemens write for him an article he would try to sell under his own name to see if it would fetch ten dollars. If his experiment worked, he promised to send Clemens the ten dollars.[13]

Some letters are amusing because their authors' attempts to be funny actually succeed. Such letters are rare, but when Clemens received one—such as a Protestant minister's complaint about his hands getting stuck to a self-pasting scrapbook—he was not above recording his appreciation.[14] However, most readers' attempts at humor fail dismally. A common thread running through many is lame attempts to amuse or provoke Clemens by throwing his own words back at him—typically in the form of puns. The frequency of letters playing on "Innocents Abroad" and "Roughing It" alone must have become irksome, and more than a few letters offered weak puns such as "Clemens-y."

The letters can also be read as mirrors reflecting the images Clemens cast on the world. Clemens worked hard at crafting his own public image and must have been gratified by the obviously sincere affection many readers expressed. An 1877 letter from a Pennsylvania man asking for help in getting published in the *Atlantic Monthly* expresses a reaction to Clemens's writings that many other readers felt: "I have not thought of preparing this request to any one else, and hardly know why I have ventured to thus address you—except it is, that I like you—through your writings and sayings—so suggestive of the man behind them."[15] One of the currents running through this collection is how closely readers associated Clemens the man with Mark Twain the writer.

The genuineness of readers' affection for Clemens is undeniable, but he sometimes found the fulsome admiration he received cloying, and it may even have engendered in him a degree of arrogant contempt. The letters also may have made him more cynical about the intelligence of his readers and human beings in general even as they fed his ego. Nevertheless, comments he recorded on the letters and their envelopes occasionally reveal his appreciation of intelligently expressed praise and criticism. Because Clemens was acutely aware of the value of pleasing the book-buying public, we can be certain he paid attention to what his readers told him.

CATEGORIZING THE LETTERS

Readers wrote to Clemens for an astonishing variety of reasons, putting him in what his biographer Paine called "a constant state of siege, besought by all varieties and conditions of humanity for favors such as only human need and abnormal ingenuity can invent. His ever-increasing mail presented a marvelous exhibition of the human species on undress parade."[16] Another biographer, John Lauber, outlined a rough typology of the correspondents: appreciative fans, inspired readers, question askers and suggestion offerers, complainers, religious cranks, aspiring writers, beggars, and hoaxers. To this list might be added categories such as condolence givers, commentators sending real-life examples of Clemens's fictions, and exaggerations and tourists reporting on how they used his travel books during their own travels. Rigid categorization may be a mistake, however, as many letters would fall into more than one category and some might not fit any.[17]

Autograph requests may have been the most common type of letter nineteenth-century authors received from readers, and Clemens probably got more than his share. In an 1882 reply to a persistent young autograph hound, Clemens claimed that he received one-half dozen such requests per week, "three hundred letters a year!"[18] His estimate is probably exaggerated, but he doubtless received a great number of requests. He wearied of their dreary sameness early in his career but became more amenable to responding favorably during his last years. He especially disliked autograph requests accompanied by demands for special "sentiments." In 1882, for example, a Pennsylvania journalist sent him a politely worded request for an autograph but foolishly added, "Will you kindly preface your 'auto' with a 'sentiment' of some kind?" That mistake moved Clemens to comment, "From some low-bred & unrefined son of a bitch in Pennsylvania." The supplicant's unused self-addressed and stamped envelope is still filed with his letter.[19]

Clemens also received many requests to supply biographical information or pithy messages from members of literary societies scheduled to present papers on him at meetings. Such petitions were akin to autograph requests—of which they may occasionally have been disguised forms. The fact that these letters meant that Clemens was the subject of appreciative discussions flattered him, but being repeatedly asked the same questions wore him down. In September 1879, he wrote to his *Quaker City* friend Mary Mason Fairbanks that he was so tired of his correspondence that "I went to Europe mainly to get rid of my inane, brain-softening letter-answering." He continued, "These letters are compliments, consequently one cannot disrespect them. But constantly answering the very same questions in the very same way is another form of climbing a treadmill—you seem to be nearing the top, but you're not."[20] The following year, he wrote on one such request, "A heavy curse fall on the particular devil who invented this most offensive form of persecution."[21]

Clemens received scores of requests for advice on writing and getting published. Some were long, detailed descriptions of books the correspondents had written or intended to write. Others simply wanted him to read their manuscripts or intervene with publishers on their behalf. Clemens struck many as a successful writer who had built his own career from unpromising beginnings, and he also projected the image of a warm and generous person willing to offer help. Moreover, any assistance writers could get from someone as famous as he was might set them on their own roads to success.

Many letters tried to soften up Clemens with lavish praise of his talent and with appeals to his generous nature. In 1890, for example, a Baltimore man signing himself "Ajax" wrote, "I come to you and throw myself at your feet, as it were, because you are a benefactor." His long, tedious letter goes on to explain his frustrations over not getting published and asks Clemens—or "some friend in your line of business"—to intervene in his behalf. Clemens was especially impatient with would-be writers seeking shortcuts to success. His curt comment on Ajax's envelope sums up his attitude toward such writers: "The same old thing. Man wants to know the royal road, & would like help—"[22]

Although Clemens generally declined or ignored requests for writing and publishing help, he occasionally did make a difference in another writer's career. A prime example occurred in 1884, when a young Kansas journalist, Edgar W. Howe, sent him a copy of his privately printed novel, *The Story of a Country Town*. Howe included the usual praise: "I regard you as the foremost American writer." He then meekly added, "I would greatly prize an opinion from your pen, but I suppose this is asking too much."[23] Not only did Clemens read Howe's book, he also responded with generous praise and suggestions for improvements, gave Howe permission to use the "public" part of his letter as he pleased, and even invited Howe to visit him.[24] Later, he gave Howe the names and addresses of other literary figures who might help.[25] Armed with Clemens's warm endorsement and similar praise from W. D. Howells, Howe later published his novel in a trade edition that enjoyed considerable success.[26]

Clemens's initial reply to Howe reveals something about why he responded favorably to that writer's request and unfavorably to most others. The big difference was Howe's sending him a *printed* copy of his book. Clemens remarked,

"I can tell hardly anything about a book which is written in an unfamiliar hand; & so, lest I express a lame & unjust opinion, I express none at all." He concluded: "Out of the six & thirty million times I have been asked for an opinion about a book, I believe this is the first time I have ever furnished one—not that I am loathsome & unsympathetic, but because the books were worthless." That last remark seems to contradict his point about handwritten manuscripts but probably expressed his true feeling.

Another reason Clemens avoided answering requests for advice was the danger of being drawn into unproductive arguments with writers dissatisfied with what he might tell them. In 1902, he made the mistake of telling Mary A. Geisse, an aspiring poet, that her work showed talent but lacked the genius that makes a poet a success. Geisse then expressed her disappointment:

> Having learned this by experience, and knowing that you must have a large acquaintance among those interested in our leading magazines I thought perhaps if I told you of my hard struggle, and *you saw any talent in my work you might be willing to speak a word for me.* But if I have erred in my judgement, I can only regret it, as it has entailed trouble upon you and been a keen disappointment to me.

In the margin of Geisse's letter, an exasperated Clemens wrote, "I tried to make this fool understand (without saying the naked brutal words) that she has neither talent *nor* genius with this damned result."[27]

The most detestable communications Clemens received must have been begging letters, which developed into an art form in Great Britain and the United States during the nineteenth century. He was the target of a steady stream of pleas for financial aid that ranged from invitations to invest in dubious schemes to artfully worded appeals for loans and requests for outright gifts of cash. At least seventy-five such letters have been preserved. Their details vary enormously, but most follow a predictable formula. After opening with a warm compliment or two, they recount their supplicants' misfortunes, offer a cannot-miss plan for recovery, allude to Clemens's alleged wealth, remind him of how he had once struggled, and offer impressive references. They then typically claim there is no one else to whom they can turn, specify what they want from him, and assure him of their undying gratitude.[28] After his publishing company declared bankruptcy in 1894 and his own financial problems were publicized, such dried up.

Clemens almost never responded to these letters. In at least one instance, however, he did write a reply (but may not have mailed it) that reveals his feelings about beggars. In 1874, a writer signing her name Mrs. Mary Margaret Field wrote him a long letter asking for a loan.[29] It opens in the usual manner: "I write to you, because I have read sketches of y^r life, and it seems to me, that, as you have raised yourself from obscurity and poverty, by your own talents and energy, you may feel some interest in the struggles of a Woman, who has supported herself, entirely, creditably, and honorably, by her pen."

Field goes on to narrate the history of her financial problems, adding that she had "written to four of our leading prose writers, stating my case," before asking Clemens for a one-hundred-dollar loan. She mentions a number of valuable assets she still owns, including some real estate. Her conclusion also follows a familiar pattern:

> I cannot tell you how earnestly I pray that your heart may be moved to assist me.—In your happy home,—wealthy, fortunate, famous and beloved, as you now are, you may have forgotten the old days of struggle.—Yet call them up once more, for a moment, to your mind, & for their sake, & because of the knowledge of suffering they gave you, have compassion on me,—for indeed, my distress is very deep, & genuine, and I know not which way to turn for relief.

Clemens was, in fact, moved:

> Madam: Your distress would move the heart of a statue. Indeed it would move the entire statue if it were on rollers. I have ~~seen~~ looked upon poverty & its attendant misery in many lands, & in my own person I have suffered in this sort: but I never have heard of a case so bitter as yours. Nothing in the world between you & starvation but a lucrative literary situation, a few diamonds & things, & three thousand seven hundred dollars worth of town property. How you must suffer. I do not know that there is any relief for misery like this. Suicide has been recommended by some authors.

Clemens went on to upbraid Field for shamelessly claiming poverty. "Madam," he wrote, "I receive a good many letters like yours, & they all have one family feature. That is, they all show the presence of a mean, pitiful sham which the writers take for 'pride,' & the utter absence of a redeeming shame." He went on to suggest Field apply for a bank loan and pledge her real estate for security

> instead of writing ten pages of "agonies of distress" to a stranger to prove that you are as unworthy a mendicant as ever went on the highway. In the days of my ~~very~~ hardest fortune, when I envied the very dogs their dinners, I would have starved before I would have ~~beg~~ humbled myself to beg the help of a stranger—so you can easily fancy the amount of grim compassion I feel for you, & your "pride," & your ~~lacerated~~ imaginary "poverty."

THE CORRESPONDENTS

Clemens knew almost nothing about most of the readers who wrote to him beyond what their letters revealed, and a large majority wrote to him only once. There can be little doubt, however, that he would have found many of their lives interesting, especially if he could have known what became of them in later years. To say that other people's lives fascinated Clemens would be an understatement.

Words he put in a fictional character's mouth in 1906 aptly express his fascination with human beings: "a man's experiences of life are a book, and there was never yet an uninteresting life. Such a thing is an impossibility. Inside of the dullest exterior there is a drama, a comedy, and a tragedy."[30]

The essential truth of that remark can be found in the life stories of many of the strangers who wrote to Clemens. Compared to the noted authors, cultural figures, business moguls, politicians, and royalty with whom Clemens often mixed, his readers led ordinary lives. Some did enjoy notable careers in various fields, but most were obscure—children, housewives, farmers, bookkeepers, railroad clerks, telegraph operators, schoolteachers, and backcountry attorneys, doctors, journalists, ministers, and the like. Nevertheless, beneath their ostensibly dull exteriors, a great deal of drama, comedy, and tragedy can be found, as annotations to their letters show.

Previously published books containing letters and extracts from Clemens's readers have said almost nothing about the correspondents that is not in their letters. Procuring even minimal data on them would have required digging deeply into widely scattered census records; government birth, death, and marriage records; military records; passport applications; contemporary newspaper stories and obituaries; city directories; and countless other publications. To make matters even more difficult, it is not always possible even to identify some correspondents confidently. Now, thanks to the recent explosion in online documentary resources, it is becoming possible to assemble at least fragmentary histories of the lives of all but a minority of the correspondents (see "Note on Sources," pages 271–273). When the letters are read in conjunction with their authors' stories, they take on greater poignancy and deeper meaning.

VOLUME OF CORRESPONDENCE

The total number of letters Clemens received from readers can be only crudely estimated. The files of the Mark Twain Papers contain about 12,500 letters addressed directly to him. Spaced over the five decades between 1861 and 1910, that figure averages only 250 letters per year, but Clemens probably received many more than that figure. The great bulk of preserved letters are from close friends, relatives, and business associates.[31] The rest are from more casual acquaintances, tradespeople, and strangers. Fixing a number on how many items might legitimately be called reader letters is difficult. However, a rough estimate based on the examination of the files undertaken while selecting letters for this book would put that figure at something well over one thousand letters.

In an article Clemens wrote early in his career, when his only major publication was *The Innocents Abroad* (1869), he complained "that if there is one thing in the world more hateful than another to all of us, it is to have to write a letter."[32] He went on to describe the tedium answering his mail brought to each day and said he "never" answered "more than nine; usually only five or six." As unanswered letters piled up, they "would shortly begin to have a reproachful look about them, next an upbraiding look, and by-and-by an aggressive and insolent aspect; and when it came to that, I always opened the stove door and made an example of them." Although Clemens's article contains burlesque elements—such as his responding to a Kentucky boy who offered to send him his wildcat by suggesting he instead send it to Henry Ward Beecher—it no doubt also contains elements of truth. It confirms that he received many more letters than are now preserved and that he did not keep many unanswered letters. It is reasonable to assume that most unanswered letters were from strangers. If Clemens did consciously destroy or discard letters, the first to go were probably those he found least interesting, such as autograph requests.

Another indication that Clemens's correspondence files are incomplete is the uneven chronological distribution of preserved letters.[33] The years during which he was out of the United States show marked drops in numbers. For example, an average of 169 letters per year from 1875–1877 are preserved. In contrast, the average for 1878–1879, during most of which he was in Europe, is only 90 per year. The average for 1880–1890, when Clemens never left the country, is 390 letters per year. Through most of the 1890s, he was again out of the country, and the average again drops to 90 per year. While Clemens was abroad, readers probably wrote fewer letters to him because they did not know how to address them or feared their letters might not reach him. Also, when Clemens traveled he probably was less careful about saving letters—particularly those from strangers he had no intention of answering.

During the last decade of Clemens's life, the volume of incoming letters reached its highest levels—an average of 589 preserved per year.[34] During 1905–1909, it averaged 922 per year. During his last decade, Clemens was in the news almost continuously, and many letters responded to published stories about him. Tellingly, begging letters virtually stopped coming—doubtless because of news stories about his financial problems.

More concrete evidence of missing letters can be found within letters that have been saved. Just as some correspondents acknowledge receiving letters from Clemens that are now lost, others mention having sent him letters now missing.[35] In addition, some letters Clemens saved seem to have disappeared after he died. Responsibility for some losses should probably fall on Paine, who had sole custody of Clemens's papers for a quarter century. A number of letters he discusses in *Mark Twain: A Biography* cannot now be found.[36]

SELECTION CRITERIA AND ORGANIZATION

The question of how representative of "average" readers the letters in this volume are must be addressed by explaining the three-stage selection process through which the letters have gone. The first stage was the correspondents' own self-selection. It is reasonable to assume that those who did write letters were at least a little better educated than the average reader and a little more self-confident. The significance of the latter point is evident in the deferential and often apologetic tone that pervades the letters. As warmly as many correspondents felt toward Clemens, they were nevertheless uneasy about writing to him (but probably less uneasy about writing to him than to other authors). It is thus not surprising that many who did write to him were in professions such as law, medicine, journalism, education, big business, and religious ministries. These correspondents could not have been average readers. Nevertheless, large numbers of less educated and less accomplished readers also wrote to Clemens.

The second selection stage was at Clemens's end. As has been shown, although he preserved a surprisingly large number of letters from strangers, he did not save everything. Evidence for his intentionally discarding letters is mostly circumstantial, but his scattered comments on the letters he kept suggest that he favored those offering reasoned praise and those with unusual properties.

The final selection stage was the choosing of the previously unpublished letters to go in this book. Because what friends, relatives, and others who personally knew Clemens thought of him is already well documented, a high priority has been given to previously unpublished letters from correspondents who were essentially strangers to Clemens—people who knew him only through his writings or public reputation at the time they wrote. A second equally important, but more difficult to define, priority favored letters revealing as much as possible about Clemens himself.

Another important goal is variety of all kinds. Although recurrent patterns and subjects run through many letters, jarring surprises tend to pop up every few pages. At least one example of almost every type of letter Clemens received is in this volume, and redundancy in unrelated but similar letters has been minimalized. The collection also includes at least one letter about every specific book, story, or article that was the subject of *substantive* comments. Most letters discussing *Huckleberry Finn* are included because of that work's special importance and because there are fewer such letters than one might expect. Another form of variety is geographical, so letters from readers outside the United States tend to be favored. The collection's single letter from a South American is not especially interesting, but as it is virtually the only letter from a South American, it is included.[37]

To help maximize variety, only one letter from each correspondent is included. When multiple letters from the same correspondent would make suitable entries, the first letter is usually selected. Exceptions include several cases in which later letters are the first to which Clemens replied. In most cases of multiple-letter correspondents, the writers' other letters are discussed in annotations.

Intrinsically interesting and amusing letters generally have been favored over duller ones. Also, correspondents with interesting life stories tend to be favored over those with less interesting stories. As these criteria tend to favor correspondents whose lives are better documented, they also tend to favor the successful over the unsuccessful and, therefore, the exceptional over the average.

Letters that Clemens annotated or answered generally have been favored over others, especially when his comments and replies reveal his attitude toward his readers. This point touches on another central question to ask of these letters: how they affected Clemens himself. Only a small percentage of the selected letters moved Clemens to reply, but in all cases in which his replies have been preserved, they are printed here in full. Most of his letters in this volume are published here for the first time.

Most reader letters Clemens dismissed with simple descriptive comments or biting sarcasms jotted on backs of letters or, more frequently, on the letters' envelopes. All such comments are printed here, immediately following the readers' letters. When letters are not followed by Clemens's comments, it can be assumed that he either recorded none or that they have been lost.[38]

A central goal in the arrangement of this volume is to recreate for readers, so far as is reasonably possible, the experience that Clemens himself had in reading his mail. To that end, the letters are arranged in strict chronological order. As precise dates on which the letters reached Clemens are not always known, the arrangement is based on the dates when the letters were composed or postmarked.

NOTES

1. Some correspondents were explicit about this. John Irwin, for example, wrote, "I am ashamed of this Beging Letter But Expect It will go Into waste Basket and no one But you will see It" (Irwin to Clemens, 13 May 1883; all letters cited here are in the Mark Twain Papers at the University of California's Bancroft Library).

2. See especially chapters 40, 105, and 127. The extracts scattered throughout Paine's 1,719-page biography are not easy to find. Most are neither identified by correspondents' names nor indexed. An example is an extract from a February 1901 letter from a "Boston school-teacher" (p. 1133). The writer was a woman named Alice May. She might well have objected to seeing her name in print next to her statement about being "filled with shame and remorse" for having once invited Clemens

to speak to a teachers group—especially as her words were followed by a savage rejoinder from Clemens.

3. Notable examples include John Lauber, *The Inventions of Mark Twain* (New York, 1990), 131–134; and Ron Powers, *Mark Twain: A Life* (New York, 2005), 398–401. I am indebted to Lauber's book for giving me the idea for the present volume.

4. The volumes of *Mark Twain's Letters* edited by the staff of the Mark Twain Project and published by the University of California Press since 1986 include—in annotations—only those reader letters to which Clemens's replies are presented. Clemens answered only a small percentage of readers' letters, and not all his replies are preserved, so the first six volumes of Clemens's letters (through 1875) contain few reader letters.

5. Clemens himself considered publishing some of the letters he received. He and P. T. Barnum shared an interest in what they called "queer" or "curious" letters, and they discussed collecting interesting specimens in a book that Clemens would edit. As a prosperous and famous showman whose name was associated with oddities, Barnum probably received even stranger letters than Clemens did. A. H. Saxon discusses examples in his magisterial biography, *P. T. Barnum: The Legend and the Man* (New York, 1989), 258–260. On 31 July 1874, Barnum wrote to Clemens that he had "destroyed *bushels* of curious begging letters. Hereafter they shall be saved for you." The following March, he said, "It *is* a shame I have wasted so much good stuff for your collection. I hope at a proper time you will publish many of the letters. They will form almost a *new* page in the volume of human nature." On 17 September 1875, Clemens wrote to William Wright (Dan De Quille), an old friend from Nevada, about his interest in begging letters. He mentioned "how rich my collection of this sort of literature is becoming, from reading some of those that Barnum sends me every month" (Michael B. Frank and Harriet Elinor Smith, eds., *Mark Twain's Letters*, vol. 6 [Berkeley, Calif., 2002], 535). In his autobiographical dictation of 23 March 1906, Clemens wrote, "A good many years ago Mrs. Clemens used to keep as curiosities some of the odd and strange superscriptions that decorated letters that came to me from strangers in out-of-the-way corners of the earth" (*Autobiography of Mark Twain* [Berkeley: Univ. of California Press, 2010], 436). Barnum sent Clemens batches of letters over the next several years and corresponded with him until 1881, but Clemens's interest in the letters book died at some point. Saxon suggests that he may have resented "Barnum's persistent attempts to draft him into the circle of his publicists as a continuing minor nuisance" (ibid., 261). It is not known what became of the letters Barnum had forwarded to him, but after Barnum died in 1891, his family tried to reclaim them. Their failure evidently led to "some unpleasantness" between them and Clemens. It appears that poet Joel Benton, who would later write a biography of Barnum, also wished to publish some of the letters (Saxon, personal communication, 17 October 2012; see also Saxon's *P. T. Barnum*, 260–261, 395, and his *Selected Letters of P. T. Barnum* [New York, 1983]; and *Mark Twain's Letters*, vol. 6, 369–371).

6. *Letters to Sherlock Holmes*, ed. R. L. Green (New York, 1985), resembles a collection of letters to Santa Claus in that most of its letters were addressed to an imaginary character; however, it also contains a handful of real letters to Arthur Conan Doyle. Children frequently address letters to Mark Twain in the North Pole of Twaindom, Hannibal, Missouri. Henry Sweets, the curator of Hannibal's Mark Twain Museum, thoughtfully answers each of them.

7. "The Inimitable Becomes the Inimical: Dickens's Bonfire Destroys Literary Heritage," www.web40571.clarahost.co.uk, accessed 21 Apr. 2011. Another writer who consigned his correspondence to a bonfire was Henry James (Greg W. Zacharias, editor of *The Complete Letters of Henry James*, personal communication, 4 Feb. 2011). Anthony Trollope also destroyed most of the letters he received (N. John Hall, personal communication, 2 June 2011; Hall's *Correspondence: An Adventure in Letters* [Boston, 2011] is an engrossing epistolary novel revolving around correspondence between a fictional nineteenth-century American and Trollope and other Victorian writers).

8. Stephen Michaluk Jr., "The Autographic Legacy of Jules Verne," *Autograph Times*, Oct. 1996, 1.

9. William Butcher, author of *Jules Verne: The Definitive Biography* (New York, 2006), personal communication, 25 Jan. 2011; Brian Taves, Library of Congress, personal communication, 31 Jan. 2011. No generally accepted theory about what became of Verne's letters has been formed.

Another writer whose incoming letters have been preserved is Henry Wadsworth Longfellow, most of whose correspondence is housed in Harvard's Houghton Library. According to Sydelle Pearl, the Hougton files include a substantial number of letters from Longfellow's readers (personal commuications, 17–18 November 2012). Pearl's recently published *Dear Mr. Longfellow: Letters to and from the Children's Poet* (New York, 2012) is not a collection of correspondence but rather a biography that draws heavily on letters Longfellow received from children.

10. Since Paine's death, stewardship of the Mark Twain Papers has passed through the hands of five scholars. It now rests with Robert Hirst, general editor of the Mark Twain Project at Berkeley's Bancroft Library.

11. See Clemens's annotations to letters 135 and 142. Citations to letters in the present collection are followed by the letters' numbers; other cited letters are not in this volume.

12. Carl Jensen to Clemens, 17 Oct. 1879 (letter 30).

13. A. G. Heizerton to Clemens, 21 April 1888. Clemens's response is unknown but can be imagined.

14. J. W. Sandborn to Clemens, 21 Jan. 1878 (letter 28).

15. W. I. Gilbert to Clemens, 19 Dec. 1877.

16. Albert Bigelow Paine, *Mark Twain: A Biography* (Philadelphia, 1997), 563.

17. Lauber, *Inventions of Mark Twain*, 131. A difficult-to-categorize example is a letter about a young girl returning from a German art gallery and announcing that she had seen a painting of "Cleopatra going to meet Mark Twain," evidently confusing Clemens's pen name with that of the artist, Hans Makart (Blanche Willis Howard to Clemens, 8 Apr. 1888).

18. Clemens to Edward W. Bok, 24 Feb. 1882. Autograph collectors also besieged poet Walt Whitman, who said that 60 percent of his mail came from them. He burned such letters but made a point of having his facsimile autograph printed in his books (Susan S. Williams, "Authors and Literary Authorship," in *A History of the Book in America: Volume III: The Industrial Book, 1840–1880*, edited by Scott E. Casper, Jeffery D. Groves, Stephen W. Nissenbaum, Michael Winship [Chapel Hill, N.C., 2007], 109). Facsimiles of Clemens's "Mark Twain" autographs appeared several of his first editions and later in many Harper editions of his books.

19. C. H. Wells to Clemens, 29 May 1882.

20. Clemens to Fairbanks, 23 Sept. 1879. Clemens eventually began replying to letters asking the same questions with preprinted letters of his own. See Powers, *Mark Twain: A Life*, 398–399.

21. Emma J. Stafford to Clemens, 18 March 1880. Stafford asked for "a letter to be read at the Literary Union of our Church."

22. Ajax to Clemens, 19 Dec. 1890. "Ajax" was Samuel Crapin Appleby (c. 1855–1923), an engraver who later became a Baltimore *Sun* reporter and editor. He may have adapted his pseudonym from the name of his father, Andrew Jackson Appleby (obituary, Baltimore *Sun*, 18 July 1923).

23. Howe to Clemens, 2 Feb. 1884.

24. Clemens to Howe, 13 Feb. 1884.

25. Clemens to Howe, 28 Mar. 1884.

26. Lauber, *Inventions of Mark Twain*, 132.

27. Mary A. Geisse to Clemens, 24 May, 1902. Geisse's original letter and Clemens's reply are lost. Two years later, Geisse published a volume titled simply *Poems* under the pseudonym Felix Connop. Its "Author's Preface" may have targeted Clemens: "Let the critics have their fling, | Since it pleases me to sing. | I shall blithely go my way | Heedless of the things they say."

28. Another writer besieged by begging letters was Charles Dickens, who published an essay titled "The Begging-Letter Writer" during the 1850s. His model of typical begging letters so closely resembles letters Clemens later received that Clemens might have written the same essay himself. See also Algernon Tassin, "The Craftsmanship of Begging-Letter Writing," *Bookman* 36, no. 3 (Nov. 1912): 246–254. Scott A. Sandage analyzes patterns in begging letters sent to the industrialist John D. Rockefeller in "The Gaze of Success: Failed Men and the Sentimental Marketplace, 1873–1893," in *Sentimental Men,* ed. Mary Chapman and Glenn Hendler (Berkeley, 1999), 181–201.

29. Field to Clemens, 21 July 1874. Field's entire letter appears in an annotation to Clemens's reply in *Mark Twain's Letters,* 6:199–201. Unsuccessful efforts to identify Field suggest that she may have used a pseudonym.

30. "The Refuge of the Derelicts," in *Mark Twain's Fables of Man,* ed. J.S. Tuckey (Berkeley, 1972), 197.

31. An easy-to-use and regularly updated online database of these correspondence files is linked to the Mark Twain Project Web site at www.marktwainproject.org.

32. "One of Mankind's Bores," *Galaxy,* Feb. 1871.

33. Of the c. 12,500 preserved letters addressed to Clemens, 9.5 percent are from 1871–1880, 32.6 percent from 1881–1890, 7.2 percent from 1891–1900, and 47.1 percent from 1901–1910. Another 3.6 percent are from before 1871 or are undated.

34. The family was out of the country from late October 1903 through mid-July 1904. Otherwise, Clemens was abroad for only brief periods during this decade.

35. See, e.g., letters 17, 27, 75, and 81.

36. An example is a letter from a Duluth man who sent Clemens an Allen revolver (Paine, *Mark Twain: A Biography,* 564–565).

37. See Carmen Ramos to Clemens, 22 Nov. 1906, letter 170.

38. Clemens usually saved envelopes, but after 1902 the proportion of letters with envelopes drops precipitously. Consequently, few letters from after that year bear his comments. The disappearance of envelopes probably had something to do with changes in his secretarial help.

Note on Texts

The two hundred letters addressed to Samuel L. Clemens in this volume are arranged in chronological order, based on the dates their authors supplied or their postmarks, and are numbered sequentially. Dates of some letters have been estimated. All incoming letters and Clemens's replies come from the collections of the Mark Twain Papers at the University of California's Bancroft Library in Berkeley. The bulk of the collections' letters are original, but a few used in this volume are copies. Searchable catalogs of the complete correspondence collections are accessible online at bancroft.berkeley.edu/MTP/databases.html.

All letters are rendered in their entirety; the ellipses appearing in a few letters are original to the texts. To approximate the experience Mark Twain had in reading these letters, as little editorial intervention as possible has been made. Transcription presented some difficulties, as the vast majority of the letters are handwritten, with no two incoming letters composed by the same person. Most spelling and punctuation errors have been left uncorrected. When individual characters or punctuation marks could not be identified with certainty, the characters most likely to be correct were selected. Omitted words have not been supplied, but in a few instances missing dates and places of composition and omitted quotation marks have been supplied within editorial square brackets. (Note that the correspondents themselves sometimes used square brackets; e.g. letters 1, 38, 142, and 145.) Periods and commas following quoted matter in the letters have been placed inside terminal quotation marks, regardless of their original positions. Vertical pipes (|) indicate line breaks.

Words that correspondents struck out in revising their letters are omitted, except in a small number of instances when the canceled words, shown ~~like so~~, may help reveal the writers' thoughts ("I give the poor lunatic credit"). Words that correspondents added during revision, often between lines of text, have been silently placed where the correspondents intended them to go, except in cases where, shown ˄like so˄ the fact of insertion is needed properly to understand the revision ("your no doubt probably stupid children"). Repeated words have been silently omitted when such repetition was obviously unintentional and when words ending pages were intentionally repeated to open the next manuscript pages but would confound a reader when transcribed. Most errors in typewritten letters have been treated the same as errors in handwritten letters. However, purely typographical errors such as unintentionally run-together words and unnecessary spaces between characters have been silently corrected.

All printed letterheads, regardless of their original formatting, are centered and rendered in small caps. A few very lengthy letterheads are truncated. Surviving notes on the letters written or dictated by Clemens are shown immediately following the letters' texts. Replies written or dictated by Clemens, when included, follow the letters or his comments. Transcriptions of his writing follow the same standards as those applied in the Mark Twain Project's editions of his letters, and all transcriptions have been vetted by the Project's editors.

The letters in this volume are grouped in decades separated by pages containing time lines highlighting events mentioned in the letters that follow. As the contents of these brief time lines are closely tied to the subjects discussed in the letters, they do not cover every important event in Mark Twain's life and writing career. For fuller coverage, see the chronology in R. Kent Rasmussen's *Mark Twain A to Z* or *Critical Companion to Mark Twain*. The latter work, which is an expanded edition of the former, extends the chronology to encompass posthumous events.

1861–1870

15 May 1861	Twenty-five-year-old Samuel L. Clemens (SLC) ends his piloting career on the Mississippi one month after Civil War begins
June 1861	Campaigns with Missouri militia unit for two weeks
July–August 1861	With brother Orion crosses plains to western Nevada, where he will prospect and work at various jobs
20 September 1862	Becomes reporter for Virginia City's *Territorial Enterprise*
3 February 1863	Signs pen name "Mark Twain" for the first time
29 May 1864	Relocates to San Francisco, where he will later report for the *Morning Call* and write for literary magazines
December 1864–February 1865	Prospects in California's Tuolumne and Calaveras counties
November 1865	"Jim Smiley and His Jumping Frog" appears in New York's *Saturday Press*
March–July 1866	SLC spends four months in Sandwich (Hawaiian) Islands, writing travel letters for the Sacramento *Union*
2 October 1866	Delivers first public lecture, on Sandwich Islands, in San Francisco, then lectures in California and Nevada
15 December 1866	Leaves San Francisco for New York by sea
March–April 1867	Lectures in Midwest and revisits his Hannibal, Missouri, home
8 June–19 November 1867	Sails to Europe and the Holy Land on the *Quaker City* cruise and writes travel letters for American newspapers
November 1867–January 1868	Serves as Nevada senator William M. Stewart's private secretary in Washington, D.C.
11 March—6 July 1868	Returns to San Francisco and works on book about *Quaker City* voyage; lectures in California and Nevada
17 November 1868	Begins four-month lecture tour in the Midwest and East
July 1869	*The Innocents Abroad* is published
August 1869	SLC Settles in Buffalo, New York, as part-owner and editor of the *Express*
1 November 1869	Begins three-month lecture tour throughout the East
2 February 1870	Marries Olivia (Livy) Langdon in Elmira, New York
May 1870–April 1871	Writes a monthly column for *Galaxy* magazine
7 November 1870	Birth of son, Langdon Clemens, who will live eighteen months

1

Virginia, Feb 9, 1863.

Mark Twain: I received so good a compliment for you this morning that I am bound to communicate it to you. John Nugent inquired of me who Mark Twain was, and added that he had not seen so amusing a thing in newspaper literature in a long while as your letter in the Enterprise this morning. I gave him an account of you "so far as I knew." I suppose you know that Nugent was John Phoenix's most intimate friend. While we were talking about you, Mr. Nugent showed me an unpublished letter of the great humorist who is now in heaven.

I didn't suppose it was necessary for me to write this to you but I thought I would, because praise from Nugent is "praise from Sir Hubert Stanley," as it were. [Oh! the last three words are original with me, you know.] But considering the *critique* of the *Union* on you the other day, I thought I would administer to you a strengthening plaster, if you felt like weakening, you know.

Yours, hoping you will not weaken,
"Isreal Putnam."

Clemens first signed "Mark Twain" to his second "Letter from Carson," which appeared in the Virginia City *Territorial Enterprise* on 3 February 1863. Putnam's letter is the earliest surviving one addressed to that pseudonym. Ironically, its own author has not been identified because he used a pseudonym himself. "Isreal Putnam" may have been a play on the name of the Revolutionary War leader Israel Putnam (1718–1790). It could also have been a pun for "Is real Putnam," in reference to Clemens's *Enterprise* colleague Charles Putnam.

There is a problem with the letter's date: 9 February was a Monday—a day on which the *Enterprise* was not published. Putnam probably alludes to the 8 February issue, in which another "Letter from Carson" appeared. It contains a burlesque account of a wedding at which a rival reporter, "the Unreliable" (Clement T. Rice), supposedly made an ass of himself (H. N. Smith, ed., *Clemens of the Enterprise* [Berkeley, 1857], 57–61).

John Nugent (1821–1880) was the former owner-editor of the San Francisco *Herald* and was a federal agent in the West during the early 1860s. John Phoenix was the pen name of George Derby (1823–1861), a humorist who had built his reputation in California. The phrase "Praise from Sir Hubert Stanley" comes from a line in a play by Thomas Morton (1764–1838): "Approbation from Sir Hubert Stanley is praise indeed." The *Union* was another Virginia City daily with which the *Enterprise* had an ongoing rivalry.

2

Nov 15th 1869

Mr Samuel L Clemens, "Mark Twain"
Honored Sir

I trust you will excuse the liberty I now take in thus intruding on your notice as I wish to ask you for your *Autograph* also Nom de plume

I am getting a Collection and should be *very much pleased* to receive *yours,* for I should *prize it* highly, as I *admire* your humorous *Lectures and Writings.* They contain so much *genuine wit,* and such *fine ideas,* your description of Places and Persons being so *correct* and *expressed* so *prettily.* A *few lines* with your Name would be *very acceptable.*

With many kind wishes for your continued Success and hoping you may be pleased to grant my request,

I remain Sir, very respectfully
Mrs. Wm. W. Pearce
Providence, R.I

This may be Clemens's earliest preserved autograph request. Newspaper publication of his *Quaker City* voyage letters in 1867 gave him a national reputation, but much greater fame would come from publication of *The Innocents Abroad* in July 1869. An 1870 census report for Providence, Rhode Island, lists thirty-two-year-old Harriet H. Pearce as the wife of William W. Pearce, a jeweler.

3

New York, 8th July '70

Mark Twain, Esq.

My Dear Sir,

I regret exceedingly that your agricultural editorship has not been appreciated. Other laborers in that field have met with the same ingratitude from
an ignorant community. Some years ago one of the governors of Indiana
devoted himself to the improvement of the stock in that benighted state
shortly before a general election. A constituent addressed him a note inquiring what he thought of the hydraulic ram? Mr Governor immediately and
properly replied that it was better than Southdown for mutton & equal to
Merino for wool, and would you believe it—the prejudices of the people were
such that he lost his re-election.

Very truly yours,

Virgilius

Readers enjoyed telling Clemens about real-life oddities resembling his fictional
inventions. This letter responds to his July 1870 *Galaxy* sketch "How I Edited an
Agricultural Paper Once," a burlesque account of a newspaper publishing nonsense
such as claiming turnips grow on vines. The letter alludes to Joseph A. Wright
(1810–1867), the governor of Indiana in 1849–1857, who was publicly embarrassed for
suggesting that the "hydraulic ram" (a water pump) could improve sheep breeds
(Ouachita, Ks. *Telegraph,* 12 Feb. 1870; D. J. Powers and E. W. Skinner, eds., *The Wisconsin Farmer* [Madison, 1856], 40). Wright did not run for reelection in 1856 but
was later appointed to fill an empty U.S. Senate seat. The anonymous correspondent's pseudonym, "Virgilius," recalls the medieval European grammarian Virgilius Maro Grammaticus and the ancient Roman poet Virgil, who was also known
as Virgilius.

4

McBean p.o. Richmond Co Georgia

August 23, 1870

Mark Twain Esq

Sir—I am an old man, a farmer, and an invalid of two years standing. My
occupation if I may call it so, is reading the papers and Magazines, of which
together I subscribe to eighteen—among them the Galaxy, next I think in its
standing to Appleton's Journal—I write to thank you for filling a void in the
Galaxy, which I have long felt in the literature of the day. The mind is like the
body, it needs relaxation and rest—for it is hard labour to read continuously the
stilted sentiment of the time and of the hundreds of books & papers I have read

during several years back, excepting Mr Dickens works. I do not remember
to have seen humour enough in any one to excite a laugh, until yr appearance
in the Galaxy—It is a great feature in the work, with me at least, and poor
down trodden devils as we are, it must be genuine humour that can produce a
cachinnation in a Southern gentleman—I trust you will continue this department, with profit to yrself and benefit & amusement to yr readers—For God's
sake dont think I have written this to have it published—it is for yself alone—I
dont know even yr real name—

Very respectfully yr
obt servt
A C Walker

Clemens's comment: Letter from a Southern Gentleman.

> *Galaxy* was a New York monthly for which Clemens wrote a monthly column in
> 1870–1871. *Appleton's Journal* was another New York monthly. The correspondent,
> "Colonel" Alexander Curran Walker (1816–1883), was a lifelong Georgia resident
> married to a New Yorker. A farmer, he was later eulogized as "a gentleman of the old
> school, scholarly and cultured, public spirited and bold" (obituary, Augusta, Geor-
> gia, *Chronicle,* 12 Jan. 1883). In 1856 he used the pen name "Viator" when he published
> "The Night Funeral of a Slave" in the northern magazine *Home Journal* (W. A. Clark,
> *A Lost Arcadia, Or, The Story of My Old Community* [Augusta, Ga., 1909], 12). In-
> spired by Walker's grief over the death of a slave, the widely reprinted story con-
> cluded with a northerner observing that "the negroes of the south are the happiest
> and most contented people on the face of the earth." When Walker's friend the future
> Confederate vice president Alexander H. Stephens resigned from the U.S. Congress
> in 1858, Walker declined the offer of the nomination to succeed him. After the Civil
> War, Walker successfully applied to the Union government's pardon and amnesty
> program, swearing he had opposed secession and had never served the Confederate
> government.
>
> Walker wrote to Clemens again on 6 February 1880, but Clemens then responded
> less charitably. Evidently thinking that Clemens edited a Republican newspaper,
> Walker compared *The Innocents Abroad*'s attacks on the Roman Catholic Church
> with Republican editors' attacks on the South, adding that the "only thing is, that I
> cant conceive how Mark Twain can edit a republican paper." Despite these criticisms,
> he invited Clemens and his wife to be his guests in Georgia for an extended stay.
> Unimpressed, Clemens simply noted, "From an ass."

5

Hartford (*one* of 'em) Aug 30th/70

"HOGWASH."

In a late number of the Galaxy you give an interesting specimen of this class of literature with an expressed desire for *Some more.*

First let me give you my experience with that same article—After carefully reading it over twice, in silence, I tried it upon a somewhat romantic and sensitive young lady friend (of course, omitting your introductory remarks)— before I had reached the end of the twaddle her eyes were "bathed in tears"

Woman like, she had got a long way ahead of the story—had identified herself with the poor sorrowing creature—so miserable with all her luxurious surroundings—had doubtless conjured up no end of Bluebeard or other troubles—(heaven knows what—I didn't cross examine)—Here was a good, earnest, modest girl, with a fair share of common sense, as well as educational advantages—

Now I wish to call your critical attention to *Lippincott for August* "The hungry heart"

The animus of the whole thing you will find on the first page of the story—

"Every woman in these days needs two husbands—one to fill her purse and one to fill her *heart*" (whatever *that* may be)

As to J. W. De Forest—he may be a woman or she may be a man—things get terribly mixed up now-a-days—

Any how, the principles instilled are those of that old hermaphrodite—*The Atlantic Menstrual*—Boston—

J. W. De F. wants taking down a peg or two—bad—and you are the man "*as can do it*"

Yours very truly
Thomas Swift, M.D.

To/Mr Mark Twain

Clemens's "Hogwash" editorial in the June 1870 *Galaxy* quoted a reader's letter he called a "miracle of pointless imbecility and bathos," offering it "for competition as the sickliest specimen of sham sentimentality that exists." The present letter's writer, Thomas Swift, responded to this challenge by describing—fairly accurately—a magazine story by the New England author John William De Forest (1826–1906). De Forest served in the Union Army during the Civil War, which is the setting for his best-known novel, *Miss Ravenel's Conversion from Secession to Loyalty* (1867). De Forest himself wrote to Clemens on 31 July 1874, proposing they publish a joint collection of sketches. He suggested that Clemens select from his (De Forest's) previously published sketches, throw in some of his own, and "add some machinery of story-telling tourists to string the narratives together." Clemens evidently ignored this offer. Swift uses *"The Atlantic Menstrual"* as a sarcasm directed at the prestigious Boston literary magazine *Atlantic Monthly*. Nineteen U.S. states have towns named Hartford. Because Swift's letter was postmarked in New York City, it is not certain in which Hartford he lived. Clemens himself did not settle in Hartford, Connecticut, until 1871, so the name had little significance to him in 1870.

1871–1880

March 1871	Clemens family moves from Buffalo to Hartford, Connecticut
16 October 1871	SLC begins fifteen-week lecture tour in eastern states
February 1872	*Roughing It* is published
19 March 1872	Daughter Susy Clemens is born in Elmira, New York
June 1873	SLC patents self-pasting scrapbook
August 1872–January 1874	Travels to England three times
December 1873	*The Gilded Age*, coauthored with C. D. Warner, is published
8 June 1874	Daughter Clara Clemens is born in Elmira
6 July 1874	"A Curious Pleasure Excursion" appears in New York *Herald*
September 1874–January 1875	John T. Raymond portrays Colonel Sellers in a *Gilded Age* play with which he will tour for twelve years
January–June, August 1875	"Old Times on the Mississippi" is serialized in the *Atlantic Monthly*; articles will later be used in *Life on the Mississippi*
July 1875	*Mark Twain's Sketches New and Old* is published
May and September 1876	*Ah Sin, the Heathen Chinee*, coauthored with Bret Harte, plays in New York City
December 1876	American edition *of The Adventures of Tom Sawyer* is published six months after the English edition
May 1877	SLC makes his first extended visit to Bermuda
April 1878–August 1879	Tours western Europe with family, gathering material and beginning to write a new travel book
March 1880	*A Tramp Abroad*, which includes "The Awful German Language" and the bluejay yarn, is published
26 July 1880	Daughter Jean Clemens is born in Elmira
September 1880	"Mrs. McWilliams and the Lightning" appears in the *Atlantic Monthly*

6

T

Astoria [Queens, New York] April. 9. 1874

Dear Sir

Please send me your autograph and greatly oblige your young friend

Winthrop Turney

S. L. Clemens Esq

Clemens's comment: A Curiosity | (The initial.) | (A boy who manufactures his own).

Winthrop Turney (c. 1864–1905) was only nine or ten when he wrote this letter. He later graduated from Yale and became part owner of a valuable mine in Sonora, Mexico. At the age of forty-one, he was found dead in Winsted, Connecticut, where he apparently shot himself after despairing over his poor health ("Mine Owner a Suicide," New York *Times,* 7 July 1905). The block *T* monograms Turney drew atop his letter and on the back of his envelope evidently impressed Clemens.

7

OFFICE OF THE
BOARD OF COMMISSIONERS OF PILOTS.
NO. 40 BURLING SLIP.

NEW YORK, July 6, 1874

Mark Twain Esq—
Dear Sir

I have read with great interest your having leased the comet and would be delighted if you would employ me as the navigator

Of my qualifications in that capacity I can speak as I swore to them a few months since on a cross examination permitted by a young judge Daly by a lawyer who know all about me.

You do not permit me then to say that I am not a therometrical navigator I am a practical one I read the proofs sheets of Bowditch's Navigator more than thirty times and there is not a problem or logarithim in the book but what has been knocked into my head by my father who was a printer before I was ten years of age

I have been a sailor and a nautical surveyor understand the use of instruments and can work any problem in navigation I will agree to keep the position of the comet and lay it down accurately on the chart

I have opposed the polar expeditions for the last forty years as an unnecessary exposure of life without adequate results as your expedition is entirely practical I should like to go

If Mayor Havemeyer could be induced to go as chaplain it would add much to the pious part of the excursion

Respect
Geo W Blunt

This letter responds to "A Curious Pleasure Excursion" in the 6 July 1874 New York *Herald*—a burlesque sketch advertising a luxury cruise aboard a recently discovered comet that Clemens maintained he and P. T. Barnum had leased. The writer, George William Blunt (1802–1878), was well qualified to serve as a navigator. His father, Edmund M. Blunt (1770–1860), had been a leading authority on navigation, and he himself began working on nautical publications at nineteen, remaining in that profession until 1866. He had also held several public offices relating to navigation ("Death of Geo. W. Blunt," New York *Times*, 20 Apr. 1878). Blunt's remarks about "Bowditch's Navigator" are not exaggerated; he helped his father edit numerous revisions of the standard navigational work for calculating latitude and longitude named after its original author, Nathaniel Bowditch (1773–1838).

Under fire for his appointments of corrupt officials, New York mayor William Frederick Havemeyer (1804–1874) would live only a few more months. Blunt probably mentioned Havemeyer because Clemens's comet sketch announced the awarding of "complimentary round-trip tickets" to several controversial politicians. The sketch also helped attract attention to Clemens's recently published political novel, *The Gilded Age*.

Always hungry for publicity, the showman P. T. Barnum also appreciated Clemens's sketch. On 16 July 1874, he wrote to Clemens, "I owe you a thousand thanks for taking me into partnership" and invited him to visit his home in Bridgeport, Connecticut.

8

Philadelphia Aug 10th

I have read it through—& what have you done? Instead of a choice slander on English manners & their infernal "I beg your pardon" &c, it is an unjust libel on the fairest government on which the sun ever shone (which is not saying too much) And who in heavens name is your "colleague" Some ——— who no one ever heard of whose name has been made illustrious by coupling it with yours,—& to what purpose To ruin your brilliant reputation There are in the book 3 good articles—for these I give *you* credit. There are 997 wretched infernal stupid idiotic ones for which I give the poor ~~lunatic~~ credit. The rest of the book was manufactured by a carpenter—or a chinee or worse.—

Respectfully yours
J. J. Winthrop.
Phila. Pa

Clemens's comment: Offensive postal card about Gilded Age.

This postcard responds to Clemens's first novel, *The Gilded Age* (1874), which he coauthored with Charles Dudley Warner (1829–1900). The unidentified writer objects to the novel's biting satire on greed and corruption in American politics.

9

Centerville, Meagher. Co. M.T.
Feb. 6th 1875.

Mark Twain,

Sir. I have just been reading Your "Roughing it," And I have laught untill the tears run down my cheeks at your confounded Oddities and lies. Beemis'es adventures with his Buffalo bull, fir-instance And Jim Blaines story of the Old ram Oh! get out, its enough to make a monkey laugh—And that land slide case

FIGURE 1. Markiss the Liar in *Roughing It*, 557. Collection of the author.

of Hyde and Morgans its bully. But I was sorry that you hadent got a little "tighter" and spun us a good yarn about the "maid of the milky way" or the "man in the moon" Their courtship fir instance. Or a yarn about the "Mermaid and Man"—You could have dovetailed them in somewhere and made it interesting, but never the less you will have his enough to account for any how. *God have mercy uppon your soul.* But I am afraid Mark you are a poor Reformer you aint good at the stick, witness when you threw away your pipe in the snow drift with poor Bllou and Ollendorff—But you aint alone in that respect. Then I think you are a very little lazey, or else you would have done that days work, and been a "Millionaire" If I were "Cal Higbie" I would curs you as long as I lived.—Mark do you think you would know a "Genuine Mexican Plug" from an American if you were to see one now? Ha, ha, ha. Oh! my buttons, Well Mark, to sume you up all in all, I think you have depicted yourselfe pretty well on page 557—*God have mercy on your Soule*

Your discription of California Life and cenes are good, I am an Old California Tramp myself and can appreciate the "eternal fitness of things" to a nicety— Your Old Friend Claggett is over, in Deer Lodge, Mining and lecturing once in a while, if he dident freese to death last winter.—Now Mark I want you to send

me your Autograph and Likeness, that I may have it to say: that I have the
Picture of the funniest man and the D——Dest liar in the World—

Lew. Griswold

P.S. I had to swallow two Whales an a young Porpoise to get up Brain material
for this effort, and if I dont get that Picter I shall weep and (Whale) for a
thousan years.

L.G.—

Excuse pencil, had no ink in cabin

Clemens's comment: Respectfully declined

An account of Clemens's years in the Far West, *Roughing It* (1872) is filled with tall
tales and embellishments of his actual experiences. The illustration to which Griswold alludes (figure 1) depicts a man hanging by his neck from a tree, wearing the
label "LIAR."

William Horace Clagett (1838–1901) was an attorney whom Clemens had befriended in Nevada. He later settled in Montana and served as the territory's delegate
to Congress. Chapters 27 and 29 of *Roughing It* mention him.

———

10

Medford, Mar. 15, 1875

Mr. Saml Clemens
Dear Sir:

A few young people in town are about forming a literary club, and as we
cannot decide upon a name, it was proposed that I should write to you and ask
your advice.

The object of the club is improvement combined with pleasure.

At our meetings we have an entertainment about an hour long, consisting of
declamations, readings, music &c., and then the rest of the evening is spent in
social amusements.

Several names have been proposed, but we cannot find an appropriate one.

If you will help us out, provided it does not inconvenience you too much, we
shall feel greatly indebted to you

Very truly yours,
S. P. Moorhouse
Sec.

Please address
S. P. Moorhouse
Box 956
Boston P.O.

Clemens's comment: This is the worst piece of cheek of all.

> Clemens hated being asked for biographical information and tips for talks at literary
> society meetings. His comment on this letter shows he tired of such requests at an
> early date, but his anger here may have been fueled by his suspicion that the letter was
> a disguised autograph bid. Its seventeen-year-old author, Stephen Percival Moor-
> house (1858–1928), was living with his father in Medford at the time of the 1880 cen-
> sus. He later worked as a bookkeeper and as credit manager in a dry goods store (U.S.
> Census reports [hereafter USCR]).

11

Chatham, Pittsylvania Co. Va.
March 18, 1875.

Mr. Clemens:
Respected Sir:—

Will you please become a kind patron to a young man, and send him to the
Art School at Munich for a season? I would be the happiest young fellow in the
world if you were to consent to do this. I believe I have in me the elements of a
first rate artist, and could demonstrate it if I but had the means to obtain a short
schooling, at least; and further think that in a year or so after leaving the
teacher I could repay you in part for your kindness.

I know that a smile will spring to your face upon reading this, but it is from
one who is using his best endeavors to find a way of reaching an academy where
the labor is of the severest kind, and where the most patient and studious young
artists go. To do this, is entirely beyond my means, and as I lack that quality of
assurance essential for the making of acquaintances who are socially above me,
can see no way of getting there.

My home is in Indianapolis, Ind., where my father, James Milleson, is
living. Of course I could not expect you to give this proposition any serious
consideration, until you knew something of the writer, but if you think
favorably of it, I would respectfully refer you to Mr. J. T. Elliott, Aetna Building, or to Mr. Robert Browning, Wholesale Druggist, 7 & 9 Washington St.,
both of Indianapolis.

The height of the absurdity in this letter (to the author of "Innocents Abroad" from an obscure stranger), may seem, to one disinterested, great; but my desire to attend a school of art is greater.

Respectfully, Your obedient Servant,
Royal H. Milleson
Chatham, Pittsylvania County, Virginia

Mr. Samuel L. Clemens,
Hartford, Conn.

Clemens's comment: Wants to be sent to Munich Art School.

Clemens received few letters soliciting patronage of the type requested here. He apparently ignored this appeal, but he did later support the European training of sculptor Karl Gerhardt (1853–1940). The present supplicant, Royal Hill Milleson (1849–1936), began his career as a journeyman printer on midwestern newspapers, eventually shifting to illustration and later to painting. By 1900 he was studying art at an academy in Chicago, where he achieved some success as a landscape painter ("Royal Hill Milleson—Painter," www.scanlanfinearts.com; accessed 22 April 2011). In 1912, he published *The Artist's Point of View*, an informal guidebook for aspiring painters; it contains an offhand mention of Mark Twain (p. 26). The brief book frequently discusses the importance of formal training and European views on art but never hints that Milleson himself studied art in Europe.

Milleson's letter enclosed a newspaper clipping about American artists in Munich that included a summary of expenses students could expect. The article was from a series of New York *Herald* articles on Munich art schools published in January–February 1875 and reprinted in other papers.

12

Poughkeepsie, N.Y.
2nd April, 1875.

Hon. S. L. Clemens.
Hartford, Conn.

Dear Sir:

As I am about to take a trip to Europe, where I expect to remain some two years, and will be a correspondent for a paper; I have taken the liberty of writing to you, as to whether you would object, to my using "*Col. Sellers*," for an assumed name; and, also, if you could give me some advice, as you have "gone through the mill," (*excuse* the *expression,*) and perhaps discovered some ideas, that would help one who has had but little experience. I have written before Debating Societies, (Essays) and all have been well received. Have read quite a number of Books on Travels, and, am only 20 years of age. Speak the German, Spanish, (or rather Mexican not a pure Spanish) Hungarian, (native language) and can read French but can not converse, but it would require but a very short time to acquire it in Paris.

> Hoping this has not inconvenienced you any,
> I beg, leave to remain
> Your Most O'b't servant
> Ladislaus W. Madarász
> 348 Mill. St.
> Po'keepsie, N.Y.

P.S. I took the name Col. Sellers, from your "Gilded Age," a splendid book, have read your "*Roughing it*," will read "*Innocence abroad*"

> L. W. M.

Clemens's comment: Wants to use "Col. Sellers" as a nom de plume.

> This request to borrow the name of a fictional character in *The Gilded Age* (1874) is unusual. The more so here, perhaps, because Colonel Sellers is a flamboyant optimist prone to failure. However, because John T. Raymond's *Colonel Sellers* play was much in the news during 1875, the name would have been an attention-getter.
>
> The letter's Iowa-born writer, Ladislaus William Madarász (1854–1900), belonged to a Hungarian American family centered in San Antonio, Texas. During the early 1870s, he studied at New York's Cornell University (*Ten-Year Book of Cornell University* [Ithaca, 1878], 92). His brother Louis Madarász (1859–1910) won some renown as a calligrapher (*The Madarasz Book* [Columbus, Ohio, 1911]). Ladislaus wrote to Clemens again on 7 April to thank him for granting the permission he had requested and invited him to visit San Antonio. Clemens's letter has not been found. In 1893, Madarasz married into a merchant family in Denver, Colorado. He died in Argentina seven years later (*The Genealogy of the Descendants of Henry Kingsbury* [Hartford, Conn., 1905], 456–457).

13

> Philada., PA., April 5 1875

DEAR SIR:

I am collecting the autographs of Men, prominent in the history of our Country, and you will confer a personal favor by enclosing me yours in duplicate, on the accompanying cards, which I shall ever appreciate with feelings of gratitude.

> Yours, Respectfully,
> A. J. Sellers
> No. 257 North Third Street.

To

S. L. Clemens, Esq'r

Please accept the accompanying p'c of Music with my compliments. A great amount of sport at my expense have you been the occasion of; *but I forgive you,* since there's "millions in it."

A J. S.

Clemens's comment: From Col. Sellers

> Most of this letter is a printed autograph request of the kind Clemens normally detested, but its handwritten postscript probably amused him. Clemens's fictional "Colonel Sellers" was a burlesque character in *The Gilded Age* (1874) whose trademark line was "There's millions in it!" Albert Jacob Sellers (1836–1908) was a real "Colonel Sellers." He had served in the Union Army during the Civil War, winning the Congressional Medal of Honor for heroism at Gettysburg and later earning promotion to brevet colonel. Afterward, he worked as a store clerk and bookkeeper in Philadelphia (militarytimes.com/citations-medals-awards, and U.S. Civil War Soldier Records and Profiles, Ancestry.com, both accessed 10 June 2011). The music and cards to which this letter alludes are now missing, so Clemens may have signed and returned Sellers's cards.

14

NEW-YORK TRIBUNE.

NEW YORK, Ap'l 7th 1875

My dear Mark:

You will look at the signature, and wonder who the audacious man is that addresses you as though he were an old friend. Well, I *am an old friend,* and you cant help yourself, though you never saw me.

But you will see me, Mark, as this is a year of jubilee with me and I am around among the people.

During the past *twenty years,* I have delivered over *600* public lectures in the different states of the Union upon the "improper use of hemp,"—otherwise called *Capital punishment.* And the *capital* part of the punishment was, that for the *six hundred lectures,* I received—the *applause* of the people, and that is more than many lecturers can do.

But then I made it lively for the hangmen. Those professional neck-breakists have "gone from our gaze" in Wisconsin, Iowa and Michigan, and they are begging for mercy in Minnesota, Illinois and Indiana, where they are forbidden to separate the "spinal column" of any individual unless the twelve men "good and true" (good as putty usually, and true to their stupidity) shall *unanimously recommend* the separation of soul and body. The good work goes on. But I am calling upon my brother lecturers with *vigorous* good nature. I pass the hat, I've got a large one. Hundred dollar bills changed, if requested—into *twenties* and all put in the hat. Geo William Curtis sends $25. Frothingham won't be outdone by Curtis and he sends his cheque for $25.

Mark: you need n't *send* any thing. I had rather call and receive it. I can't help it if I do love you. You shouldn't be so attractive. But I have a little prejudice against you after all. When you were abroad, report has it that you played "old Sledge" on the "grave of Adam" and euchred the Pope at Rome, by "dealing Jacks off the bottom of the pack" the same as we do in the West.

But I'll call and see you the latter part of the week. Ever thine,

Marvin H. Bovee.

I lecture in Boston the early part of next week.

Clemens's comment: From some bore who wants to destroy the death penalty— with an eye to his own future, doubtless.

A Wisconsin farmer who served one term in his state senate, Marvin Henry Bovee (1827–1888) began a nationwide campaign against capital punishment in 1859. He saw legislative victories in several states but was ultimately worn out by his reform efforts (Elwood R. McIntyre, "A Farmer Halts the Hangman: The Story of Marvin Bovee," *Wisconsin Magazine of History* 42, no. 1 [autumn 1958]: 3–12; *Dict. of Wisconsin History* online; accessed 5 May 2011). He apparently never met Clemens but wrote a second letter on 10 February 1876, restating his appeal. This time, Clemens commented: "From that inextinguishable dead beat who has infested legislatures for 20 years trying to put an end to capital punishment. | No answer"

George William Curtis (1824–1892) and the Reverend Octavius Brooks Frothing- ham (1822–1895) were contemporary lecturers. Bovee's letter also alludes to the tear- ful visit of *The Innocents Abroad*'s narrator to Adam's grave in Jerusalem's Temple of the Sepulchre (chapter 53). That passage does not mention "Old Sledge," a card game also known as seven-up. *Innocents* mentions euchre games in several chapters but nowhere in reference to the pope.

15

ATLANTA, GA. April 12th 1875

Mr. Clemens—
Dear Sir—

As this letterhead will tell you, I am on the ragged edge of sending a book of nonsense to the nonsense reading public. Being my first, with only a few years reputation as a humorous writer to back it, it needs all the stimulus possible. I

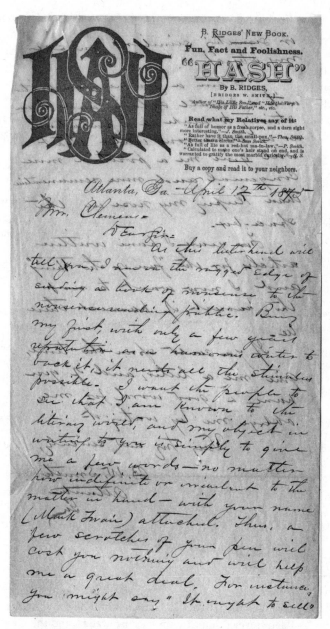

FIGURE 2. First page of letter from B. W. Smith. Courtesy of the Mark Twain Papers, Bancroft Library, University of California, Berkeley.

want the people to see that I am known to the literary world, and my object in writing to you is simply to give me a few words—no matter how indefinite or irrevelent to the matter in hand—with your name (Mark Twain) attached. Thus, a few scratches of your pen will cost you nothing and will help me a great deal. For instance, you might say "It ought to sell" or something similar—You see my object—

I am a journeyman printer with a small salary, and I am striving to make a reputation as a humorous writer that will give me a position more congenial and more remunerative than keeping my nose in the space-box.

For years I have written articles for the "fun of the thing" and I now want to reap the harvest, if harvest there be.

If you could spare the time, give me a letter, and if you have a good word for me, oblige me by writing it—

Very truly and sincerely,
B. W. Smith
Atlanta
Ga

Clemens's comment: From some unknown person who probably has brains & modesty in about equal proportions.

Clemens received many letters similar to this one. Its author, Bridges W. Smith (1848–1930), was a Confederate Army veteran who enjoyed a long career as a Macon, Georgia, *Telegraph* editor and also served as a judge and the mayor of Macon ("Bridges Smith, After Fifty Years of Newspaper Work," Macon *Telegraph,* 19 Oct. 1919; obituary, Augusta *Chronicle,* 8 Oct. 1930). During Smith's later years he wrote a daily column for the *Telegraph,* "Just 'Twixt Us," which occasionally mentioned Mark Twain. He published *HASH* under the name "B. Ridges" and probably designed his decorative letterhead (figure 2) and envelope himself, as he was an artist and collector of unusual envelopes.

16

Pittsburgh April 29th 1875

Sam'l L. Clemens Esq
Dear Sir—

I am very much indebted to you, in round numbers I should say about $50,000, and I wish I could pay you—It all comes of "Old times on the Mississippi"—I had traveled some on the western waters, and the same propensity that always lifted me to the top of a stage coach, carried me to the Pilot house; and I have been renewing my youth in your papers—

It will be no compliment to you to say that your reproduction of those scenes and characters is simply wonderful, but it may be when I tell you that I am laboring hard to convince my wife that it is not pure and unadulterated fiction—Woing her was easy work in comparison—

Very Respy yours,

T. B. A. David

Clemens's comment: About River Sketches

> This letter responds to Clemens's memoir of his apprentice steamboat piloting days, "Old Times on the Mississippi," serialized in the January–June and August *Atlantic Monthly.* Its author, Thomas B. A. David (born 1836), who had probably visited steamboat pilot houses only as a passenger, was born in Pittsburgh, Pennsylvania, and began working in a telegraph office at thirteen. At seventeen, he became manager of a Wheeling, Virginia, telegraph office, and he held a similar position in the Union Army during the Civil War (W. R. Plum, *The Military Telegraph during the Civil War in the United States* [Chicago, 1882], 145–146).

17

S. L Clemens,

Dear Sir

Altho' I have not the honor of yr acquaintance, I, take the liberty of remonstrating against yr refusal to contribute to the "Spirit of 76."

You sent me word that you are called upon "every day" for similar purposes. I reply that you cannot be aware of the nature of this application—for you have *never* been so called upon and never will be again. In fact you are called upon *thus* but Once in a *hundred years!*

I know not if Conn. be yr native state—(it is not mine)—yet being yr adopted home you should be as jealous of its honor and credit as if you were the 'child of the soil.' It is to this sentiment that our Journal must appeal, and I ask you to remember that it can be sustained only by the free will offerings of our literary and scientific men. If all these were to follow yr example—where wd the paper be. (I omit, from politeness, the adjective 'selfish' which I was going to put in before example!)

Of course you are busy!—what literary man is not?—If you were not busy you wd not be asked to write for this Journal.

I think, however, that you magnify the favor asked of you, and the time & labor it wd involve. There are to be but 12 numbers of the S of 76, and but two will be issued this summer. Then it will be regularly sent out from Feb to May 76, and the remaining numbers in July and Oct of that year.

If you cannot find 10 min for each number then do us the favor of finding it for the first number (June 1st) and afterward give us what you can, and allow me to put yr name upon the list of contributors.

Trusting that you will consent and give me a favorable answer—I am

Very respy,

Mrs John. S. Beach

124 Temple St

City.

May 14th 75

Contributors already *secured*

Revd Leonard Bacon

T D Woolsey

Prof Hoppin,

D Cady Eaton

Prof Nier

Revd Dr Harwood

Clemens's comment: From a coarse, impertinent woman with a patriotic mission.

Clemens received many requests to contribute cash or services to various causes. No other record of the 1876 Centennial project this letter discusses has been found, but Clemens evidently spurned an earlier request for help and may not have answered this letter.

Rebecca Gibbons Beach (1823–1893) married the prominent New Haven, Connecticut, attorney John Sheldon Beach (1819–1887) in 1847 (*Biog. Encyc. of Connecticut and Rhode Island* [New York, 1881], 359; "Died," New York *Times,* 7 Sept. 1893). Most of the "contributors" she names had Yale connections: Leonard Bacon (1802–1881) taught theology and church history there; Theodore Dwight Woolsey (1801–1889) was a former university president; James Mason Hoppin (1820–1906) taught homiletics and later art history; and Daniel Cady Eaton (1834–1895) taught botany. The Reverend Edwin Harwood (c. 1822–1902) was rector of New Haven's Trinity Church. Prof. Nier has not been identified.

18

Warrenton Ga

Nov 17th 1875

Salm. L. Clemens Esqr

Dear Sir:

Excuse the liberty I take in writing to you but I must give way to my "whim" and write.

I have read two of your works viz, "Inocents Abroad" and "Roughing It." I am pleased with both and often have cried while reading it. For instance, In the latter book when yourself & companions were lost in a snow storm and asked each other to meet you in Paradise, I could not refrain from giving vent to tears. In your quaint style of writing one moment I would be in tears while the next in laughter

Now, Mr. Clemens, I hope you do not think me a *"non est"* or *"non compos mentis"* but I must ask you to write to me. Tis true we are unknown to each other yet when I intend making a tour around the world I will pay your expenses to have the felicity derived from you as a companion

I have not yet finished my college course yet can find sufficient time to devote to you and your letters.

Let me hear from you soon stating I can claim you as a correspondent

Truly yours

Thos. S. Hubert

Box 7B

Warrenton Geo

Warren Co

Even younger at the time than his letter suggests, Thomas Shivers Hubert (1860–1953) became a Protestant minister at nineteen. He later graduated from Vanderbilt University and was a Baptist pastor in Alabama, Kentucky, Georgia, and Florida (www.floridabaptisthistory.org/biographies, accessed 30 April 2011). His letter alludes to a passage in chapter 32 of *Roughing It* in which prospectors repent of their vices when they seem certain to die in a blizzard, only to relapse the moment they are saved.

19

Union Springs, Ala.,

Nov. 21st:/75.

Sir:

I have written a book and can't get it published. What, do you suppose, is the cause of my failure? It is a novel—the *book* I mean—and is sensationally perfect. In fact, it is so far ahead of most of the "roughing it" species of publications, that I am amazed beyond measure, at the refusal of the publishers to issue it. How did you manage to get your first work before the public? It is a "dark and bloody mystery" to me; and I would like you to explain. Perhaps if you let me into the secret I may succeed with mine. My cousin Willie (I live with him and his wife) says it is because your writings are sensible; which is a polite and delicate way he has of expressing his opinion of my own. He paid me a dubious compliment the other day. I happened to quote you on something we were discussing; and he said I was the only woman he knew who had sense enough to appreciate Mark Twain.

Where are Dan and Jack? Are they married? If not, I will send them a valentine if you will tell me where and how to direct, and keep the secret. I don't want to get up a flirtation. I am not sweet sixteen. I am practical twenty-six; but I like a little innocent fun; and a valentine from this far-a-way place would puzzle them. Moreover, I am sorry for Dan; he's so awful ugly; and there is a bond of sympathy between Jack and I, on account of that turtle. I found him a fraud, too. Why didn't you favor(?) the public with a likeness of yourself? My cousin's baby cries sometimes, and I always make the nurse get Dan's picture, and show her. It scares her into silence. I often wish I had yours.—

To be serious, I really like your works. How I wish I could have gone with you to the old world; but as I could not, I would like you to know how much I thank you for writing out your trip. I plead guilty to being romantic; but I believe I am more ambitious than romantic; and I wish you *would* help me with a little advice about my book. I am not able to pay beforehand, for its publication, and I don't know whether I could do anything with it, unless I had money. Can I, do you think? Please be so obliging as to tell me. I have no friend who is informed in such matters.

Are you going to the Centennial? Then, come to see us. We are only forty miles from Montgomery. An amusing incident occurred while you were in the latter city; and as it relates to yourself, you might like to hear it; but my letter is already too long.

I shall be glad to have you reply, if not too much trouble. I am quite considerate. I do not want to give any one trouble.

Respectfully
Louise Rutherford.

P.S. Direct in care W. C. Bower, or in care "*Bower and Pitts.*"

L. R.

Beg pardon. My respects to Mrs T.

Clemens's comment: From a muggins in Alabama.

This request for advice on getting published is typical of many that plagued Clemens. Its author, Louise Rutherford, is difficult to identify beyond the fact she was born in Alabama around 1850 and probably lived with a cousin named William C. Bower (1839–1905), a dry goods merchant. Her professed fascination with the "Dan" and "Jack" frequently mentioned in *The Innocents Abroad* (1869) is also difficult to account for, as little about Dan's picture in the book (figure 3) should have appealed to a young woman. Dan and Jack were Clemens's *Quaker City* companions Dan Slote (c. 1828–1882) and Jack Van Nostrand (c. 1850–1879). Chapter 47 of *Innocents* describes

DAN.

FIGURE 3. Dan in *Innocents Abroad*,
288. Collection of the author.

Jack clodding a Holy Land mud turtle for not singing, because of his misconstruction
of the biblical passage about "the voice of the turtle [being] heard in our land" (Sol.
2:12). Rutherford's mention of Clemens's having visited Montgomery is puzzling, as
Clemens never set foot in Alabama.

20

Middletown, Conn. Jan. 25/76.

Dear Sir

I have taken the liberty to forward to you by mail, a little book, not as a
sample, nor for review exactly, but to do as you please with. I do, however, desire
to say a word on business. I have spent several winters in Florida, and have seen
the tourist and native elements in all their phases, and am confirmed in the
opinion that the pen that produced the "Innocents Abroad" should write up
Florida. It is the richest field now open to such a pen, and the harvest is ripe for
the sickle,—or thereabouts.

What I would like to propose is, to be brief, that you take a tour down there
this winter—3 or 4 weeks will do if you do not wish to stay longer—and write a
book on Florida, and I should like to assist and take a certain share in the sale
of the book. There is plenty of material and a large market, and the assistance I
could give would be to furnish information of incidents and localities to be put

into shape by you. You will very naturally think this proposition presumptuous, but I simply wish to say that I am willing to take the risk of the sale of the book for my remuneration, and have no doubt of a satisfactory adjustment of what that share should be. I can give you plenty of crude material. I would undertake the publishing of the book, or have it published by any house you choose.

I am not a literary man, as you see, but could be of assistance in the way indicated.

It is a good thing. Messrs. Burr Bro⁵. of the Hartford Times, and especially Mr. Frank L. Burr, can tell you all about me.

Will you be kind enough to answer; and if you should entertain the subject I can come to Hartford at any time to see you farther about it. Would like to come anyway, but do not wish to bore you uselessly. If you wish to go to Florida, and are willing to go by water, and can go within say a fortnight (just in time for the heighth of *the season*) I could furnish you with a ticket from N.Y. to Palatka & return, free; but I have no doubt you could go by either route on the same terms, if you chose. An early answer will greatly oblige

Yours very truly
C. C. Hubbard
Middletown, Conn.

S. L. Clemens, Esqr.
Hartford, Conn.

Clemens's comment: No

Clemens received frequent proposals to collaborate on publishing projects, but this one is more concrete than most and came from a man clearly capable of backing it up. A prosperous Connecticut hardware manufacturer and politician, Charles Carroll Hubbard (1832–1898) was mayor of Middletown at the time he wrote. Earlier, he had served in both houses of the state legislature and was elected state comptroller. He was later appointed collector of the port of Hartford by President Grover Cleveland (obituary, Hartford *Courant*, 1 Oct. 1898). During the mid-1870s, the Middletown *Daily Constitution* reported at least three extended trips Hubbard made to Florida with his family.

Alfred E. Burr and Frank L. Burr were coproprietors and editors of the Hartford *Courant*. Apart from a brief stop at Key West during an 1866–1867 sea voyage, Clemens's only visit to Florida occurred in March 1902, when he rode a train to Miami to meet his friend Henry H. Rogers's yacht *Kanawha*.

21

Cambridge May 17, 1876.

Mr. Clemens,
Dear Sir,

I am going to make bold to ask of you a great favor. I wish to publish a small sheet, say, about 16x22 inches—divided into four pages of three columns each.

And I wish your permission to use the title (Mark Twain) as editor. I want you to furnish such matter as would in your own opinion, be suitable, for such a paper, as I wish to have this filled with your fun and sentiment. I, shall, if you oblige me, sell them at Philadelphia, this summer, and I assure you that everything shall be conducted in such a manner as you would agree to. There shall be no advertisements in the paper—but all space shall be filled with reading matter. Paragraphs can be selected from other Authors, which will lessen your labors, somewhat. The matter need not of necessity, all be fresh, but of course you will use your own judgment in that matter.

I am aware that in presuming to ask such a favor of you, since your time must be so completely occupied that I am rather audacious, and perhaps, impertinent. But if you can possibly find it in your power to grant me the request—I shall consider it a great—and lasting favor, for which you will have my sincere thanks.

I will allow you what remuneration you consider just and right, either paying you a certain sum at the start or allowing you a percentage on the sales—

If you think it best and necessary I will come to Hartford and see you, about the plan. I hope and trust that you will grant me this favor, and greatly oblige,

Your Obedient Servant
Charles. S. Babcock.
53. Holyoke st. Cambridge
Mass.

P.S. Please drop me a card giving me your own opinion in the matter.
Respectfully,

C. S. B.

Clemens's comment: From a muggins

This letter's eighteen-year-old writer, Charles S. Babcock, was the son of John Martin Luther Babcock (1822–1894), a printer, former Unitarian minister, and radical Free Thinker who published *The New Age,* a newspaper focusing on social and labor reform issues ("Burned Alive: Rev John M L Babcock Meets with a Horrible Fate," Boston *Journal,* 4 April 1894; "John M. L. Babcock," *Groton Historical Series* [Groton,

1899], 281–282). On 22 May, the younger Babcock again wrote to Clemens, who had evidently replied to his first letter by postcard. Babcock's second letter added details about his plan, pressing Clemens to respond quickly. This time, Clemens remarked, "This is the Orion style of ass"—doubtless thinking of his brother Orion's many failed schemes for making money. No record of Babcock's magazine's being published has been found.

22

WOODRUFF & STEWART,
ATTORNEYS AT LAW,
ODD FELLOWS' TEMPLE.

COLUMBUS, O., June 14th 1876

Samuel L. Clemens Esq
Hartford Conn

Sir:

I trust you will pardon an entire stranger for intruding upon your attention but I cannot send you the enclosed paper without an explanation.

I am the fortunate possessor of a copy of your book called "Roughing It" in my library; and having within a year moved into a new neighborhood, have had the privilege of loaning the most of my books to my neighbors. Among others I loaned "Roughing It" and in due course of time it was returned. I may here state that I am living in a portion of the city which is mostly inhabited by Quakers. Last Sunday was the first time I had looked at the book since it had been returned, and I opened it to the find upon the fly leaf the enclosed commentary upon the book. Knowing that as an author you would appreciate honest criticism upon your writings I tore out the fly leaf and take the liberty of herewith presenting it to you. The names signed to it are those of the principal Quakers in my neighborhood, who are doubtless very much concerned for my welfare, since reading "those lies." Again hoping that you will pardon me for thus addressing you

I remain
Yours
Gilbert H. Stewart

P.S. Supposing that up to this time the fly leaf is mine you have my full permission to print it in any future edition of "Roughing It" among the recommendations.

Gilbert H. Stewart
Columbus Ohio

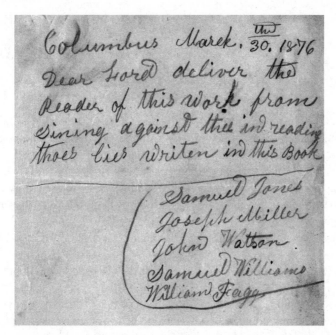

FIGURE 4. The suspicious flyleaf from *Roughing it*. Courtesy of the Mark Twain Papers, Bancroft Library, University of California, Berkeley.

This letter seems to involve a hoax, but its perpetrator is difficult to identify. The letter is accompanied by an ostensible flyleaf from *Roughing It* (figure 4) on which is penciled: "Columbus Marek. 30th. 1876 | Dear Lord deliver the Reader of this work from sining against thee in reading thoes lies writen in this Book | Samuel Jones | Joseph Miller | John Wattson | Samuel Williams | William Fagg." Census reports list working-class men with these names in Columbus, but precise identifications are not possible. Clemens did not annotate the letter but may have suspected the flyleaf message was a hoax, as its message and signatures were apparently written by the same hand. Moreover, the note's 30 March date suggests that whoever borrowed the book may have intended for its owner, Gilbert Holland Stewart Sr. (1847–1912), to read the note on April Fools' Day. Stewart himself seems an unlikely hoaxer. A prominent Ohio attorney, he would later be elected a circuit judge and serve as chief justice of the Circuit Court of Ohio. He would also teach medical jurisprudence at a Columbus medical school and publish several books on law ("Gilbert H. Stewart, Sr.," *Ohio State Bar Assoc. Mid-Winter Meeting, 1913,* 156).

23

149st near Courtland Ave. N.Y. City.

7th June. 1877.

Mr. Samu'l Clemens,

Dear Sir:

I have a book, like and unlike, the Pilgrims Progress, and call it, "Entranced, a Romance of Immortality." I am a poor Presbyterian minister, for whom you once brought a watch from George MacDonald.

I recently read aloud the story in your last book, of the boy who took a whipping for a girl at school, and it was Sabbath Evening, in the family of Mr Wiles up the Hudson River, where I was preaching, and we all cried over it, before prayers.

I thought you might like mine, and get that great Am. Publ. Co. to like it too.

Very. Rev. A. P. Stanley, of Westminster, wrote me a good letter about it, when he read it, and so did Dr Loyden of Bradford.

P. W. Zeigler of Pa, agreed to take it, but is not able to do so now. If you just *would* read it, it might make me *almost* as famed as you are. *Yes,* on a postcard, and I will tell Dr Rand, of Am. Tract Society to send it to you.

Respectfully.

Henry W. Cleveland.

Clemens's comment: No *sir!*

This is the first of six preserved letters from Henry Whitney Cleveland (1836–1907), whom Clemens came to regard as a pest. In his 9 August 1877 letter, Cleveland offered "to be the Slave of the Lamp . . . to only be your clerk and humble helper, with only such pay as you please." That letter also suggested that Clemens publish in his own name a play Cleveland had written, "if you will write some fun in it." His later letters became so annoying that Clemens eventually dismissed him as the "Reverend D—d tramp." Cleveland's August 1877 letter also describes his long struggle to find success, claiming he once owned fifty thousand dollars in property, became a Presbyterian minister, edited newspapers, practiced law, served in the Confederate Army, and was a friend of the Confederacy's president and vice president. Whatever the truth of his claims, he was also a struggling writer whose most notable publication may have been a poem in the October 1875 *Atlantic Monthly.* He later became well known as an autograph collector (obituary, New York *Tribune,* 21 March 1907). In the present letter Cleveland compares his unpublished book "Entranced" to *The Innocents Abroad,* whose subtitle was "The New Pilgrims' Progress." Cleveland pitched his same book to Clemens again on 20 September 1888.

George MacDonald (1824–1905) was a clergyman and writer whom Clemens befriended in 1873. Cleveland's allusion to the watch is cryptic, but his tendency to drop names familiar to Clemens may have been an attempt to suggest an intimacy that did not exist. The whipping story Cleveland mentions is from chapter 20 of *Tom Sawyer* (1876), in which Tom saves Becky Thatcher from punishment by confessing to something he did not do. Cleveland also mentions Arthur Penrhyn Stanley (1815–1881), the Church of England's dean of Westminster; P. W. Zeigler & Co., a Philadelphia publishing firm; and William W. Rand, secretary of the publishing committee of the American Tract Society, which distributed Christian literature.

24

Dennis, Mass. Aug 27, 1877

Mr. Sam¹ L. Clemens
otherwise Mark Twain;
Dear Sir

We are two sin twisters (we meant to write twin sisters) of Cape Cod, have lived here all our lives with a few interruptions; we never went to a big city, never saw a publisher, are afraid of big cities and publishers. But something happened in this locality a while ago that we have written into a book and want dreadfully to publish. So we want to know if you will let us send you the M.S.S. and read it and approve it and send it to that unknown animal the publisher and tell him to put it in print. We should not know what to say to one, we should feel as scared as you did the night of your first lecture as described in "Roughing it." Now we haven't any one to laugh for us unless you will laugh, and we haven't anyone to pound our genius into the publisher's brain, unless you will pound. Will you laugh? While you pound? (Tears of entreaty fall at this point) and *will* you answer this brassy epistle? (We acknowledge it is brassy "should not have written in this style to Mark Twain one of the Authors of Ah Lin—and lots of other sins" I hear you say.[)] however we humbly implore your pardon and on bended knees and awful big tears beseech you to answer by return mail.

We read "Roughing it" all last Winter wept each time we came to the end—if you had only kept on writing more of it, it would have been the best book in the World it beats Dickens works all "holler."

Will you have the kindheartedness and disinterestedness to ask Mr Bret Harte if he will send us his parody on the May Queen as we lent our copy to Aunty Carber and she's lost it—it is so tremendously pathetic we cannot possibly live without it, and we should admire a copy of the "Gilded Age" but I dont know as the publishers give you an extra one? do they?

Our Book is not very long but very remarkable like your play Oh! that we could see *that play.* We cant write any more for we've both got the "Epic-zootic." Dont forget to answer.

The ardent admirers of "Roughing it"—"Innocents Abroad" &c &c.

S. T. Crowell,

E. Gayle

(Innocents at Home)

Please direct to Dennis—Cape Cod, Mass.

Clemens's comment: Villains

This letter's allusion to Clemens's fright before his first lecture reflects his embellished account in *Roughing It*, but the actual lecture was a great success. The correct title of the play the letter mentions is *Ah Sin, the Heathen Chinee*, which Clemens coauthored with Bret Harte. It had a one-week run in New York in May 1876 but ran for four weeks several months later. Harte published his poem "The May Queen (Adapted to a Backward Season)" in 1875. *Epizootic* was a term for physical ailment.

The authors of this letter have proved elusive. One may well have been the Sarah Thomas Crowell (1842–1924) of Dennis, Massachusetts, listed in 1860–1880 and 1900–1920 censuses as the wife and later widow of grocer Uriah Howes Crowell (1843–1872) and mother of four. However, an 1870 census report for nearby Boston lists another Sarah T. Crowell (born 1841) as the wife of mariner Dennis Crowell and the next-door neighbor of an Emma Josephine Thomas Gale. An 1880 census report lists that Crowell as a widow living *with* Emma Gale, who is described as an "authoress" (USCR; Findagrave.com).

25

SANCTUM OF WILL CLEMENS.

FOREIGN STAMP DEALER

NEWSPAPER CORRESPONDENT. EDITOR OF THE SUNNYSIDE.

AKRON, O., Nov. 26th 1877.

To "That Uncle of mine"

Dear Mark;

I have just finished the "Gilded age," for the second time, and I am determined to write to you, not, for the sake of the book but to form an acquaintance with yourself.

I am a young man of 18, or a boy in his teens, just as you like it.

As you will perceive I belong to the band of rising young journalists that infest this land of wine and women. I am also an author just budding you know, and my favorite style is the humorous, but this I cannot help for "They all duet," the Clemens' I mean.

FIGURE 5. Cover of Will Clemens's *Mark Twain*. Courtesy of
Kevin MacDonnell.

I have published a minature journal for boys & girls but it has gone where the
potato vine sprouteth. But of all this nonsense I am through, and I earnestly
wish you will answer one who bears your name.

Very truly Yours
Will Clemens, Akron, Ohio.

Clemens's comment: ~~an~~ curiosity | No answer required

This is the first of at least thirteen letters William (Will) Montgomery Clemens
(1860–1931) wrote to Samuel L. Clemens between 1877 and 1909. Although Will's letters were always respectful, his persistent attempts to capitalize on Clemens's famous

name became increasingly annoying. On 7 January 1881, for example, he capped a long account of his struggles as a writer with the suggestion that Clemens hire him as "a private secretary in the broadest sense that the name implies. It would not only be a God send to me—give me a chance at fame (as it were)." His introduction to his book *Famous Funny Fellows* (1882) tells how after Clemens declined his invitation to write a brief introduction, he quoted Clemens's letter within his own introduction without permission. Will also published his second book (figure 5), *Mark Twain: The Story of His Life and Work* (1892), without Clemens's approval. That book further irritated Clemens, who was protective of his personal biography, but Will was not done trying to exploit Clemens's name.

In a 13 June 1900 letter to his friend Henry H. Rogers, Clemens said of Will, "Clemens can't write books—he is a mere maggot who tries to feed on people while they are still alive." In his 28 July 1900 letter to Samuel E. Moffett, his nephew by marriage, he called Will "that singular tapeworm who seems to feed solely upon other people's intestines & who seems to be barren of any other food-supply," and he added, "I wonder what this bastard's real name is." When Will wrote to Clemens on 19 September 1907, Clemens wrote on his letter, "This is that Will M. Clemens who was born a fraud & will remain one." No kinship between Will and Samuel Clemens can be established, but the fiction that Will was Clemens's nephew was repeated in Will's published obituaries.

A native Ohioan, Will Clemens was a journalist, genealogist, and hack biographer. After graduating from college, he had a twenty-year career on newspapers in Pittsburgh, Cleveland, Los Angeles, and San Francisco. His later years he devoted to founding and editing magazines and writing articles and books, including biographies of Theodore Roosevelt and Admiral George Dewey ("W. M. Clemens Dies; Kin of Mark Twain," Trenton, New Jersey, *Evening Times,* 25 Nov. 1931; "W. M. Clemens Dies," New York *Times,* 25 Nov. 1931; *Who Was Who in America,* vol. 1, *1897–1942* [Chicago, 1942], 230).

26

Elkhill Saline Co Missouri

Dec 4th 1877

"Mark Twain"

Dear Sir,

Is there the slightest probability of your writing and publishing any other books. "Innocents Abroad" "Roughing It" & "The Gilded Age" have about up-set our youngest brother Frank (the youngest of nine)—a youth of seventeen, now six feet two in his stocking-feet, and like yourself, a "Missouri puke," "and to the manner born."

If you contemplate issuing any more books like those above mentioned please let us know in due time in order that we may get him out of the way— send him to Patagonia—or some other region where access to them will be impossible. Some time since—the Judge—*pater familias*—gave him ten dollars to invest in books to suit his own fancy. At first he thought of buying an illustrated copy of Bunyons Pilgrims Progress, but on reflection, being religiously inclined, gave your works the preference. He has since read them forty times, and then re-read them backwards and cross-ways. He has literally read them to peices. It would, or ought to, do your heart good to see them,—the books, He is so chuck-full of them, that no matter what may be under discussion in our familiar after-supper controversies,—whether, law, politics, literature, or divinity, the Holy land, the life of Christ, or the silver bill,—five minutes cannot elapse without his putting in, "Mark Twain says so & so &c &c,"—a delightful grin immediately enlightening his countenance. He is worse than old Claude Halcro, and his immortal John Dryden.

To cap the climax he has begun writing a book of his own, and takes yours for his models. Can't you wean him from his folly, "We feel hot."

Let us hear from you.

> Yours excitedly
> John Napton.
> H. P. Napton.
> C. Mc. Napton.
> L. W. Napton

N.B.
Seriously,—we all read and like your books almost as much as Frank. Our Address Marshall Saline C°. Mo

Clemens's comment per Fannie C. Hesse: Curiosity | answered Dec 9th 1877
Clemens's comment on envelope back: John Smith et al

The signers of this letter were sons of the Missouri state supreme court judge William Barclay Napton Sr. (1808–1883), after whom Napton, Missouri, is named (C. Phillips and J. L. Pendleton, eds., *The Union on Trial: The Political Journals of Judge William Barclay Napton* [Springfield, Mo., 2005]). The father may have been a Clemens fan, too. A law journal editorial applauded Napton's ruling in a riparian rights case, remarking that "the formation of alluvion by 'avulsion' reminds one too much of the land slide in Mark Twain's book, where one man's ranch slid down the mountain and covered up another's, the avulsionist all the while sitting on his gate-post, waving his hat at his unfortunate neighbor" (*Central Law Jnl.* [St. Louis, 10 Dec. 1875], 1; see also *Roughing It*, chapter 34).

Judge Napton's nine children included seven sons who eventually relocated to the Far West. Frank Napton (1860–1938)—the subject of this letter—later became city clerk of Polson, Montana, before settling into ranching in Oregon. He apparently never published the book to which the letter alludes. John Napton (1843–1917) briefly ranched with two brothers in Montana before resettling in Missouri as a farmer. Harry P. Napton became the law partner of another brother, Thomas Lanier Napton (1841–1888), in Montana. Charles McClung Napton (1847–1907) also practiced law in Montana before settling in St. Louis, Missouri. Lewis William Napton (1857–1938) became a farmer in Idaho (Phillips and Pendleton, *The Union on Trial*, 572–573).

Claud Halcro is a character in Walter Scott's 1821 novel *The Pirate* who shares his enthusiastic reminiscences of the poet John Dryden (1631–1700).

————

27

Florida Mo Jan 20th—78

Mr Saml Clemens—

At the solicitation of my two little girls I send you a picture of your birth-place cut by them from my county map. They say they are certain you will send them, each one a nice Chromo & also a photograph of yourself, in return. I knew you when you were a boy & remember hunting with you at your uncle's John A. Quarles'—The old man is, as I suppose you have probably heard, dead,—has been dead about a year. He failed in business & lived for many years in a state of poverty. None of his family ever did very much in business, Ben & Polk are still living Jim is dead, Tabitha or Pap youngest daughter is living—

Florida boasts greatly of being your birth-place & there has been of late quite a little discussion in the Co papers as to what part had that honor. Your letter to Mr Holliday of St Louis of course settled the question—It was published in the papers.

Florida jogs along after the same old style & sits like Rome on her hills,—always the same. The picture of your old house is true to nature & it is to this day the same as you see in the picture to the minutest particular. It is now occupied by the village shoe maker—there is no telling what *other great man* may go forth from beneath its eaves—The man in the street is intended to represent you off on your pilgrimage after style of your speech at meeting in honor of poet Whittier. The little girls say dont forget *those pretty Chromos* for they will wait with patience to hear from you. I live at & own the mill owned by Boyle Goodwin on the north fork of Salt River.

Yours truly

Joseph G. Hickman

In 1906, Clemens remarked that for thirty years he had received a dozen letters a year from strangers claiming to have known him as a boy, but he rarely remembered any of those people. He may have exaggerated how many such letters he received, but the present letter was from an authentic resident of his Florida, Missouri, birthplace. Joseph G. Hickman (born c. 1838) owned a prosperous Florida saw mill his family had purchased from a man named Boyle Goodwin around 1852 (USCR; *History of Monroe County,* chapter 6, "Jefferson & Indian Creek Townships" [1884; at www.rootsweb.ancestry.com/~monroe/history, accessed 20 May 2011]). In 1878, Hickman's daughter Betty was about thirteen and his daughter Frankie about eleven. He also had a younger son, Willie. Hickman's enclosures are lost, and the county map from which he cut a picture of the house in which Clemens was born has not been identified. A house believed to have been his birth home is now preserved inside a museum in Florida's Mark Twain Birthplace State Historic Site. John Quarles (1802–1876), the brother-in-law of Clemens's mother, owned a farm outside Florida where Clemens spent most of his summers as a youth. Mr. Holliday's identity is uncertain.

Hickman's remark about Whittier alludes to the seventieth birthday banquet for John Greenleaf Whittier on 17 December 1877 at which Clemens delivered a burlesque speech recalling an imaginary visit to an isolated Nevada miner who had recently encountered three uncouth ruffians posing as Ralph Waldo Emerson, Oliver Wendell Holmes, and Henry Longfellow.

Clemens may not have replied to this letter, but a letter he wrote to Hickman on 24 July 1881 has been preserved. It is a belated reply to another letter from Hickman, now lost. Clemens sent Hickman a twenty-five-dollar donation to the "Florida Literary Association" along with information on cheap books the association could buy.

28

[Gowanda, New York?]
Jan. 21.

Mark Twain,

Dear Sir;

I got hold of a Circular which advertised your Scrap Book, and by it I was enveigled into sending for one; It arrived today. I've used it. I am a plain minister of the gospel, and I wish to say, *I never swore any more in my life than I have today.* I am as fond of fun as you are, but when it comes to be so serious a matter—this Scrap Book affair—*I* must pause. Certainly your Scrap Book with nothing but gummed lines is a very funny book—probably the funniest book you ever made, but, my dear Twain, why didn't you tell folks not to moisten your gummed lines with their fingers. I got stuck to those *gummed lines.*—I cant help emphasizing *gummed*—I have about three hundred sympathizing parishioners, counting men, women and babies, and they've all been in—every one of them, with lots of their neighbors, to get me away from your awful Scrap Book; but I am stuck fast. For two hours and nine minutes I have been flying about this house frantically and fruitlessly endeavoring to get loose from your *gummed lines.*

Already your Scrap Book is advertised all over this town and my greatest fear is that somebody else will get fast!

Why did n't you tell people how to handle the dangerous thing? I've an engagement to lecture to-morrow night, and, unless I break loose, I shall have to carry this product of your wicked brain to the very platform. If I must, I must, but be assured I shall flutter this horrid leech of a Scrap Book in the face and

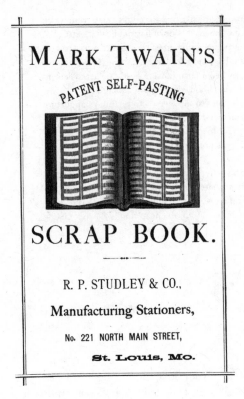

FIGURE 6. Advertisement for Mark Twain's self-pasting scrapbook. Courtesy of Kevin MacDonnell.

eyes of my audience, and say, "This, my friends, is Mark Twain's Patent Scrap Book."

Yours, etc.
John Wentworth Sanborn.

Clemens's reply:

Hartford, Jan. 24.

'Sh! Dont say a word—let the others get "stuck." I'll tell you privately, to use a wet rag or brush—but let us leave the others to get into trouble with their fingers. Then they will abuse the Scrap Book everywhere, and straightway everybody will buy one to give to his enemy, and that will make a great sale for the inventor, who will go to Europe and have a good time.

Yours truly,
Mark Twain.

Clemens tinkered with several inventions, the most successful of which was the self-pasting scrapbook he patented in 1873 (figure 6). Sold in a variety of sizes and formats, the scrapbooks had pages with printed glue strips users dampened to mount pictures and clippings. It is easy to imagine someone getting a hand stuck on a page—at least momentarily. (See also letter 143.)

John Wentworth Sanborn (1848–1922), a Methodist Episcopal minister until 1908, was known as an authority on Indian culture after doing missionary work among the Seneca in Western New York. He published poetry, books on American Indians, and textbooks on classical languages ("Meet Methodist Minister John Wentworth Sanborn," www.smethporthistory.org, accessed 13 June 2011). He later gave Clemens copies of his *Legends, Customs and Social Life of the Seneca Indians of Western New York* (1878) and *The Method of Teaching the Elements of the Latin Language* (1881). Both Sanborn's and Clemens's letters are known only from Sanborn's self-published book *Distinguished Authors Whom I Have Known* (Friendship, N.Y., 1920). Sanborn wrote at least five more letters to Clemens through early 1882.

29

Hartford
March 12th 1878.

Dear Mr. Twain! Friends good & true,
  With blood more thick than water,
Have heard what you intend to do
  And think you had'nt ought to.

We prize you highly as a man,
  And as a Citizen.
We make you happy as you can
  Why will you quit us then?

The Foreigners may not afford
  To meet you with such cheer.
And spread your Inner-sense abroad
  So see do—far and near

Sweet Mrs. Twain—to you we come
  And ask your Clemency,
Do'nt leave the charming, lovely home,
  Where the little Clemens' be.

If all our pleading is in vain,
  And fails to reach your pity.

In losing Twain, we must remain
A broken Heart
ford City.

Clemens's comment: Scrapbook it

> This anonymous message was probably sent by a Hartford resident who knew the
> Clemens family would depart in April for a long European trip. The message was
> written on the same day that the Middletown *Daily Constitution* reported the fami-
> ly's imminent trip.

30

To
Mr. Samuel L. Clemens alias Mark Twain:

Please to excuse that I fall with the door in the house, without first to begin
with the usual long ribble-row. I want to become the autograph of the over alle
the world well known Mark Twain, whose narratives so apt have procured me a
laughter.

If you will answer this letter, I will be very glad. Answer me what you will;
but two words. If you not will answer me other so write only, that you do not
like to write autographs.

Your
Carl Jensen

Ans.
C. Jensen, custom officer
Stubbekjobing in Falster
Denmark
Europe

Clemens's comment: Preserve this remarkable letter.

> Clemens probably appreciated this letter, postmarked 1 October 1879, because of its
> curious syntax. Jensen's command of English was obviously limited, so he probably
> read Danish translations of Clemens's books. Between 1875 and 1879, Danish editions
> of *The Innocents Abroad, Roughing It, Tom Sawyer,* and *Sketches New & Old* were
> published in Copenhagen. In 1880, Danish editions of new Clemens titles began ap-
> pearing during the same years the books were published in the United States (Kevin
> Mac Donnell, personal communication, 10 June 2011).

31

E. P. DORR. JR

Buffalo New York
Sunday
November 16th

Dear Mr Clemens I have been wating for you to come home from Europe to write to you for your autograph I am ten years old I have a Colection of stones shells and autographs and I would like yours very much I have just been looking at one of your books I think the pictures are very funny My Grandpa just came home from California and brought me some more Curiosities one of them is a square peice of white stone with a fish petrified on it. and he brought me a lump of salt from the mines I have just got over the measeals I have not been to school for nine days.

Eben P Dorr
314 Niagara Street
Buffalo New York

PLEASE WRITE SOON

Clemens's comment: A boy's letter.

Clemens returned from Europe in September 1879. Eben Pearson Dorr was a member of a Buffalo, New York, family with a distinguished New England pedigree. He later worked for the Buffalo *Times,* published poetry, and was president of a naturalist club (*Magazine of Poetry* [Chicago], January 1894, 18). He is listed as a brass-bed salesman in a 1910 Chicago census report and as an "investigator" for the United States in a 1920 report. His "Grandpa" was Captain Ebenezer Pearson Dorr (1817–1881), a former Great Lakes mariner and leading figure in Buffalo's insurance industry, in which Eben's father also worked (Buffalo *Express,* 30 Mar. 1881). The illustrated book to which young Dorr alludes may be *Sketches New and Old* (1875), whose pictures later frightened young Fannie James (see letter 111).

32

My dear Sir
    Will you have the goodness to send me as fully as you may be able the history of y'r pseudonym—"Mark Twain." How it was originated when you first used it, & in what connection on all these points I sh. be exceedingly glad to be informed.

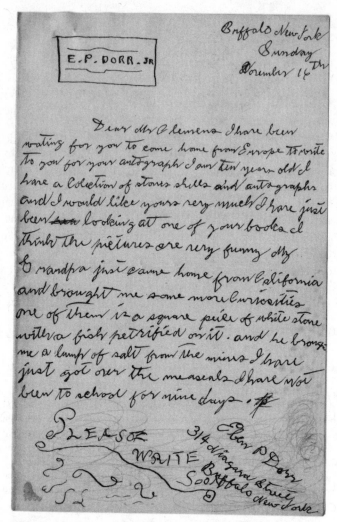

FIGURE 7. Letter from Eben P. Dorr. Courtesy of the Mark Twain Papers, Bancroft Library, University of California, Berkeley.

I am preparing a handy book on pseudonyms—to include the history of the more important ones—wh. the Harpers are to publish—and it is extremely desirable th. I have the information for wh. I ask.

With the hope th. I am putting you to no great inconvenience
Believe me Dear Sir
to be faithfully:
Rev. J. Dewitt Miller.
34 West—24th St
New York City,—

24 Nov. 1879

Clemens's comment: From an ass—Not answered

> Clemens usually simply ignored requests to explain his pseudonym. His evident irritation at this letter may be partly attributable to its insistent tone and annoying use of abbreviations.
>
> Jahu Dewitt Miller (1857–1911), was a freelance journalist, seminary teacher, and lay Methodist minister who became a popular lyceum lecturer and serious book collector. The fate of his pseudonym handbook is unknown. Clemens had sent Miller a photograph of himself in 1874; Miller's request for it is lost (Clemens to Miller, 2? Dec. 1874, *Mark Twain's Letters* [Berkeley, 2002], 6:302–303; L. H. Vincent, *Dewitt Miller: A Biographical Sketch* [Cambridge, Mass., 1912]).

33

New York City
Feby 6th/80

Mr Samual. L. Clemens
Mark Twain—
Dear Sir

It is well know among the colored People throughout the county that you have always spoken a word of kindness for them A few weeks ago i called upon you to secure if—Possible your cooperation with other men of Standing in the work of missions which we as a religious denominations are engage in throughout New-England States we have 24 places called mission fields. they afford religious instruction to our race. for in many places where there is but few or not more then a half dozen persons the access to white churches is easy and Desirable But if there be more then this number they are Timid—and the most of them will imagine that they are not wanting now. Sir the uneducated State of our people and there peculiar religious notions warrant us to secure places of worship, of our own, for the present. again our People could not get all perhaps that they might demand in white Churches more especially where there rented pews—

Under this Plane truth regarding my race, we call upon Christian friends and all others of the Amarican People throughout good Old New-England to help us bear this burden. beside this home work we have 200,000 Souls beyond the line who oftimes cry to us for help but those that clame our home attention throughout the State need our first care if nothing more then to arrest the young—I am pleased to inform you Sir the Mr. Thomas. Smith Esqur has head my list Followed by the Governor of the State and a large number of your Influenchel Citizens. I called upon you but family Sickness called you out of Town. I now ask your name donation to our cause which have been so willinglly aided by the Friends of Hartford. as you have always manifested true friendship for our race that has been wonce oppressed but now free, thank God, we know that so great Mani in the Litteray world as yourself will help our cause My head quarters is at Rv. R. R. Morris Pastor of Pearl St African M. E. Church No. 17, S. Am. St who will give your all Satisfaction as he is the Bishops. Secty

Direct to Rv. Thos. A. Davis
157, W. 24th St

I purpose of Publishing a rool of honor attached to our appeal

Res 157, W. 24th St

N.B. on account of Sickness i have been *unable to* move to my destrict

Clemens was inclined to be sympathetic toward African American correspondents, but the black pastor who sent him this and at least seven other letters between 1880 and 1889 tried his patience. On 7 February, Clemens forwarded this letter to Connecticut governor Charles B. Andrews (1834–1902), remarking, "I have been so often duped by strangers who used people's names without authority, that I [am] become cautious by compulsion. Will you kindly re-enclose the letter to me & tell me if you know Rev. Mr. Davis to be a responsible person?" Andrews replied four days later, saying he knew nothing of Davis.

An African Methodist Episcopal Zion Church pastor in New York City, Thomas A. Davis was born in Nova Scotia in c. 1837. Enclosed in his letter is a printed appeal for donations to his church. He later wrote from parsonages in Trenton, New Jersey, and Baltimore, Maryland. Whatever replies Clemens sent him have not been found, but Davis's 28 April 1887 letter acknowledged receipt of books from Clemens and asked for an additional cash donation. This later letter Clemens annotated "Rev. Davis the beggar."

The Friends of Hartford was a philanthropic organization that later helped preserve Clemens's Hartford home, which is now a public museum and research center. Davis's 17 March 1881 letter identifies the Reverend Morris as his cousin. The African Methodist Episcopal Church was another primarily black Protestant denomination not directly related to Davis's church.

34

Lancaster February 11th 1880.

Dear Mark.

I sit down to write to you once more.

In the Name of the Father and of the Son, and of the Holy Ghost, this is the third time I have written to you, and dont know whether you have received any or not. In my last letter I mention to you that it was your duty to let me know whether it was divine inspiration or the influence of the devil made me Address a gentleman I dont know However I am writing this through the influence of two stars, which I am going to tell you by and by if you have Patience to read my scribbling. I must tell you first Dear Mark, the substance of the first and second. The first I wrote some seven years ago and nailed it on the court house door. In said letter I beged of you to send me five dollars to use it in honor of the Blessed Virgin Mary.

And in my second letter I asked you to send me five dollars to buy a turkey and other eatables to make up a Plain dinner that I would cook, myself. Now Please dont laught sir. Although I am from the starving country, I don't want to eat myself God forgive me for laughing over this. Mark, I told you in my last letter that I want to cook a Plain dinner and invite the Rev. Bishop Shanna, the Rev. Henry Ward Beecher, the Rev. Father Hickey and the Rev. Doctor Green Wald, to take dinner together. As I am under the impression if the Reverent gentlemen mentioned be united the People all would be come blessed by John Wilkes Booth's Aid, and the information I have in Store to give John, which the People ought to know long before this. It is now too weeks next friday, since I Posted the letter and you didn't do your duty if you received the letter didn't answer it [canceled word] matter how bad it was written, I told you Jesus is my teacher So now although I have shed bitter tears often for the last week through the distress of my Poor country, I am not in despair as I am going to stay with Miss Miller until I will have the price of the dinner together if god leaves me my hearth, and may be He will as it will be for His own benefit Mark I have to invite seven. I have mention four, and 3 more which I have divine Authority to invite. And let them refuce to come if they think Proper I have to do my duty to invite President Hayes. As I have something important to tell President I have to invite Doctor Charls Nicholas Superintendent of Washington insane asylum to whom I gave a note which contained the words Jesus did speak on this Earth in St Louis 3 months before President Lincoln's death So if Doctor Nicholas isnt living Doctor Franken will do. So Mr Twain, I want you if you have no objection to head the table and carve the Turkey. I suppose I want two everything is convient in Mr Millers house, to entertain the best of People. all is needed is the eatables.

So now as I am not sure to whom I am writing I cant mention about the stars, as I have to tell John Wilkes Booth alone, about the tree, the star, and Jesus. Which will complate all, and if John wont come soon the tree is over right the room I am writing this in, will be soon, cut down as there is a new street to be made. However last night after I was done washing the supper dishes I came in this little room I am writing this in to get the lamp, as it was rather cold in the room to sew and I didnt want to burn, the gas in the kitchen anyhow as I came in the room I went and sat at the Window in the dark to look at the stars two in Particular which is the greatest importance about, the night before last in looking at the too stars I was inspired to write to you Mr Twian so last night as I sat down at the Window in the dark as I have said A cat came scraping at my aporn. So strange and didnt know what it was at first. It seems God orderd this for His own wish end, in the after noon.

As I came up stairs a cat came in the room what I never seen there before and I couldnt get Her out I didnt think no more about the cat until the cat came about me in the dark and through how strange she acted I would get very much frightened only I thought the instant she touched me it was the same cat. So at the same moment I was reminded of the night I came to know and feel how Jesus feels when He Afflictes any of His children through you Mark Twain, and A cat, I hope you will not be offended, sir.

It is now eleven o.clock at night oh Jesus have mercy on the souls in Purgatory

Amen

Feb. 12th. It is now about 3 o.clock in the after noon, and I hear shooting which brings to my mind Easter Monday sixty five I heard the sound of a cannon at four o.clock in the morning and my brain was that far gone that I felt if I heard the sound the third time I couldnt live and I said oh stop that. And as luck happend I didnt hear the sound of a cannon no more I thought the shooting was for Joy, that the Person that was accused of President Lincoln's death was taken up. oh Jesus how did you support me that time. Ah Mark Dear how did I get up that morning and got through my work, with my head bandaged & Mark why did I suffer for two gentlemen I didnt know or why did suffer so much in trying to get the work ready for Abraham Lincoln, and after Pledge my life for the man is accused of His death. And is firm still of necessity requires to die for John Wilkes Booth. If the People thinks He is guilty of President Lincoln's death after I shall tell the manner in which Jesus, did appear, and the words our blessd Redeemer, did speak. Now Mark, I am scribbling too much. I wish some Person, would take my case in hand and give me chance to Prove that I did see Jesus not for my own good but for the benefit of the People. Ah Mark, how different the People would live if they did see the sad face of Jesus, in sixty five when the North and the South were in their glory acting the fool, or how different the

People would live if they did see the Picture of Jesus, taken along with the Picture of Abraham Lincoln, in the manner in which both did appear in St. Louis in sixty five & Mark, how the little room I am writing this in brings to my mind the room Jesus did appear 12ᵗʰ of January 1868. And the room President Lincoln's vision did appear Easter Sunday night the same year the third day after His death. And how is it that I didnt know that I did see this vision for two weeks after, &, Mark, like the cat the night before last you ordered it so. As He know that I am not strong minded enough although I must say in makeing images and banners, that I did often see great miracles and had no Person to tell about it only to relieve my mind by sheding tears. And is it Possible that I have now to give up the thoughts of learning to draw and heir out for low wages, and leave the images and banners with so much importance blank. Shame on the People didnt give me room, to bring all my work together at blessd Virgin Mary intercede for me to God to have Patience May be the time didnt come. Now it is five oclock I must go and sitt the table and leave the explanation of you dear Mark and the cat and how I came to know the feeling of Jesus, through both. Now Mark, you may laugh or get offended, at how I am writing this what is the reason all the Roosters in the Nieghbourhood or crossing this moment which brings to my mind the unbaptised children. I shall take this to the express office to morrow on my way to church. Although I feel I should take it this evening to send it to you at this instant there is bells ringing and horns blowing and seem to say hurry Just as if the day of Judgement is at hand Mark dear try and come to see me I am not afraid of the Gentlemen

Your true friend Mary

Clemens's comments: From my lunatic. (Sent her the $5 | Feb. 21/80.)

Clemens's reply:

FARMINGTON AVENUE,
HARTFORD, CONN.

Feb. 21, 1880.

Well, Mary, my friend, you must think I am a slow sort of correspondent, & the truth is, I am. You must forgive this fault; it is one which I have never been able to correct. I am a pretty busy person, & a very lazy one; therefore I am apt to let letters lie a long time before I answer them. However, once a year, on or about Washington's Birthday, I rake together all the unanswered letters & reply to them. I meant to answer the letter you sent me some weeks ago, but waited for Washington's Birthday to come. Write to me when you feel like it, Mary, but don't you feel hurt if I keep you waiting till the next Washington's Birthday for an answer. I do not feel half so much hurried & bothered when I have a year to answer a letter in as I do when people expect an answer right away. I only send money to people once a year, too, & that is on Washington's Birthday, so you see if I had answered you earlier I could have not sent you the five dollars until now.

Take this check which I enclose, & go to the bank with Mr. Miller, & he will tell the banker you are the person named in it, & will give you the money, or if you choose, you can mail the check (after writing your name on the back of it), to Messrs. George P. Bissell & Co., Hartford, Conn., telling them to send you a postal order, & they will send it by return mail. I think your idea of getting those clergymen together at a dinner table is a very good one. They will have to put up with each other's society a good long time in heaven, so they may as well begin to get used to it here. Besides, I think, as you do, that their coming together in a friendly spirit will have good influence on other people. I am much obliged to you for asking me to be present & carve the turkey, but I must not go. Always when I carve a turkey I swear a little. (All people do to themselves—but I swear right out. I never could help it, though it has cost me many a pang). I think a person ought not to swear where clergymen are, unless they provoke him. Well, I couldn't be there, anyway, because I have to stay at home & stick close to my work, else this nation would become so ignorant in a little while that it would break one's heart to look at it. No, you & I have our separate duties in this world, Mary— your line is to humanize the clergy, & mine is to instruct the public. Let us not interfere with each other's functions. I have a most kindly sympathy towards you & your work, & perhaps that is a better contribution than mine would be. You say "Pity me"—indeed I do, & that is a true word. I wish I could tell you whether those are genuine visions & inspirations you have written me about, but I cannot be *absolutely* certain. They seem to me to be just like all the visions & inspirations I have ever heard of, & so I think you may *rest assured* that yours are as perfect & true & genuine & trustworthy as any that have ever happened in the world. Now let that comfort you, Mary, let that give peace to your troubled spirit, &n believe me your friend.

S. L. [Clemens], (Mark Twain.)

Clemens received many strange letters but few like those of Ellen (Mary) Keily (c. 1816–1901), a resident of the Lancaster, Pennsylvania, county alms house and insane asylum. Between 1880 and 1884, Keily sent him at least twelve letters, of which this is the second and the only one he is known to have answered. It repeats the main points of her letter of 27–29 January 1880 and alludes to another letter she had nailed in a public place seven years earlier. Despite the number and great length of Keily's letters, her life story is hard to reconstruct. Her letters are difficult to decipher and understand, and the only other known evidence comes from scattered census reports, brief mentions in the Lancaster *Daily Intelligencer,* and a terse obituary in the 21 August 1901 *Intelligencer.* What drew Keily to Clemens is unclear, but she may have attended his 19 January 1872 lecture in Lancaster and later miscalculated what year she had posted her public letter.

Evidently born in Ireland, Keily was a devout Roman Catholic, as her letters constantly show. By her own evidence, her madness went back to the mid-1860s, possibly while she lived in St. Louis, Missouri. Her letters also allude to her spending time in Washington, D.C.'s federal insane asylum. That institution was founded and supervised by Dr. Charles Henry Nichols (1820–1889) from the early 1850s through the late 1870s (obituary, *Evening Star*, 18 Dec. 1889). An 1870 census report for Lancaster describes Keily as "insane" and lists her living with her brother, James Keily (c. 1817–1904), a contractor, at 611 East Orange St. In 1872, James married a second time, to a much younger woman—also named Mary—who soon lost patience with Keily's religious mania and threw her out. From that date, Keily permanently resided in the county asylum, less than a mile east of her brother's home. She evidently enjoyed considerable freedom of movement outside the asylum and occasionally had long stays in her brother's home.

Keily posted her letters to Clemens with the help of *Intelligencer* editors (her envelopes are addressed in several different hands). That may explain how Clemens's reply to the present letter got published in the 10 March 1880 *Intelligencer* and reprinted in other papers (the text used here comes from the newspaper version). The story accompanying his letter describes Keily as the "banner woman," a harmless eccentric: "For years she has been wont to see visions and dream dreams of a condition of universal peace and social harmony . . . and a restoration of the 'era of good feeling' in church and state, when heretics and saints, Republicans and Democrats, lawgivers and lawbreakers, shall be reconciled and meet in one communion." To that end, Keily made banners "with characteristic inscriptions and endless decorations, which she hangs in public places, and writes lengthy epistles to the newspapers and to public men." Whatever letters Keily wrote to others are not presently known, but "Dear Mark" figured prominently in her notions of God's plan. She was obsessed with the idea that Abraham Lincoln's assassin, John Wilkes Booth, would succeed John the Baptist. On 30 July 1880, she suggested to Clemens, "May be Mark you could change your Name to St John the Baptist."

Keily's devotion to Booth is difficult to explain, unless it had something to do with Booth's shooting Lincoln on Good Friday, two days before Easter Sunday in 1865. Here and in other letters, Keily alludes to having been in St. Louis on that date. Within this letter she mentions her distress for "My Poor country." Her empathy for Booth suggests she may have meant the South, but she herself was a resident of the North. Ireland (the starving country) was probably the country of her birth, but she never states that explicitly in her letters. She may have meant that the United States as a whole was experiencing a spiritual crisis.

In the present letter, Keily's central wish was for Clemens to preside over a banquet for religious leaders. The guests were to include Jeremiah F. Shanahan (1834–1886), the Catholic bishop of Harrisburg, Pennsylvania; Henry Ward Beecher (1813–1887), the famous Congregationalist pastor of Brooklyn's Plymouth Church; J. C. Hickey, a pastor in Keily's local Catholic church; and Emanuel Greenwald (1811–1885), pastor of a Lancaster Lutheran church.

If Clemens knew that Keily's letters passed through the hands of newspaper editors, he may have written his carefully crafted reply expecting it might be published. Clemens doubtless invented his story about catching up on correspondence around Washington's birthday to explain why he had not replied sooner. Nevertheless, several people who read his letter in newspapers may have taken him seriously. For example, on 30 March 1880, Edson O. Beebe of Montrose, Pennsylvania, wrote to ask his help on a school essay because he had helped Keily. Beebe added his wish that Clemens would not wait until Washington's next birthday to reply. On 27 March 1880, two Michigan schoolteachers expressed a similar concern. Curiously, in the same letter in which Keily suggested Clemens change his name to John the Baptist, she also mentioned she was now able to "give Washington the title of a Saint" (30 July 1880). Another letter reports her posting a banner "on St George Washington birth day" (7 Apr. 1881). Keily wrote her last known letter to Clemens in May 1884. In August 1901, at the age of eighty-five, she died in the asylum from dysentery.

35

UNIVERSITY OF KANSAS,
CHANCELLOR'S OFFICE.
LAWRENCE, KANSAS.

3. 21 1880

Dear Sir:

The "Sticks"—an organization that meets once a fortnight to discuss American authors—have placed your name upon the list for the 19th of April. We would be pleased to hear from you in any manner that you see fit. Were it not that modesty forbids I would ask whether it is true that you never went to a circus, nor fell in love with some other fellows girl, nor played "hookey," nor wrote poetry. Delicacy also forbids my asking whether the rumor that you are investing your surplus funds in raising a new species of tadpole for the Boston market, is a true one or not.

I enclose stamp for reply, partly because Postmaster General Keys clerk recommends it and partly because it is a good custom; one handed down from antiquity.

Respectfully
W. H. Simpson
Secy
Box 751

Samuel L. Clemens Esq
Hartford, Conn.

Clemens's comment: And a curse on him.

This is a saucy example of the type of "literary society" letter that Clemens loathed, and its silliness probably added to his irritation. Only a few days earlier, he had received a similar request from a woman named Emma J. Stafford. Despite her note's more polite and sober tone, he commented, "A heavy curse fall on the particular devil who invented this most offensive form of persecution." The young author of the present note was at a turning point in his life. A recent University of Kansas graduate, William Haskell Simpson (1858–1933) worked in the university's chancellor's office until the following November (*Graduate Magazine of the Univ. of Kansas* 1, no. 6 [March 1903]: 216). A year or two later, he began a fifty-one-year career with the Santa Fe Railroad, in which he rose to a high-level position (obituary, New York *Times*, 13 June 1933). In later years, Simpson became a noted patron of New Mexico art. He also published poems, including one betraying a Clemens influence that begins, "Pauper or king—as up and down swift slips" (Hattie Horner, comp., *Collection of Kansas Poetry* [Topeka, 1891], 150).

36

Detroit, Mich.,
Apr. 17th, '80.

Mr. S. L. Clemens,
Dear Sir,

It is possible that you may remember that you received, some time ago, a letter requesting your advice upon the subject of publishing a little book to be entitled "College Tramps." You were so condescending as to notice the request, and to write quite a lengthy letter in return; but, before the kind advice contained in it could be acted upon, it had already been placed in the publishers' hands, and has since been published. You have, doubtless, ere this, discovered that there is such a thing existing in this world as *ingratitude;* and I fear that you will consider yourself as having met with another instance of the same in my inflicting upon you, in return for your kindness and courtesy, a copy of my first-born, "College Tramps." It has thus far met with an amount of success not yet great enough to enable me to decide that the literary world is my oyster, and that I must open it with my pen; but, for the present, I consider this book as but a fresh-water clam opened by the wayside. It has however made me very desirous of entering one of the New York publishing houses, and I am going to storm them soon. With many thanks for your kindness, and hoping that you may find time and inclination for the perusal of a few pages of the accompanying crude literary effort, I remain

Respectfully Yours,
F. A. Stokes,
41 Adelaide St.,
Detroit, Mich.

Clemens's comment: Not much of a book.

Clemens received more requests for writing and publishing help than he could answer, but this letter shows he did occasionally help young writers, although his message to this correspondent is lost. The correspondent's book, *College Tramps: A Narrative of the Adventures of a Party of Yale Students during a Summer Vacation in Europe* (New York, 1880), is written in a style obviously influenced by *The Innocents*

Abroad. For example, its chapter on Venice mimics *Innocents* by having a traveler ask a guide if the great San Marco, "ze patron of Venezia," is dead. The guide grows livid and asks, "Is you call Marco Twain?" The traveler replies, "No . . . my name is not Mark Twain." Mollified, the guide then mutters, "Zat Marco Twain hav made one big fool of ze guide profession in Italia, and all ze guide have conjurationed to keel him, soon as he come once more!" (p. 191).

Frederick Alexander Stokes (1857–1939) toured Europe with friends before graduating from Yale in 1879. After briefly studying law, he joined the publishing firm of Dodd, Mead & Co. A year later, he founded his own firm, Frederick A. Stokes, which he directed through the rest of his life. Among the thousands of books his firm published were Archibald Henderson's *Mark Twain* (1911) and Cyril Clemens's *Mark Twain Wit and Wisdom* (1935) ("F. A. Stokes Dead," New York *Times*, 17 Nov. 1939; *The House of Stokes, 1881–1926: A Record* [New York, 1926]).

37

Haverhill (Mass) 4–18–80

Mr. Clemens,
Gracious Sir;—
You are rich. To lose $10.00 would not make you miserable.
I am poor. To gain $10.00 would not make me miserable.
Please send me $10.00 (ten dollars).

Very respectfully yours
Ola A. Smith

Clemens's comment: O my!

A member of a family that originated in Maine, Viola (Ola) A. Smith (born c. 1854) had an older brother who was an artist, and her father, Benjamin F. Smith (born c. 1809) was an artist and photographer (not to be confused with the more famous artist Benjamin Franklin Smith [1830–1927]). Smith was living with her parents in 1880 and apparently never married. In 1930 she was again living in Maine, as a boarder (USCR).

38

Buffalo April 27th

Dear Mr Twain
I've read right along for two days & nearly reached the Appendix 'till I came, [at 4.30 P.M.] to "; dusted with *fragrant* pepper;" So I just put a hairpin in the book for a minute, while I ask you where you get yours, the pepper I mean. I broil my steak on a gridiron, its better than frying on a griddle, stew the

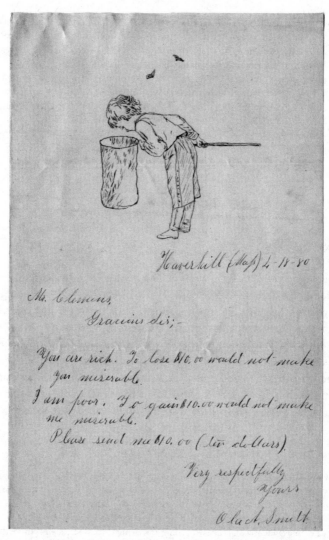

FIGURE 8. Letter from Ola A. Smith. Courtesy of the Mark Twain Papers, Bancroft Library, University of California, Berkeley.

mushrooms separately & pour over. The archipelagoe'd be just as geographically delineated.*

> Please answer about the pepper
> E. S. A. plain cook
> 468 Pearl St.

*& taste better.

This letter was probably sent in April 1880 because it responds to *A Tramp Abroad*, which was published earlier that year. Its quotation (including the semicolons) is from a passage explaining how to cook porterhouse steak in chapter 49. The letter also paraphrases Clemens's line about "precious juices of the meat trickling out and joining the gravy, archipelagoed with mushrooms." "E. S. A." was Evelyn S. Allen (1839–1889), the wife of Buffalo banker William K. Allen. Active in church and charitable work, she was also an officer in the Association for the Advancement of Women (USCR; "Death of Mrs. William K. Allen," Buffalo *Express*, 28 Nov. 1889; *Report of the Assoc. of Women: Sixteenth Women's Congress* [Detroit, 1889]).

39

Natick Mass. July 15—1880.

Mr Clemens

Dear Sir

Have just read your "Edward Mills & Geo Benton" in Augst Atlantic. I am a church member, a deacon, ex-S.S. Supt., ex-Y.M.C A. Prest &c &c(!) but I want to thank you for the story, all the same. It is *capital, perfect*. You have builded better than you knew. I only wish it might have been written by a man "inside the fold," with a little different motive than a desire to get off a good joke, but whatever the motive the story is true, my only fear is that the officers & members of the "Prisoners Friend Society" will not read it. I am a hearty & sincere believer in the church, its work & above all its Master & only regret that there should be facts in existence to sustain such a "Tale" but it *is* a success.

Yrs E. H. Walcott

Clemens's comment: About "Mills & Benton—a Tale."

"Edward Mills and George Benton: A Tale," about foster brothers who meet opposite ends, epitomizes Clemens's famous quip, "Be good & you will be lonesome." The industrious and honest Edward comes to grief, unappreciated and ignored, while the lazy and dishonest George is rescued from trouble by Christian do-gooders. The story's theme evidently hit home with some practicing Christians, such as this letter's correspondent, Erwin Herbert Walcott (1846–1913). In 1884, Walcott relocated to Vermont, where he edited newspapers until around 1892, when he moved to Boston. There he became secretary of the Boston Merchants Association. He spent his last five years as honorary consul for Japan in Boston (obituary, St. Johnsbury, Massachusetts, *Caledonian-Record*, 10 Dec. 1913).

40

R. M. GRISWOLD, M.D.
PHYSICIAN & SURGEON.

NORTH MANCHESTER, CONN. July 29 1880.

Samuel L. Clements,
Hartford, Ct,

Dear Sir:

I wish to tender you my sincere thanks for your article in the last Atlantic, "Edward Mills & George Benton." The article should be printed for distribution in every temperance, benevolent, and church organization in the land,

Very Truly Yrs,
R. M. Griswold.

Clemens's comment: Benton & Mills—a tale.

Roger Marvin Griswold (1852–1935) practiced medicine for fifty years in New England, including eleven years in Manchester, Connecticut. He was also a regular contributor to medical journals ("Dr. Griswold, 82, Dies in Berlin Home," Hartford *Courant,* 29 Apr. 1935; *Distinguished Successful Americans of Our Day* [Chicago, 1911], 567–569).

41

Petrolea Aug. 7 '80

Mr Clemens

Dear Sir,—What will you charge to write me a lecture. One that will take about 1¼ hours to deliver it. Humorous and stirring, but not too pathetic. An early answer will very much oblige

Yours Respectfully
R. T. Lowery
Petrolea
Ont
Can.

Clemens's comment: Ass.

This unusually brazen request came from a moderately successful Canadian humorist. Nicknamed the "Colonel," Robert Thornton Lowery (1859–1921) wrote on Western topics and won favorable comparisons to Clemens. He later edited newspapers in British Columbia (A. Pervin, *Wit and Wisdom of the Wild West* [Bloomington, Ind., 2010], 76; "'Colonel' Robert Thornton Lowery," Sandon Historical Society, www. sandonmuseum.ca, accessed 14 Apr. 2011).

42

Winsted Aug 18th 1880.

Horrid man! how did you know the way I behave in a thunder storm? Have you been secreted in the closet? or lurking on the shed roof? I hope you got thoroughly rained on!—And worst of all is that you made me laugh at myself: my real terrors turned round and grimaced at me: they were sublime, and you have made them ridiculous. Just come out here another year and have four houses within a few rods of you struck, and then see if you 'll write an article of such exasperating levity. I really hate you, but you *are* funny. How I should love to see you in a real hail and lightning jamboree just for once,—only I should never dare to look on!

I am not Mrs Mcwilliams, only
Rose Terry Cooke.

P.S. My husband says, "Tell him—'Bully for you! it's so, every bit of it.'" but he's a man, too!
P.P.S. Don't do so any more please!

Clemens's comment: Rose Terry Cooke

This letter responds to Clemens's "Mrs. McWilliams and the Lightning," a gentle sketch about a housewife with a preternatural fear of lightning published in the September 1880 *Atlantic Monthly*. The correspondent, Rose Terry Cooke (1827–1892), was a prolific New England poet and prose writer whose local-color stories Clemens admired (Clemens to W. D. Howells, 4 July 1877, *Mark Twain–Howells Letters*, ed. H. N. Smith and W. M. Gibson [Cambridge, Mass., 1960], 1:187). Cooke apparently did not meet Clemens until sometime after she wrote this letter.

43

CHARLES W. RHODES.
EXPORTER,
CHEESE, BUTTER AND PROVISIONS,
28 & 30 WHITEHALL ST.

NEW-YORK, Dec 13 1880

Mark Twain
Hartford Ct

Dear Sir.

I have read "Roughing It" "Innocents" "Gilded Age" "Scetches Old and New" and am just finishing the "Tramp Abroad" What I want to know is by what rule a fellow can infallibly judge when you are lying and when you are telling the truth. I write this in case you intend to afflict an innocent and unoffending public with any more such works. I would suggest the next volumn be published with the truth printed in italics. They usually have small fonts of these in printing offices

Yours Truly
C. W. Rhodes.

Clemens's comment: Ha!—ha! | captured another idiot. SLC

Perhaps Clemens was thinking of this letter when he later wrote, "I never could tell a lie that anybody would doubt, nor a truth that anybody would believe" (*Following the Equator* [1897], chapter 62). Charles W. Rhodes (1846–1916) was a New York City cheese merchant throughout his adult life (USCR).

1881–1890

1881–1890	Clemens family lives in Hartford, Conn.
November 1881	SLC visits Montreal to secure Canadian copyright for *The Prince and the Pauper*, which is published in United States in December
April–May 1882	Travels on the Mississippi River to gather material for a new book
June 1882	*The Stolen White Elephant* is published
May 1883	*Life on the Mississippi* is published
March 1884	George Washington Cable organizes April Fools' Day hoax
May 1884	SLC forms the publishing firm Charles L. Webster & Co. to produce his own books, Ulysses S. Grant's *Memoirs,* and works by other authors
5 November 1884	Begins fifteen-week "Twins of Genius" lecture tour with Cable
December 1884	Extract from *Huckleberry Finn* appears in *Century Magazine* and complete book is published in England; American edition follows in February 1885
16 July 1885	"On Training Children" letter appears in *Christian Union*
30 November 1885	SLC celebrates fiftieth birthday
December 1885	"The Private History of a Campaign that Failed" appears in *Century Magazine*
April 1887	"English as She Is Taught" appears in *Century Magazine*
November 1889	Extract from *Connecticut Yankee* appears in *Century Magazine*; book publication follows in December
November 1890	Jean Clemens is diagnosed as an epileptic

44

OFFICE OF WALLACE MUZZY,
DEALER IN
STAPLE GROCERIES, CANDY, TOBACCO, STATIONERY, &C.

Bristol, Conn. 7th Mch 1881

S. L. Clemens,

A skillful pilot, once, you were, but see how an honest tale shall make you blush. You gave the beef contract to that clerk; I am his attorney. We mistrusted you were the scalper of Makinzie, and have been shadowing you ever since, and now you have endorsed—(Do try—ON ME. = Deuteronomy)—Reka's poem, which verifys the Indian, and tomahawk; my client receiving $1,000,000,—my half 500,000—and you pull hemp, with Kingshorn, the State street paper firm, also, have a little *acct* against you. Dear Friend, be there peace between us. It was simply a question in chemistry, or algebra, but it vexes me; perhaps you would be kind enough to dissolve the puzzle $= Ko_1Fo_2O_3\bar{T} + Ag$ $H4NO, FE_2O_3\bar{T}+4Ag$

Ever Your Friend
W. W. Muzzy

Clemens's comment: The idiots seem to be uncommonly thick, this year.

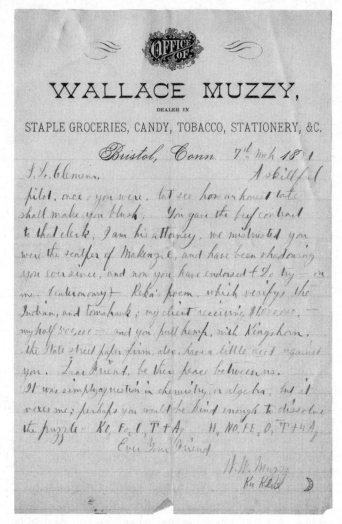

FIGURE 9. Letter from Wallace W. Muzzy. Courtesy of the Mark Twain Papers, Bancroft Library, University of California, Berkeley.

An ostensibly respectable businessman, Wallace W. Muzzy (1846–1915) wrote at least five bizarre letters to Clemens between 1881 and 1889, plus a sixth that reached Clemens indirectly, signing a different name to each. He signed the others "E. U. Reka" (6 Apr. 1881), "W. Wilkins Micawber" (24 Sept. 1883), "Muzio Clemens" (25 Sept. 1884), and "W. W. M——y" (1 Jan. 1889). In July 1882, he sent a poem about Clemens signed "S. A. Hara" to journalist Robert Burdette, who forwarded it to Clemens (letter 54). His intentions remain a mystery, and his letters may contain inscrutable puzzles.

Clemens obviously thought little of the present letter and wrote similarly scathing remarks about Muzzy's other letters. However, he evidently did not notice that all the letters were written by the same person, even though Muzzy wrote most of them on letterhead containing his real name (see figure 9).

Muzzy was born in Bristol, Connecticut, where he lived at least fifty years. A grocer during the 1880s, he also worked for the Ingraham clock works for several years, apparently during the 1890s (USCR; "Wallace Muzzy Dead," Hartford *Courant*, 24 Mar. 1915; L. Lee and S. F. Lee, *John Lee of Farmington . . . and His Descendants* [Meriden, Conn., 1897], 366). His letter alludes to "The Facts in the Case of the Great Beef Contract," a burlesque about government corruption Clemens published in the 17 December 1870 Buffalo *Express* and the January 1871 *Galaxy* and reprinted in *Sketches New & Old* (1875). The sketch tells how a contractor named John Wilson Mackenzie was tomahawked and scalped while trying to deliver beef to General Sherman's army in the West. ("Ku Klux" at the bottom of the letter was apparently added later.)

45

Cleveland, Ohio, May 5, 1881

Mr. Twain,—Dear Sir:

Perhaps you will excuse me for writing to you, when I tell you that for the last three years, although unknown to yourself, you have been one of my physicians. A physician certainly ought not take offense at hearing from one of his patients.

For the last three years I have been confined to the house with paralysis of the lower limbs, nearly two years of the time having been unable to walk. Now that I am somewhat better, I wish to thank you for the pleasure which your writings have given me. I firmly believe that the good solid laughs I have had over them, have done me more good than all the medicine I have taken. And if it be a comfort to know that you have helped a boy pass three dreary years of illness, may that comfort be yours.

Respectfully yours,
Emerson O. Stevens,
17 Webster St.,
Cleveland, Ohio.

Clemens's comment: From a lad.

Emerson O. Stevens (1865?–1900) was probably about fifteen when he wrote this letter, as he graduated from Cleveland's Adelbert College of Western Reserve University in 1888. He later taught English at Adelbert and also published occasional magazine articles, including one on Western Reserve that opens with a nod to Clemens: "The Connecticut Yankee, whether at the Court of King Arthur or grubbing stumps in the clearings of a western wilderness, is an estimable type of man"

(*New England Magazine*, April 1896, 163; obituary, *Western Reserve Univ. Bull.*, October 1900, 199).

46

"Athol Bank," Hamilton,
Ontario, Canada
20 Decem 1881

The Illustrious "Mark Twain"
Dear Sir,
    If you will allow the privileges of the "the season" to cover what at any other time might well be considered a decided liberty in a stranger and "foreigner," I will ask you accept the annexed very humble Salutation. And you will permit me at the same time, as a Canadian, to express my extreme regret that there should be anything in the laws of Canada (or any other country) to frustrate the just and reasonable object you had in view in your recent visit to Montreal.—
    However much you may have been (innocently) "abroad" on the "domicile" question, you were certainly very much "at home" in your glorious speech delivered at the Montreal banquet, so deservedly given in your honor: which speech, moreover, made all Canada more than ever at home with *you* when devoured with our breakfasts all over the land next morning.—

With much respect,
I remain, Dear Sir
Gratefully yours
William Murray.

Enclosure

"Athol Bank"
Hamilton, Ontario
Canada, 20 Dec. 1881.

"The Bard of Hamilton" presents—
    (Oh! would I were a Hemans
Or one who could at least *commence*—)
    His compliments to Clemens.

I crave your *Clemens*-y if I
    Should for a moments' pain
But Clemens never can come nigh
    The deathless name of Twain.

So, if you please, in this address
  I henceforth will refrain
From hazarding the greenest guess
  That you are less than Twain.

"Address"! said I? the nameless thing
  Already's almost done:
I simply used the word to ring
  With what I had begun.

I only wish to state my fear
  That if you, Marcus Twain,
Could ever die, we surely ne'er
  Would "see your like again";

To thank you also for the spice
  You furnish for our fare,
Which, tho' devoured and relished thrice,
  Can still destroy dull care;

And, finally, I wish that you,
  'Mid all creations' cheers,
May live—(your "Prince & Pauper" too.)
  At least a thousand years.

W^m. Murray.

Samuel L. Clemens Esqre
("Mark Twain")

An admirer of poet Robert Burns, Scottish-born William Murray (1834–1923) styled himself the "Bard of Hamilton" and "Bard of Athol," after his name for his Hamilton home. He sent similar laudatory verses to many public figures, including Prussian chancellor Otto von Bismarck, Canadian author John Reade, Canadian governor-general A. H. Grey, and other political leaders (D&E Lake catalog, www.delake.com, accessed 28 Dec. 2010). Murray immigrated to Ontario at the age of twenty and worked in the dry goods trade in Hamilton (Jeff Seffinga, "The Bard of Athol Bank" [2003], www.towerpoetry.ca/talk-bard.html, accessed 13 Aug. 2009).

Murray's letter alludes to Clemens's ongoing grievance about Canada's failure to give his books copyright protection. While visiting Canada to secure copyright for *The Prince and the Pauper*, Clemens spoke at a banquet at Montreal's Windsor Hotel on 8 December 1881 that Murray seems to have attended. Murray's poem also contains an allusion to the prolific English poet Felicia Hemans (1793–1835).

47

Baltimore, Feb. 1882.

Mark Twain Esq.

My dear Friend:

Permit me, an admirer of yours and a scribbler at times, to address you in a friendly way, for I feel that I am an intimate and long acquaintance of yours. My addressing you is to satisfy a long pent-up desire that has been filling my bosom for months—nay—years.

I have read with the keenest pleasure all the books you have written and published, I believe, and have just finished your last—"The Tramp Abroad" and was extremely edified.

Dear Mark:—I love you dearly and want you to write me an autograph letter—the subject I will leave for yourself, only let me know how Mrs. Mark and all the little Marks and Markesses are getting along.

Some of my lady friends have seen the cut of a "counterfeit presentment" of yourself in the "Tramp Abroad" and they say, that if that is anywhere near the truth, why, you are a handsome man.

This remark is written in a *whisper* with the hope, that, should it reach the eye of Mrs. Mark, no Jealousy will be created.

I am, like you *were once,* a poor, friendless orphan—an unsophisticated youth and "Innocent" down this way, and should you wander in this direction anytime, I will be glad to extend you the right hand of fellowship.

I will say in this connection, that we have lots of pretty girls in our *village,* and should you come this way, I am sure you would be treated the same as the "*Professor*" was by Mrs. Elliott's girls up in the White Mountains, so I beg of you, should you come to that determination, prepare yourself with plenty of wardrobe and an easy-fitting *pair* of *shoes.*—Shoes that won't *toast* nor *roast.*

With assurances of my highest regards, and hoping to hear from you shortly,

I remain, yours truly.

J. E. Hemmell,

134 Pearl st.

Balto. Md.

The author of this letter apparently knew little about Clemens, who had three daughters and whose only son had died in infancy in 1872. Moreover, Clemens was not an orphan, as his mother lived until 1890. Jacob E. Hemmell (born c. 1841) had a variety of occupations. Baltimore city directory and census records list him as a coachtrimmer in 1880, a journalist in 1900, and a newspaper agent in 1910. The 1920 census lists his wife as a widow.

FIGURE 10. The "counterfeit presentment." Frontispiece from *A Tramp Abroad*. Courtesy of the Mark Twain Papers, Bancroft Library, University of California, Berkeley.

48

KERRICK, LUCAS & SPENCER,
ATTORNEYS & COUNSELORS.
THOMAS C. KERRICK.
BENJAMIN D. LUCAS.
HENRY D. SPENCER. | NOTARY PUBLIC.

210 N. CENTER STREET,
BLOOMINGTON, ILLINOIS. Mar. 8th 1882

Hon. Samuel L. Clemens,
Hartford Conn.

Dr Sir:

I plead no excuse for this letter, as probably, if the truth were told, nothing but a selfish motive might be the cause of my writing.

I have read most of your publications and like great many others, have been both instructed and entertained by them. I am uncle to nine nephews and nieces to whom "Tom Sawyer" is real hero—a living character.

Last evening one of my nieces asked, "Uncle Harry, wont Mr. Twain ever tell us what sort of a man Tom Sawyer became. Wont he tell us if we ask?" I of course told her I did not know & she then said "Will you ask him"? I could not refuse & so here is the question[:] "Mr. Twain" What sort of a man did Tom Sawyer become?

I have sometime thought that a book, such as you could produce, written to satirize the young men of this age, who are not willing to commence sweeping the stores as their fathers did, but insist on being cashiers, &c, without going through the drugery of the trade; or a work treating the "aesthetic" nature of our period—using the word aesthetic in its ironical application to affected & "shabby-genteel" people—would be useful, & instructive.

I was City Editor here for nearly 7 years, and my observations have made me quite cynical, which statement may give you a clearer inkling of what I mean.

I would not suggest such a book intimating that my judgment is better than yours, or that you should do so. The request of my niece started this epistle & the suggestions of mine are "thrown in without charge." The selfishness of my motives you will perceive when you see I simply order such a book as my fancy might desire—just as a man would order a shirt—instead of writing it myself.

You scored a long mark when you presented Tom Sawyer, & if you produce a book such as I have indicated I think you should (forgive the pun) Mark Twain.

Hoping this is not the "last straw that breaks" & so forth I am
With Great Respect,
Yours Sincerely,
Henry D. Spencer.

P.S. Dont think I expect the book by return mail.

Clemens's comment: Answered

Tom Sawyer concludes with this paragraph: "Most of the characters that perform in this book still live, and are prosperous and happy. Some day it may seem worth while to take up the story of the younger ones again and see what sort of men and women they turned out to be; therefore it will be wisest not to reveal any of that part of their lives at present." Clemens wrote several sequels to *Tom Sawyer,* including *Huckleberry Finn* (1884), but never wrote about the novel's characters as adults.

A son of the distinguished Illinois attorney Hamilton Spencer (1815–1891), Henry Dwight Spencer (1854–1929) practiced law in his father's firm and was living with his parents at the time of the 1880 census. When he married in 1886, his wedding guests included Illinois governor Richard J. Oglesby ("Spencer-Rogers Wedding," Decatur *Weekly Republican,* 9 Sept. 1886; "Killed in the Street: Lawyer Hamilton Spencer's Death," Chicago *Herald,* 24 June 1891).

49

Sioux City, Ia, 3–9 1882

Samuel Clemmens

Dear Sir,

The favor of your Autograph is respectfully solicited.

Yours truly,

Clarence E. Ash.

Clemens's comment: Good God!

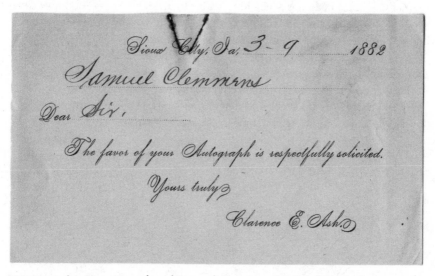

FIGURE 11. An 1882 autograph-seeking card. Courtesy of the Mark Twain Papers, Bancroft Library, University of California, Berkeley.

Few letters irritated Clemens more than printed autograph requests such as this (figure 11). Its sender, Clarence E. Ash (c. 1861–1897), sold real estate in Sioux City until 1892, when he moved to Idaho. Four years later, he settled in San Luis Obispo, California, where he owned a general merchandise store ("Death of C. E. Ash," San Luis Obispo *Tribune,* 12 Dec. 1897; "Death of Clarence Ash," Sioux City *Journal,* 12 Dec. 1897).

50

Shelby City, Kentucky,
March 31st, 1882.

Mr. S. C. Clemens:

Dear Sir:

If you please I want to get you to write me an essay (for a lady friend) on this subject "How old are you."

I want the thought to run as follows with the addition of your most excellent wit—

That we should number our years, not by the revolution's of the earth on its axis once in every 24 hours, but by the number of noble deeds and thoughts. Let the idea be that we live in acts not years, in thoughts not breaths.

As the little fellow says "if I count my age from the fun I have had, I would be an old man."

Please, let it be a mingling of sensible sound thought & your good wit and humor Of course I can not & would never try to dictate to you—You know what I want & of course you will fix it up all right. I would not want the essay to be more than five or six or seven pages of foolscap paper.

Will you write it for me, for $10.⁰⁰? I will send the money by P O Order immediately on hearing from you.

Please be so kind as to favor me with an early response.

O You must write it for me, and if not for $10.⁰⁰, please state your price & as low as you can afford it. Again let me insist, you reply immediately.

Address me
W. T. St. Clair,
Shelby City,
Boyle, Co.} Kentucky.

(over)

P.S. This is a very urgent matter with me, and it will be such a favor, to receive a favorable response.

Please write soon.

Yours' Truley
W. T. St. Clair.

Many correspondents pressed Clemens to reply quickly, but William Thomas St. Clair (1859–1910), this letter's author, was unusually insistent. When Clemens did not answer him, he wrote again on 3 April, repeating his request and adding, "I don't want you to fail me—I am so anxious to get her something *fine,* and have her excel all the other girls." St. Clair wrote a third time on 10 April, acknowledging receipt of a letter (now lost). He now modified his request: "Will you give me a few ideas—say only a couple of pages—just a few ideas so as not to intrude on your time: I will send you $30.^{00} IMMEDIATELY, if you will be so Kind as to accommodate me." Clemens noted that his wife, Livy, answered this third letter.

St. Clair's letters hint that he had an obsessive-compulsive tendency. After graduating from Centre College in Danville, Kentucky, in 1880, he taught math at Louisville's Male High School, where he later headed the Latin department. His publications include *Medical Latin . . . for Elementary Training of Medical Students* (1897) and *Caesar for Beginners: A First Latin Book* (1899). A year after first writing to Clemens, St. Clair married Mary P. Shelton (Stanford, Kentucky, *Semi-Weekly Interior Jnl.,* 27 July 1883). In May 1910, he was committed to the Kentucky Eastern Asylum in Paris, where he hanged himself six months later (USCR; "Asylum Inmate Commits Suicide," Paris *Bourbon News,* 15 Nov. 1910).

———

51

Private

Fremont, O.
6 Apr 1882

Dear Mr Clements:

The children of all ages, of my numerous household, have enjoyed your new book so much that I must thank you on their and my own behalf.

The child in his eighth year and the child in his sixtieth, and all between them in age and of both sexes were equally hearty in their applause and delight. The Prince and The Pauper is as entertaining as Robinson Crusoe to the Young Folks, and the older ones see in it a most effective presentation of the inhuman criminal laws, hardly yet wiped out, of English jurisprudence, and the only defence, or explanation rather, of the Puritan Codes of our New England ancestor.

I congratulate you on your great success in this admirable book.

Sincerely
R. B. Hayes
Mr. S. L. Clemens
Hartford

Ct.

Clemens's comment: From Ex-President Rutherford B. Hayes

Clemens's reply:

Hartford, April 10th, 1882.

Dear Mr. Hayes:

An odd thing! We had two or three old friends to dinner, & were discussing your administration; & had just arrived at the verdict that its quiet & unostentatious, but real & substantial greatness, would steadily rise into higher & higher prominence, as time & distance give it a right perspective, until at last it would stand out against the horizon of history in its true proportions, when your most welcome letter was brought in! And previously we had been discussing a paper which I am ^to^ read before a Club of young girls in Boston next Saturday, entitled "Mental Telegraphy," wherein I use, as an illustration, the fact that an approaching letter often foreshadows its coming by flinging its writer into the mind of the person who is about to receive it! [[One will never believe how frequent an occurrence this is, until he begins to watch for it & take note of it: I began six years ago.]]

I am deeply gratified by the happy reception which the book has enjoyed at the hands of your household; & I am peculiarly grateful to you for telling me the pleasant news, when, if you had so chosen, you could have followed the world's wrong custom & refused to take the trouble. Such an attention, coming from you, has a value which I do not underestimate; for whereas, coming from an ordinary source, it might be considered in some vague nebulous way a sort of duyty, no such duties attach to one who has worn the purple of sovereignty—it is then an act of grace, & its worth is multiplied accordingly.

Thanking you again, I am, with great respect,
Sincerely Yours
S. L. Clemens

I never thought of it before, but it seems strange that there should be no title for an ex-President but plain Mr. Still, it is reasonably conspicuous, since in our day pretty much everybody else is Esq.

Former U.S. president Rutherford B. Hayes (1822–1893) composed this letter just over a year after leaving office. Clemens had supported his election in 1876 and had written to him several times but had not yet met him. Hayes's letter has been published before but the children to whom he alludes were not identified until now, perhaps partly because the word "sixtieth" had been mistranscribed as "sixteenth." The "child in his sixtieth" year must have been Hayes himself, as he would turn sixty the following October. The other children he mentions were not members of his own family. His diary reveals that in late March, the family of the attorney John Grant Mitchell (1838–1894) were his houseguests. When Hayes's wife went out of town, she instructed him to entertain the children. As his own family was in the habit of reading books aloud, it is probable that Hayes himself read *The Prince and the Pauper* to Mitchell's four children, the youngest of whom would turn eight in October (Tom Culbertson, Rutherford B. Hayes Presidential Center, personal communications, 14 Dec. 2010). That child, John Grant Mitchell Jr. (1874–1957), later became a character actor in Hollywood films, including *The Man Who Came to Dinner* (1940), in which he played the harried Ohio husband, and *The Grapes of Wrath* (1940), in which he was the kindly manager of a government camp for migrant workers (see figure 12).

Hayes's 14 February 1890 diary entry records that he had finished reading *A Connecticut Yankee in King Arthur's Court* (1889): "Instructive; not equal to 'Prince and Pauper.' Sound on the question of wealth and poverty. No rule, just and wise, except the rule of the whole people. Our danger is the rule of the few wealthy. These are the serious points of the book" (www.ohiohistory.org, accessed 14 Dec. 2010).

52

Flint, Mich., April 19 [1882]

Mr. Mark Twain,

I have read your Tom Sawyer and am very much interested in it. Wont you please tell me whether Tom and Huck Finn had the initiation that night. If you have the time. We have all of your works. Papa said he knew you once, his name is Gorge L Walker. Tom must have had a hard time to keep still with the spirit of three boys in one, was Huck Finn composed of two or three boys. If you have time please answer my letter as soon as soon as you can. You must be a ever so nice because you write such nice books

Yours Truely.
Jennie S. Walker
Flint, Michigan

Tom Sawyer begins planning his gang in chapter 35 of *Tom Sawyer* (1876), but its initiation does not occur until chapter 2 of *Huckleberry Finn* (1884). The notion that Tom was "three boys in one" comes from Clemens's preface to *Tom Sawyer,* which calls him "a combination of the characteristics of three boys."

FIGURE 12. Grant Mitchell as the kindly migrant camp caretaker in a still from the 1940 film *The Grapes of Wrath* (Twentieth-Century Fox). Collection of the author.

Jane Seville "Jennie" Walker (1870–1947) was twelve when she wrote this letter. By 1900 she had the married name of Durfee but was still living with her parents in Flint, with no occupation listed. In 1897, she married attorney Irving William Durfee (1868–1946) but never had children and had no occupations listed in census reports. Nothing found outside this letter links Clemens to Jennie's father, George L. Walker (1838–1909), a prominent Flint businessman who later helped organize the Buick Motor Co. (USCR; findagrave.com; E. O. Wood, *History of Genesee Co., Michigan* [Indianapolis, 1916], 509, 527–528).

53

West-Point, Miss. July 20th 1882

Mr Mark Twain
Hartford Conn.

Dear Sir,

I am taking a great deal of interest in your collection of long German words.
I send you hereby "noble" specimen, at the condition that you will send me
your autograph, an autograph written by *you* not by your secretary.

I see you accept the condition as I take your silence for an assent. This word
is genuine. I have seen it in one of my travels on a sign in Genève.

Vierwaldstätterseesalonschraubendampferactienconcurrenz-
gesellschaftsbüreau   ah!!

Remember I send you this C.O.D. Be kind enough to remit the amount.

Yours thankfully
Louis Chable
West-Point
Miss

Clemens's comment: Long word.

Chable's German tongue-twister translates as "Office of the Vierwaldstättersee
propeller-steamer stock company ... ah!!" If the author of this letter was the Louis
Chable (1863/64–1935) who was president of New York's American Paper Exports Co.
during the 1920s, he was only a teenager when he wrote it (1921 passport application;
findagrave.com). An apparently different Louis Chable was clerk of the U.S. House
Committee on Commerce in 1888 (*Annual Report of the Light-House Board* [Wash-
ington, D.C., 1888], 232).

54

July 29

Dear Mr. Clemens,

It would be a shame to permit this honest & earnest worshipper to burn his
incense so far away from his most gracious majesty that it could not penetrate
the royal nostrils. With your permission therefore, I will act as his priest and
swing the censer a little nearer the regnant nose.

Ever yours
R. J. Burdette

Enclosure

Bristol, Conn. July 1882

R. J. Burdette, Esq.

You have styled M. T. "The king of humorists." This I endorse, in the subsequent poem, (sub rosa) We are a perpetual motion inventor, and now resume that occupation. "Poor Harvey is in Congress now. Who tried so hard to be a poet"

VIVE LE ROI.

Our little song, not very long, Is of the right, and not the wrong. Our hero bold, the truth has told. He is the fairest of the fold.

In forty three (?) it was that he. Was born, in fair Columbia. A Western state; we will relate. This youth appeared; Missouri great From pie at home. Then did he roam. And printer's pi, did sample some. And next afloat, in river boat. A pilot soon became of note

Then at the mines, composing lines, An *Enterprise* complete finds. The land that gold, and silver hold. Its mysteries, then did unfold

There Slade he met, and Smiley bet His frog would out-jump, any yet. Another fed and filled with lead. This frog, and wager won, 'tis said

The State did note, and then by vote Sent Mark to Sandwich Isles, remote. The costumes queer, he saw, while here. And poison centipedes appear

And then, with vim, the ladies swim He sits upon their clothes, so trim. Six months was there; a record fair Among the natives, did he bear

Around the world, his flag unfurled. On land a bicycle, he whirled. And many laughed As on a raft; against a bridge, he wrecked the craft

We read, and learn, on his return. In war paint; then did scalp and burn. In Senate, where he will repair. In '84, the seers declare.

He does reside, above the tide. Where Charter oaks grow, side by side. His mansion there complete, and fair. Built of this timber; few compare

"Innocent's" wit, and "Roughing It" are excellent, all will admit. "A Tramp Abroad," with gun and rod; And "Prince and Pauper" we applaud

> S. A. Hara
> Receptacle 266, Bristol, Hartford Co. Ct.

N.B. J. S. C. Abbot made Napoleon a saint; another author made him a demon; we have taken a middle course, and confined ourselves to facts; this is right and laudable

Clemens's comment: D——d rubbish

"S. A. Hara" was a punning name used by the Bristol, Connecticut, grocer Wallace Muzzy, who wrote at least five letters directly to Clemens during the 1880s (see letter 44). Muzzy may have sent his poem to Robert Jones Burdette (1844–1914) because of what Burdette wrote about Clemens for the Burlington, Iowa, *Hawkeye* in January 1881. In that widely reprinted article, Burdette called Clemens's Hartford home "this palace of the king of humorists." Burdette himself had met Clemens in Hartford in December 1880 and corresponded with him throughout the decade.

Muzzy's allusion to "perpetual motion" may have had something to do with Bristol's reputation as a clock-making center. "Poor Harvey" may have been former Connecticut governor and Hartford *Courant* owner Joseph Roswell Hawley (1826–1905), who represented Connecticut in the U.S. House of Representatives in 1872–1875 and 1879–1881. No other congressman had the name Harvey in 1882. Muzzy's poem contains some errors about the life of Clemens, who was born in 1835 in Florida, Missouri, not in Columbia. The poem's other allusions to Clemens's life and writings are reasonably accurate. Muzzy's postscript mentions John Stevens Cabot Abbott (1805–1877), the American author of the laudatory *History of Napoleon Bonaparte* (1855).

55

Mi Dear Sir:

I lik you Please send me yur auto graf. I am 20 old. I cant rite good. bil says I can. I dont beleive Bil Wilson. I wuz sik last winter. I hav got a Baby. Hiz nam is Mark Twain Kane cauz I lik wat you rite. bil reads to me and I laf. Send your autograf to me. more next time.

Address Miss Mollie Kane mother of Mark Twain Kane, Union Missouri. Grandma used to know your uncle. Rite soon to me and see me this summer I will feed you well spiritually and bodily.

> Your Mollie

This postcard was postmarked Union, Missouri, 7 August 1882. Mollie Kane might have been the forty-two-year-old Irish immigrant Margaret Kane listed in a 1860 census report for Kirkwood, a town about thirty-five miles northeast of Union. How-

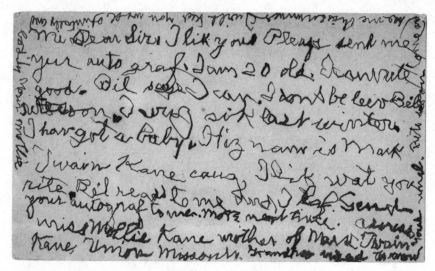

FIGURE 13. Postcard from Mollie Kane. Courtesy of the Mark Twain Papers, Bancroft Library, University of California, Berkeley.

ever, no "Mark Twain Kane" has been found, so the message may have been a hoax. Its spelling and grammar errors resemble the type of unschooled writing that humorist Petroleum V. Nasby mimicked, but internal inconsistencies may betray the hand of a more literate writer.

56

304 President St.
Brooklyn, New York
Dec'r 21st, 1882

Samuel L. Clements, Esq.
My dear Sir:—

On behalf of my young Son, your namesame, Samuel Clements Bock, I take the liberty to address you.

My boy is now two years and seven months old, and I am intensely anxious that I should possess something from your pen which my darling child my cherish long after you are dead and gone.

Will you not kindly send me a few sentiments on the cards, I beg to inclose herewith, or better still, if you can find a larger size, please substitute it for these?

Samuel is a very attractive and intelligent boy and the greatest ambition of my life is that he may possess the same brilliant intellect, royal nature and the many excellencies of his most illustrious namesake.

My unbounded admiration for you and your splendid works, induced me to name the boy in your honor, and I shall teach him to be proud of that great name, and always to respect and revere it.

I am certain that you will agree with me, that it will be a grand thing for me to possess a few sentiments from your gifted pen, which I can present to my son, when he attains a proper age, and undoubtedly they will afford him great pleasure and interest in after life.

This favor will take you but a moment, yet make us all happy and grateful, although I fully appreciate the value of an ever busy man's time, especially an author's.

May I suggest that you favor us with the following beautiful sentiments, or rather quotations,

> Beneath the rule of men entirely great,
> The pen is mightier than the (Richilieu) sword.

and

> "Leisure, without literature is death."

May I respectfully ask if you will add—both your autograph and your nom-de-plume to these sentiments, and Hartford, and "Christmas, 1882."

You cannot imagine how grateful we shall be for this great courtesy, and how much joy it will implant.

My wife joins me in this earnest appeal, on behalf of our darling and beautiful boy.

Should you not like to write these quotations mentioned for him (but I most sincerely hope and pray that you will) be so good as to substitute anything which you can think, will be interesting, or characteristic. To possess something from "Mark Twain"—one of the immortals of literature, and a man of many noble instincts—is like being the fortunate owner of a contribution from Byron or Milton to my mind.

With a thousand good wishes, and all hopes for your welfare,
I remain, Dear Mr. Clements,
Your obedient servant,
William Bock.
304 President St.
Brooklyn, N.Y.

Clemens's comment: Sarcasm?

> Clemens had good reason to distrust the sincerity of this letter: Would parents nam-
> ing a child after him have misspelled his surname? Moreover, Clemens would have
> been put off by any request to sign his name to other writers' words. In any case,
> neither William Bock nor his alleged son has been identified. (See also letter 191.)

57

6th Bengal Cavalry
Segoolie
Chumparun
India
Jan 21. 83

Dear Mr Clements,

I am half ashamed of writing to you again, but though I have never seen you,
you are about the best friend I have got. Do you remember my assaulting you
with a letter from a fever hospital about three years ago? Well now I have
changed my quarters to where we manufacture the article at first hand, there is
not a better place for smallpox and cholera in all India, than about here—

My reason for writing to you, is that I think it would please you to know how
even in this remote corner of the world your books are known and enjoyed, not
15 miles from Nipal, the other day I was attending a lady in labour, on the third
day after, I found her reading one of yours & had to inhibit it, lest she shd shake
herself loose!

The other evening at mess, I was telling the fellows of Buck Fanshaw's
funeral, and Scotty Brigg's interview with the parson, I thought they would go
to pieces—especially Major Jennings, the man who did the gallant action in
Egypt of seizing a lot of Egyptian trains in Zag-a-Zig with only a handful of sowars—

My copies of your books are worn to the bone with lending—Sir Girdlestone
the political resident in Nipal, a very scholarly man, was greatly struck with
your description of Kileauea. For goodness sake write something more, *we* are
just hungry for more, you cant think how we want to laugh in this Sun tormented fever bed of a country, I wish the Russians would take it & pension us
off. The swells from home come out in the cold weather and enjoy it immensely,
but in the hot weather, one fries in one's own perspiration, and goes mad with a
mixture of boils and a cursed malady peculiar to these climates, known as
'prickly heat' just then it takes some fortitude to see a joke!—

I apologize for troubling you, though it is done with the best intentions,

Sincerely yours
Donald M. Grant.

This illustration of Clemens's popularity among the British in India provides an insight into the success of his lecture tour there in 1896. When Donald Grant wrote to him from Ireland on 21 March 1882, he said he had read everything of Clemens's printed on his side of the Atlantic and knew most of it by heart. He also described himself as an "embryo doctor" at Dublin's Cork St. hospital. He earned bachelor degrees in medicine and surgery at the University of Dublin in 1881 (*Medical Press & Circular*, 20 July 1881, 30). Grant's 1883 post was at Sagauli near the Nepal border.

The Scotty Briggs interview Grant mentions is a mutually incomprehensible conversation between a western ruffian and a meek eastern parson in chapter 47 of *Roughing It* (1872). Major R.M. Jennings commanded a decisive cavalry action against the Egyptian railway station at Zagazig in September 1882. His "sowars" were the cavalry equivalent of infantry sepoys. Col. C.E.R. Girdlestone was the British resident in Nepal. A huge volcano on the island of Hawaii, Kilauea is described in chapter 75 of *Roughing It*.

58

Columbus, Ohio,
October 28th, '83,

Mr. Mark Twain
Hartford Con.

Dear Sir

I am a little girl nine years old. I have been reading Tom Sawyer quite a great deal and I think it is a very funny book and I now write to ask you to write a book of his manhood. I am a great reader that is I read very much, and of course I delight in all kinds books like that. We have two books that you wrote Tom Sawyer is one of them and the Prince and the Pauper is another. I delight in reading both of these books very much. I would be very much pleased if you would answer my letter. My address is Florence Cope, Corner Winner Ave. and Broad St., Columbus, Ohio. I have a brother fourteen years old and a little sister eight. I will be ten years old the 24th of next month and my little sister was 8 a few day ago. All of our family would enjoy a book of Tom's manhood and whether he turned out robber or not after all. I am in the fifth reader and enjoy those of books immensely. I would not know how to thank you enough if you would write another as good as the one about Tom and all our family would be very glad. I think Tom is just perfect. I am getting very tired so I must stop here.

Yours respectfully
Florence Dean Cope.

Clemens's comment: Praises from a small Ohio boy.

Florence Dean Cope (1873–1951) had a curious history. The head of a distinguished Columbus, Ohio, family, her father, Alexis Cope (1841–1918) was a prominent attorney and later an officer of Ohio State University. Her mother, Ione Cope (c. 1845–1923), was a first cousin of Clemens's close friend William Dean Howells. Howells and Florence Dean Cope thus inherited their middle names from the same ancestor (USCR; A. Cope, *History of the Ohio State University* [Columbus, 1920], xix–xxiv). Florence later studied journalism at Ohio State and was considered one of Columbus's most beautiful society women. In June 1899, shortly before she was to wed a former army captain, she eloped with Allen J. Seney (1875–1926). Eight years later Seney filed for divorce, charging that Cope's drinking had caused her to neglect him and her children. Seney later went on to a distinguished legal career, while Cope did some magazine writing, got into theatrical promotion, and married a man named Samuel Maurice. Late in her life, she did publicity work for the leprosarium in Carville, Louisiana, where she resided for several long stays during the late 1940s. After she died in Galveston, Texas, in 1951, her ashes were buried at the leprosarium ("Miss Cope Jilts Capt. Schurmer," Cleveland *Plain Dealer,* 25 June 1899; "Drink Brings to End an Ohio Romance," Tucson *Daily Citizen,* 7 Aug. 1907; S. Stein, *Alone No Longer* [Carville, La., 1974], 259–262).

59

Chicago, Feb. 4, 1884.

Dr. Sir,

I had just finished one of your stories and was thinking about it as I was walking down the street the other day.

All at once I was disturbed from my reverie by hearing a man say "that you deliberately murdered your grandmother in cold blood." This I could not believe and though I am only a boy I knocked the man who thus accused you, down. Was I not right?

Please answer & tell me.

Yours respectfully
W. P. Harrison

P.S. My address is:
231 Ashland Ave.,
Chicago, Ill.

Clemens's comment: Too thin

Clemens evidently regarded this letter as a transparent bid for an autograph. Why the writer invented a rumor about Clemens's murdering a grandmother is unclear. Not quite fifteen when he wrote, William Preston Harrison (1869–1940) was the son of Chicago mayor Carter Harrison Sr. (1825–1893), who would later be assassinated at the very address from which William was writing. William's older brother, Carter

Harrison Jr. (1860–1953), would also serve as Chicago's mayor. William himself later studied at the University of Chicago and in Europe and went into journalism. In 1918, he moved to Los Angeles, where he became a noted art patron and art director of the county museum (USCR; "Death Calls Art Patron," *Los Angeles Times*, 29 June 1940).

60

IMPRIMERIE ET LIBRAIRIE
POUR LES MATHÉMATIQUES, LES SCIENCES ET LES ARTS,
QUAI DES GRANDS-AUGUSTINS, 55.
GAUTHIER-VILLARS, SUCCESSEUR DE MALLET-BACHELIER, . . .

PARIS, 28/III 1884

Sir,

I found myself last year in Darmstadt, (Hesse), a small town formidably tedious as perhaps you know; it was eleven in the evening, I had made my daily round to the grills; for lack of greater fun distractions, I was disposed to go to bed, when in the room neighboring mine, I heard resound a burst of interminable laughter, which filled me with fear.—I say of fear. You know Darmstadt, you comprehend what could be the stupefication of an honest boy (me) who hears laughter in this town at eleven in the evening; note that the room from where these signs of equivocal gaiety came was occupied by a young man of Newark (New Jersey) who had only this evening drunk his daily beer.

A first explosion of laughter, another followed and then a third. "O horrible! Most horrible!" my poor Willy was becoming insane, insane fit to be tied! I knocked at his door, gently, with a dreadful palpitation.

"Can I enter, old friend Will?"

"Ye . . . ye . . . yes. He . . . he . . . in here!"

What a spectacle! The prey to an irresistible laugh, my neighbor twisted himself like an eel on his bed biting his handkerchief in vain hope of choking his joyous din, hilariously hitting his pillow.

"Ha! Ha! Ha! So queer!

"What's this?

"So funny!

"Who?

"So stunning!" So . . . twisted.

"? . . ."

Without being able to explain himself further he handed me a book signed Mark Twain.

Since that evening, Sir, I have learned to know you like Willy, I have devoured the handkerchiefs; like Willy I have rolled on my bed, but I have wanted to do more than him, and I tried to explain in some pages that I published why your humor has pleased the French so much, just like your own countrymen, "laughter is the nature of man." Even translated in French, the fragments of your works that I read at the Conference Olivaint had greatest success, a large number of my friends, on my counsel, undertook to read you, and all, all have thanked me for having introduced them to you.

But, I've been running on too long, so I'll stop. Pardon me, Sir, for only being able to say so badly what I feel so well.

Henry Gauthier-Villars fils

Clemens's comment: French translator

> Henry Gauthier-Villars (1859–1931), a French author and critic now best known as the first husband of novelist Colette (1873–1954), was the first person to publish a book about Clemens. In fact, he may have written this letter (translated from the original French) to promote that book, but no evidence has been found that Clemens replied. Not long before writing this letter, Gauthier-Villars delivered a long paper at a session of the student literary society Conférence Olivaint on humor focusing on Clemens. The same year, his family firm published the paper in book form as *Mark Twain*. After earning a law degree, Gauthier-Villars worked for his family's publishing firm, and his interests had turned to literature. A vigorous self-promoter, he published more than fifty novels under the pen name "Willy," many with the help of uncredited ghostwriters. The appearance of his pen name in his letter is a hint he was talking about himself. Indeed, the young New Jersey man he describes was probably imaginary, possibly inspired by Clemens's 1864 sketch "Aurelia's Unfortunate Young Man," whose title character is a "young man from New Jersey." Gauthier-Villars was probably also familiar with Clemens's 1872 sketch "How the Author Was Sold in Newark."
>
> Clemens may have passed through Darmstadt during his 1878 travels in Germany, but no evidence of his doing so has been found.

———

61

Box 1465
N.Y. CITY *Mar.* 31/84

S. S. Clemens, Esq.
Hartford, Conn.

Dear Sir

A friend has mentioned to me that he is about writing to you, requesting your autograph; and it occurs to me that it will be saving you trouble if I ask you to send one to me at the same time. Please write on a sheet of linen paper, not ruled, 10″ × 12″ in size, and free from blots. Arnold's writing fluid is preferred; and an original sentiment, as characteristic and humorous as possible, should

be prefixed. I should be obliged, if you would also add to your signature "Author
of the Schoolmaster Abroad."

Yrs. truly,

R. W. Raymond

This is one of at least eighty joke letters Clemens received around April Fools' Day in
1884. Many of the letters were prompted by this printed circular that George Washington Cable sent to writers and journalists:

> private and confidential.
>
> My Dear Mr.——:
>   It has been agreed among some friends of Mr. S. L. Clemens that all his friends,
> as far as they will, write to him on receipt of this circular mailing on such dates
> as to allow all the letters to reach him simultaneously on the first day of April
> asking for his autograph.
>   The consent to co-operate has been already been obtained from a number
> sufficient to make it certain that the matter will take the character intended for it,
> and this circular is now mailed to 150 persons of the literary and journalistic
> guild, in Boston, Hartford, Springfield, New York, Brooklyn, Washington and
> other cities, each of whom—with yourself—is requested to invite others, ladies or
> gentlemen, to take part.
>   It is suggested that no stamps or card or envelope be inclosed with the request;
> that no stranger to Mr. Clemens and no minor take part.
>
> Yours truly,
>
> G. W. Cable

The sender of the present letter, Rossiter Worthington Raymond (1840–1918), was
a German-trained mining engineer who also had notable achievements in literature,
law, and theology. His numerous books include *The Mines of the West* (1869), *Camp and
Cabin: Sketches of Life and Travel in the West* (1880), and *Brave Hearts* (1873), a Western novel published under the pseudonym Robertson Gray. It is not clear whether
Raymond knew Clemens personally. He may have gotten Cable's letter from Henry
Ward Beecher (1813–1887), pastor of Brooklyn's Plymouth Congregational Church, of
which he was a lifelong member. Beecher's own letter to Clemens stated, "Although I
am myself a very curmudgeon about answering autographe letters . . . I want others—
and your reputation for kindness in this respect emboldens me to ask for a *double*
one, viz your real name & pseudonym" (Beecher to Clemens, 31 Mar. 1884, MTP).

62

140 Pearl St

March 31ˢᵗ 1884

Dear Clemens

    I am acquainted with a beautiful young lady about 18 years old, who is
anxious to go upon the stage. I am too old to find out if she has other desires,
but you are about the proper age.

If by return mail you will send me your photograph and autograph, I will hand them to her, and ask for the pleasure of introducing you when you visit the city. I am

Very Sincerely
Chas Watrous.

Clemens's comment: Watrous

This April Fools' Day writer was Charles Watrous (1827–1891), a prominent New York City lumber merchant and vice president of the Staten Island Rapid Transit Co. (obituary, New York *Times*, 17 Aug. 1891). As Clemens may not have known him, he probably got his copy of Cable's circular letter from someone who received it directly from Cable.

63

Burlington, Iowa

Dear Mr Twain

I am a little girl, 8 years old and I am making a quilt with the names of all the great people in the world. Won't you please send me a piece of your clothes with your Autograph on it. I have sent for a piece of Queen Victoria and John Brown. Mamma says if you will please to write "Innocence abroad." on it. I may be sure you sent it.

Lovingly yours
Gracie Stearnes
No. 715 North 6th St
Burlington Iowa

P.S. If you know any more great persons won't you please tell me where they live so I can get peices of them. I am in a hurry to get my quilt down before the fair so I can get the premium to buy me a big doll they have the lovlyest one down town with natural hair and a diamond ring left over from Christmas. Goodbye

Postmarked 7 April 1884, this letter is of a type to which Clemens might have responded favorably, but it may have been a hoax or an adult attempt to get an autograph. Its penmanship is finer than one would expect from an eight-year-old; no "Gracie Stearnes" has been found in Burlington, Iowa; and the mention of abolitionist John Brown (1800–1859) may be a joke.

64

MO. WHEEL CO.

EXCLUSIVE AGENCY OF THE COLUMBIA BICYCLES,

. . .

210 & 212 NORTH 12TH, NEAR OLIVE STREET,

ST. LOUIS, MO., JUL 7 1884

Saml. L. Clemens Esq

Friend "Mark"

When yourself and a Companion left the "Quaker City" at Naples in July 67 and came to Rome you there met a young American who roomed at the Via Babuino #68 (Pincion Hill) it was his pleasure to show you some points of the Eternal City.

After exactly 17 years he now addresses you first to Congratulate you on your continued success and next to greet you as a brother wheelman.

By todays express I send one of our patent Duryea Saddles try it and if found worthy give us a few lines on it.

Yours Truly

Richard Garvey.

Clemens's comment: Sho!

This letter reveals something new about Clemens's 27 July to ca. 1 August 1867 visit to Rome with Dan Slote and Dr. Abraham Jackson, his closest friends throughout the *Quaker City* voyage (*Mark Twain's Letters* [Berkeley, 1990], 2:393–394). Chapters 26–28 of *The Innocents Abroad* describe that phase of his travels.

Richard Garvey (1845–1931) emigrated from Ireland to America with his parents as a young child. By 1860, he and a brother were working with their father in ornamental plastering in New York City. Garvey's letter shows he was in Rome in 1867. He cannot be found in 1870 U.S. census reports, but in 1880 he was living in St. Louis, married to the daughter of the prosperous St. Louis merchant Charles Rueppele. The April–September 1883 *Wheelman* reported that Garvey, then captain of the Missouri Bicycle Club, "has just perfected arrangements to devote all his energy to the bicycle business" (p. 313). His involvement in that business was apparently brief. The 27 August 1886 issue of *Cycle* reported him in San Diego, California, "managing a stage route and a mine" (p. 365). Garvey relocated to San Diego in 1891 and spent his last thirty-eight years in Los Angeles, where he appears to have worked in the carnival-ride business (USCR; death certificate, Los Angeles County, 13 Sept. 1931).

Garvey alludes to contemporary newspaper accounts of Clemens's learning how to ride a bicycle in May 1884. Around this same time, Clemens wrote "Taming the Bicycle," but that essay was not published until 1917. A U.S. Patent Office record dated 19 February 1884 shows that Charles E. Duryea (1861–1938) assigned one-half his rights in the "Bicycle-Saddle" to Garvey. Duryea and his brother, James Frank Duryea (1869–1967), later pioneered in the automobile industry (C. W. Carey Jr., *American Inventors, Entrepreneurs & Business Visionaries* [New York, 2002], 103–105).

. 65

S.S. "Umbria"
18 Nov. 1884

My dear Sir,

I have just been hearing you read, and my pleasure was only marred by the
regret that Scotchmen had so few chances of hearing you at any time.

Now I do not know if you care anything about lecturing but if you ever did
think of visiting my country I think you would have a very great success.
Perhaps you are aware how widely your books are read & *understood* in Scotland. I know I am not alone in having read every word you have ever published I
think; and I *know* how keenly you are appreciated in that dull witted country.

I am on my way home after 6 weeks in New York. If you think worth while to
say anything to my idea my address is .

Nunholm, Dowanhill Gardens Glasgow. I am only a Glasgow merchant, but
if you care I would gladly make all enquiries for you. I know I could guarantee
you good audiences & a pleasant reception in Glasgow. If all this is impertinence never mind. I only write because I feel that I know you: your works are so
exsactly yourself that I felt you were no stranger the moment you opened your
mouth.

Believe me, with much admiration,
Your obedient Servant
William Smart.

S. L. Clemens, Esq.

Perhaps I should say, in excuse for addressing you, that I also am a lecturer—
and, of course, never reform.

Clemens visited Scotland in July–August 1873 but never lectured there. His Scottish
correspondent, William Smart (1853–1915), interrupted his University of Glasgow
education to work in his father's threadworks mill until the early 1880s, when he returned to school to complete a master's degree. On his father's retirement, he became
a partner in the firm but was freed from that responsibility when the firm was sold in
1884. Later that year, he visited the United States to oversee his interests in a manufacturing concern. He probably heard Clemens and George Washington Cable do
readings at New York City's Chickering Hall on 18 November. In later years, Smart
became a professor of political economy at Glasgow and published extensively on
economics (Thomas Jones, "Biographical Sketch," in William Smart, *Second Thoughts
of an Economist* [London, 1916], ix–lxxix).

66

November the 23rd 1884.

Sir,

Having red your "Tramps Abroad" with the greatest interest, I feel encouraged by it, to ask for a favour, which I hope according to my high opinion of it's author will not be refused.

Your descriptions of all the interesting trips as well as the charming charachteristics of the persons you met with, pleased me in so much, that I could not but inform others of my being enchanted and cause them to read this work.—But how surprised was I to hear, that you are told to have never seen those countries, and to have nevertheless been able to give such most artistic pictures of them. Doubts about this puzzled me for a long time, in so much that I resolved to chose the directest way for hearing the fact. Hoping, that you will fulfil the wish of a young lady, who takes such interest of you, by answering very soon, I am already now very much obliged to you.

Your respectfully
Eugenie Alexander.

Clemens's comment: Bid for autograph

Eugenie Alexander was apparently a German who composed this letter in English. Clemens's suspicion of her sincerity may have been unfounded. He did visit the places described in *A Tramp Abroad* (1880), but during the early 1870s he had experimented with writing proxy narratives based on notes provided by other travelers.

Alexander's unused return envelope is addressed to 27 Bendlerstrasse, Berlin. That same address would be used as a German army propaganda headquarters during World War II.

67

Cambridge, Dec. 17th, 1884.

Mr. Samuel L. Clemens:
Dear Sir,

When my sick friend read me the passage of Emmeline's untimely promptness, and the occasion of her one deficiency, I was equally tumultuous; so, likewise, have others been, to whom I have read or repeated it.

The last stanza of my poem is an *exaggeration* of a very natural conjecture, judging all humorists by one.

With best wishes.
Very truly yours,
Charlotte Fiske Bates.

Enclosure

TO "MARK TWAIN."

How full of tears the sick man's eyes!
   His suffering must be sore,
For, though of pain he nearly dies,
   He never roared before.
Nay! he doth read of Emmeline,
   How her announcing verse
Of every death, the second sign,
   Went once, *behind* the hearse.
Yes! for a moment, wonted pain
   Left laughter full of health;
That man who goes by name of Twain
   Has done a good, by stealth.
Though men are rightly slow to mirth,
   Over their *grave* affairs;
Yet kindly humor has its worth,
   With Peril on the stairs.
But thus it crossed me while I laughed;—
   Twain has his solemn side,
And plying well Thalia's craft,
   Who knows but that *he* cried?

Charlotte Fiske Bates.

Clemens's comment: Verses—Charlotte Fiske Bates

A deceased background figure described in chapter 17 of *Huckleberry Finn* (1885), Emmeline Grangerford is noted for having dashed off funerary poems even before the undertaker arrived whenever someone died. Her fatal "deficiency" was failing to find a rhyme for "Whistler."

Because *Huckleberry Finn* was not issued in book form in the United States until early 1885, the present correspondent's sick friend must have read about Emmeline in an extract published in the December 1884 *Century*. A former schoolteacher, Charlotte Fiske Bates (1838–1916) herself published a poem in that magazine's next issue. She was also a correspondent of poet Henry Wadsworth Longfellow, whose work she helped edit. She compiled anthologies, published poetry of her own, and later taught literature in a New York school (Cambridge Women's Heritage Project, www.cam bridgema.gov, accessed 23 Dec. 2011). Her emphasis on death in the present letter is ironic because her own death was prematurely announced in newspapers in early 1890—seven years before "exaggerated" reports of Clemens's death were published ("Charlotte Fiske Bates Dead," Trenton, New Jersey, *Evening Times*, 6 Jan. 1890; "The Modern Athenian Remembers a Poet When Her Death Is Reported," Chicago *Daily Inter Ocean*, 11 Jan. 1890).

68

DEZOUCHE & ATWATER,
PIANOS AND ORGANS,
49 BEAVER HALL,

MONTREAL, Feby 19 1885

Mark Twain Esq
Dear Sir

Your "Tragical tale of a Fishwife" last night reminded me that I, too, tried to learn German. It was years ago, and when I had crept in, about up to my ankles, I discovered words which looked badly, sounded badly, and almost smelled badly. So one night when my teacher came I told him I had prepared no lesson for him, but I had worked some of the curious words into a rhyme. There & then I had to give it to him & here it is for you

THE SLEIGH RIDE

Mein Kleine Schatz, Come let us start,
You need the air to day.
We'll have a glorious Schlitten fahrt
In meinem neuen Sleigh.

She whispered me, my own sweetheart
So low, I scarcely heard,
"Mein Gott! I schmell that Schlitten fahrt
It must have been das Pferd."

Excuse me for bothering you but I would very much like to have your autograph.

Yours Truly
C. C. De Zouche

Adapted from a section of "The Awful German Language" in *A Tramp Abroad*, "The Tragic Tale of a Fishwife" mocked German's ostensibly random assignments of genders to nouns by comically mixing "he," "she," and "it." The correspondent's poem is a nonsense mixture of German and English. Rendered correctly, its German phrases should read *meiner kleiner Schatz* (my little treasure), *Schlittenfahrt* (sleigh ride), and *das Pferd* (the horse). "Schmell" is neither German nor English.

Charles C. DeZouche (c. 1830–1896) probably attended Clemens and George Washington Cable's 18 February readings at Montreal's Queens Hall. DeZouche himself was an Irish immigrant who settled in Virginia and became an officer in the Confederate Army. After the Civil War, he spent at least several years in Montreal, where he may possibly have gone before the war ended. He later lived in Baltimore, Maryland; Dallas and Waco, Texas; and Cleveland, Ohio. From the early 1870s through the 1890s, he published music and sold pianos and other instruments. In 1892, he wrote the lyrics of "Turn Texas Loose," the campaign song used in Democrat George Clark's unsuccessful run for governor (U.S. and Canadian census reports; *Encyclopedia of Music in Canada*, www.thecanadianencyclopedia.com, accessed 18 Jan. 2011).

69

Indianapolis, Ind., Feb. 25, 1885

Mr. Clemens—
Dear Sir:

Your sketches in which real characters and their varied dialects occur have interested and delighted me for many years; and in thanking you, as I want to now, I ask you to accept as well the little book of Hoosier dialect I mail with this.

Very Truly Yours,
James Whitcomb Riley.

Clemens's comment: J W Riley the poet

James Whitcomb Riley (1849–1916), the "Hoosier Poet," was on the threshold of fame when he wrote this letter. He and Clemens had not yet met, but they later became friends and regular correspondents. The book he sent was *"The Old Swimmin'-Hole" and 'Leven More Poems* (1883).

70

Cleveland Ohio 3/10/85

Dear Sir:

For Gods sake give a suffering public a rest on your labored wit.—Shoot your trash & quit it.—You are only an *imitator of* ARTEMAS WARD & a sickening one at that & we are *all sick of you,* For Gods sake take a tumble & give U.S. a rest.—

U.S.—

The blast in this anonymous postcard may have been directed against *Huckleberry Finn*, which was first published in the United States a month earlier. Artemus Ward was the pen name of Charles Farrar Browne (1834–1867), a popular humorist who befriended Clemens in Nevada in 1863 and encouraged him to write for eastern journals.

71

Fort Collins Colorado
March. 24th 1885

Mr S. L. Clemens
New Haven Conn

Dear Sir.

While confined to my room the result of a runaway accident a year ago, a young lady the grandaughter of the proprietor of the hotel, brought me your work, Tom Sawyer, to read. I read it aloud to her. it took us an awful long time to read it and—well, we are married now, & she thinks we ought to have a nicely bound copy of it on our table, as it was indirectly responsible for our marriage. not knowing where to procure it, I thought I would ask you to tell me. hoping that you will pardon me for troubling you.

Respectfully
G. W. Galloway, M.D.

Clemens's comment: Tom Sawyer

This letter's story appears to be essentially true. An Ohio-educated physician, George W. Galloway (1846–1893) practiced medicine in Mt. Blanchard, Ohio; Shawnee, Kansas; Ft. Collins, Colorado; and Trinidad, Colorado, before settling permanently in Findlay, Ohio, in 1886. His first wife died in 1880. On 10 September 1884, he married Flora M. Schneider (1860–1891) of Akron, Ohio, in Colorado. Flora's maternal grandfather, Jacob Welch, was a prosperous Ft. Collins businessman who built the town's Windsor Hotel around 1880. Ironically, Flora later died from her injuries in a horse-related accident similar to the one that had brought Galloway and her together (USCR; obituary, *Trans. of the 48th Annual Meeting of the Ohio State Medical Society* [Cincinnati, 1893], 387; Findagrave.com, accessed 27 Jan. 2011; "Mrs Doctor Galloway," Canton, Ohio, *Evening Repository*, 22 Dec. 1891; Barbara Fleming and Malcolm McNeill, *Fort Collins* [Charleston, S.C., 2010], 47).

72

THE CLINTON COURANT
CLINTON, MASS.
W. J. COULTER, PUBLISHER.
W. E. PARKHURST, EDITOR.

April 4 1885

S. L. Clemens Esq
Hartford, Conn.—

Dr Sir

Presuming on a brief acquaintance with you, formed on the occasion of your visit to our town some fifteen year ago, I made you a copy of my paper, by wh. you will see that our Library directors have decided to help your sale of ["]Huckleberry Finn" by *refusing* it a place in our library. I can assure you, that the anxiety to see and read "Huckleberry" is on the increase here; the adults are daily inquiring where "Finn" can be had, and even the children are crying for "Huckleberries"; the only way by wh. we can preserve some of our young lads in the facts of moral rectitude is a promise to give them a copy of Mark Twain's rejected "H.F."—Both as an *incentive* and as an *opiate* the *promise* of a copy of this work is a marked success.

Yours Very Truly
W. E. Parkhurst
Editor of "Courant"

Clemens's comment: Huck Finn

On 15 November 1869, Clemens lectured in Clinton, a town about twenty miles southwest of Concord, whose public library attracted national attention when it removed *Huckleberry Finn* from its shelves on 16 March 1885. Wellington Evarts Parkhurst (1835–1924) began a three-decade career as editor of the Clinton *Weekly Courant* in 1865. He also held many public offices, including several terms in the Massachusetts state legislature during the early 1890s (Edwin M. Bacon, ed., *Men of Progress . . . Massachusetts* [Boston, 1896], 245–246; Findagrave.com, accessed 4 Feb. 2011). The enclosure he mentions has been lost.

73

Bridgeport, April 23, '85.

Mr. S. L. Clemens,

Dear Sir,

The unrelenting hatred of hypocrisy and oppression that runs through all your writings encourages me to appeal to you in behalf of a cause which at present is occupying the minds of the thinking world.

Voltaire ridiculed dogmatic superstition of the 18th century out of existence. His work was more effective than all the powers of arms could have been.

Why should not Mark Twain imitate his noble example and wield his mighty pen for the abolition of Wage-slavery—the curse of the 19th century!

Make this the crowning effort of your life and generations of grateful people will bless your memory.

A Socialist.

Clemens's comment: Socialist

This anonymous letter seems unconnected to any specific work. After Clemens published *A Connecticut Yankee* in 1889, however, he received many similar suggestions to turn his pen to economic issues. Clemens was familiar with the writings of the eighteenth-century French satirist Voltaire, but his only published mention of Voltaire appeared in a quotation from James Boswell's *The Life of Samuel Johnson* (1791) in his 1891 essay "Mental Telegraphy" (Alan Gribben, *Mark Twain's Library* [Boston, 1980], 2:729).

74

Keokuk, June 8, 1885.

My Dear Brother:—

I just now met John H. Craig, the leading lawyer here, and possessing the chief local reputation as a poet and popular orator.

He says he read Huckleberry Finn through, and then reread it and studied the points. In his view Huckleberry Finn is as distinctly a created character as Falstaff. The dialogues between him and Jim are inimitable, and the dialect perfect. How you could get down to their ideas, especially Jim's of King Sollerman, and manage so many dialects he does not see His boys lie on the floor and read it, and roll over, and laugh. It is full of fun.

Tom Sawyer was read and loaned till it had to be re-covered; and Huckleberry will soon start on the same journey.

He regards Jim as a very clear-cut character; standing out with Huckleberry natural distinctness. He can see them. To him they are real characters.

The feud is a perfect picture.

I am going to take ma to the park this afternoon. The artesian well water has iron, magnesia and sulfur and other things, and seems to benefit her. It is in the park.

Love to all,
Your Brother, Orion.

P.S. Sometime ago Charley Whitney here told me he had seen the Duke and the King (whom Craig considers as wonderfully strong as samples of meanness). Whitney says a man came into the store once, where he was, and bought some bars of common washing soap, about a foot long, by an inch and an inch and a half. He cut it up into small cakes, wrapped them in tissue paper and sold them in the country in Iowa and Missouri villages at auction, for the cure of corns, to eradicate freckles, take out stains, and wash niggers white. He made 4^{50} on a box or two of that soap.

Another came since he has been in the foundry here, and got work in the moulding-room. After working a few days they discharged him. He learned from him that he had once got hard up and put out a shingle as a lawyer. Some hands paid him a hundred dollars to libel a vessel. He gave a lawyer forty dollars, and left after the trial. He procured a paper with advertisements, before he left Whitney's office, and selected the foremanship of 3 different kinds of business, for which he meant to apply in answer to the advertisements.

This letter from Clemens's older brother, Orion Clemens (1825–1897), merits inclusion here because it relates the reactions of two strangers to *Huckleberry Finn*. John Henderson Craig (1824–1893) was a native of Pennsylvania who had been admitted to the bar in 1856 while working in the law office of a Pennsylvania congressman. The following year, he settled in Keokuk, Iowa, and formed a partnership with Judge R. P. Lowe, later governor of Iowa, and John W. Noble, later secretary of the interior under President Benjamin Harrison. Craig himself retired from his practice in 1888. Throughout his legal career, he wrote unpublished poetry and prose while earning a reputation for having "fine literary taste" and being a brilliant lecturer ("John Henderson Craig," *Biographical Review of Lee County, Iowa* [Chicago, 1905], 465–468).

Sir John Falstaff was a roguish character in William Shakespeare's plays *Henry IV*, parts 1 and 2 (1597–1598), and *The Merry Wives of Windsor* (1597). In chapter 14 of *Huckleberry Finn*, the escaping slave Jim argues that the biblical king Solomon (Sollermun) must not have been wise if he had a million wives and especially not if he would "chop a chile in two." An "Explanatory Note" in *Huckleberry Finn* says that the book's characters speak in seven different dialects.

"Ma," the Clemens brothers' mother, Jane Lampton Clemens (1803–1890), lived with Orion and his wife, Mollie, in Keokuk from 1883 until she died. Charley Whitney has not been identified. The "duke" and "king" are the only names by which the scoundrels who join Huck and Jim on the raft in chapter 19 of *Huckleberry Finn* are known.

75

Detroit, July 18/85

My Dear "Mark Twain."

About fifteen years ago I was impelled by my great delight in "Innocents Abroad" to write you, which won for me in reply a little note, still kept among my chief treasures.

Since then nothing that you have written has so appealed to my feelings as this paper on the Government of Children, in the Christian Union, and before *I* cool off I want to thank you in behalf of the little innocents who are being experimented upon in so many homes to their everlasting discomfort—if nothing worse—and their parent's disgrace. Being a wife and mother I have been especially tormented by this very subject—or the discussion of it, in the C.U. and the modes of torture adopted by adult obstinates for the coercion of Infant obstinates. Imagine a mother keeping her three year old son three days in a dark room, toyless and supperless, to make him pick up a scrap of paper. I think I could have accomplished the same result in about three minutes, and had half a minute to spare for his after comforting. Only I would not have been so elated with my success that I must publish the entire story.

Your paper, so sensible, so alert, vigorous and twainy—(if I may coin a word) is delightful. My thirteen year old daughter says she cannot imagine the lazy, drawling, humorous reader of the Blue Jay writing such an article; and her mother says that you have risen head and shoulders above yourself. The great humorist is also the wise father and sensible appreciative husband. You have I think only paid an honest debt by this paper, for, in your time, you have given the boys no end of valuable hints how to become bad boys, and it is only just that you should furnish their parents with a few rules for their after control.—

Your tribute to your wife has touched me deeply. To her I am sure this bud of long silence opening to such a blossom will be an unceasing benediction. Long after Tom Sawyer and Huckleberry Fin are forgotten these eloquent and beautiful words will be quoted, and she whom you have so tenderly honored, will henceforth be placed above other wives for their love, admiration and example. You may wear your laurel wreath—Her you have "crowned with glory and honor."

May she so rear your young brood that they will be her comfort in old age, and have a reasonable respect for their Father.

Yours Sincerely
Tilla Bradshaw Swales.

Clemens's comment: Preserve it

The 16 July 1885 issue of the *Christian Union* published "On Training Children," Clemens's reply to "What Ought He to Have Done?" in the magazine's 11 June issue. Widely reprinted, Clemens's article compared the child-disciplining techniques of a man called "John Senior" in the earlier article unfavorably to those of his own wife. It elicited a variety of positive and negative reactions from readers. Clemens's wife, Livy, was not pleased with his *Christian Union* article—especially after seeing the letter he received from "Thomas Twain" (see letter 76).

Born in Ohio, Susan Matilda (Tilla or Tillie) Bradshaw Swales (1843–1916) was the wife of prominent Detroit businessman Charles Everett Swales (1840–1900), whom she married in 1871 ("Charles E. Swales Has Passed Away," Detroit *Free Press*, 30 Aug. 1900; "Mrs. Susan M. Swales Dies," *Free Press*, 13 Oct. 1916). The earlier correspondence she mentions has not been found. Her thirteen-year-old daughter, Grace B. Swales, was her oldest of three children. In 1896, Grace married the wholesale jeweler Herman A. Rolshoven and apparently never had children of her own (USCR). The bluejay yarn that intrigued Grace appeared in chapter 2 of *A Tramp Abroad* (1880).

On 16 June 1904, Swales wrote to Clemens again to express her sorrow over his wife's recent death in Italy: "The pathetic picture of you, as I read it, sitting by your beloved dead in a foreign city, has haunted me ever since, You, who have made the world laugh, weeping alone; you who so strangely seem to belong to us all . . . You have never seen my face and yet I know you well, through your books." The 1904 letter confirms that Clemens replied to her present letter.

76

Mr Mark Twain
Sir

Your opinion as to the charms and goodness of your children carries no weight. Your neighbors *may* agree with you, or they may *not*—The public do not know their private opinions. I would hope anyway that the children are an improvement on their father, that their mother has taught them what she has failed to teach her husband (probably because filthy King Solomon does not sanction corporal punishment applied to husbands) to see when they become tiresome, when they are bores, when their forced jokes and eternal straining after wit and smartness are a d——d nuisance, and when speaking generally, they should shut up, talk less about themselves, and subside. I am assuming they are chips of the old block, and require what their father clearly did not get enough of—"corporal punishment"—

But they may not be artificial fools—They may be bright, loving children, with children's imperfections, caprices, impetuosities, sensitiveness. In such case, I contest altogether the 'goodness' of either your wife or her training in "invariably letting a few hours elapse between the sentence and the execution so that no anger on her part shall enter into the matter." What sense is there in this when the sentence is passed in anger, and is irreversible even after a few hours cooling down, and is carried out with 'calm' brutality. It is clear the good woman enjoys the contemplation of the treat in store for her. But what of the child? What is its state of mental agony and fright during these horrible intervening hours? The 'torture' to sensitive children would be something damnable. Doltish, sulky, stupid children would perhaps not greatly dread the coming "calm" castigation in view of the 'taffy' and 'blarney' in which it would end. You should keep your farcical domestic discipline to yourself, and not bother the public with it. It would suit few children of sensitive, or proud, or high-spirited temperament. It would still suit fewer mothers. Your wife must be a solemn ass, a prig, a calvinistic schoolmistress of three generations back. I hate the very idea of her perambulating around thinking of the "duty" i.e. treat to come, and then with her damned "calmness" executing the 'sentence,' and requesting the child to see that it is in love and not in "anger"—Oh—damn the woman! I had such a mother, and being my mother I shall say nothing disrespectful of her except this that neither my two brothers nor myself shed a tear for her when she died, and although our sister did cry in a feminine way, she rapidly reconciled herself to the loss of the admirable disciplinarian with her irrevocable sentences, her hours of torturing delay, her calm 'execution,' and her hateful embraces and humbug afterwards which made hypocrites of all of us. It gives me pleasure to damn your wife. I feel she deserves it, and it relieves me. When our father married a second time some three years after our mother's death, our young step mother won all our hearts. No damned crocodile calmness about her. She had little bits of temper, she could give and take with her tongue, sometimes she would give us a little slap, but everything in that way was soon forgotten, she was joyous, kind, charitable, indulgent, good—She believed in bright example and good humor, & any hastiness of temper was only a summer cloud—She knew children, she loved them, she understood our minds and our imperfect point of view. She was worth 20 cartloads of stereotyped, drill sergeant mothers with their d——d organized discipline—

When you were at it, Mr Mark Twain, why did not you make a little money by a graphic description of the "scene of torture," and a full account of the modus operandi. I'll be bound admirable Mrs Twain has some special method, or weapon of her own, which she has calmly thought out and given some mind to. I'll be bound also she knows all the soft spots of a child's anatomy, and carefully notes and studies the effects as she calmly exerts herself in the "scene of torture"—Torture! Good God, and by a Christian mother!

'Suffer little children to come unto me, and after being duly 'tortured' for a space by a scientist and student in fulfillment of a promise made in anger four hours ago, but which cannot now be revoked, or modified, and then when their

flesh is quivering I will woo them back to happy heartedness and joyful spirit'—
Admirable Mrs Pecksniff Twain!

Your admirable wife be damned, Mr Twain. I only wish I had her in a room
quietly by myself and free of interruption for half an hour. I would tie her
hands, I would strap her on a table, her feet on the floor, making a fine half
crescent at a certain part of her body, convex side upper-most, I would bare her
to the skin, and then proceed to ply a stout leather strap with knotted tails to
her buttocks. Heavens! I enjoy the very idea of it! There would be no delay
between sentence and execution. I would consider my anger righteous. But in
the tempest, torrent, whirlwind of my passion I would beget a calmness of
scientific application. I would study the torture and I would rejoice with
exceeding joy as I saw the blisters and welts accumulating under my scientific
handling. Then I would untie Mrs Twain, and lead her to the sofa, and then in
less time than it takes to tell it "love her back into happy heartedness and a
joyful spirit"!

Mr Twain. You are getting to be a bore, a nuisance, an intrusive fool. We
dont look to you for wisdom, or guidance in matters domestic, national, or
educational. So please shut up. Dont bother us with your wife. You are bore
enough. Kindly read the enclosed cut from today's paper. You will see your
wife's admirable methods although they may suit your ~~no doubt~~ probably
stupid children, wont apply everywhere. Good bye Twain. I dont read anything
you write now, but happened to read a paragraph summarizing your blowing
letter about your wife and children & I thought it as well to let you see there
were two sides to the question, & when your children grow up unless they turn
out solemn fools, prigs, asses, they will shew you Ha!

Yours till we meet across the Jordan

Thomas Twain

Clemens's comment: Letter—evidently from "John Senior."

Postmarked New York City, 21 July 1885, this letter responds to "'What Ought He to
Have Done?': Mark Twain's Opinion," an article by Clemens in the *Christian Union*
replying to an earlier article about child discipline (see letter 75 above). Its "Thomas
Twain" signature is an obvious pseudonym. Clemens suspected the writer was the
father called "John Senior" in the original *Christian Union* article. His own article
had compared Senior's disciplinary methods unfavorably to those of his wife, Livy.
The letter's description of Clemens's remarks about his wife's disciplining methods
are broadly accurate, but in calling her "Mrs Pecksniff Twain," the letter equated her
with a character in Charles Dickens's *Martin Chuzzlewit* (1843–1844) whose name
became synonymous with hypocrisy. The letter's sadistic fantasy may make it the
nastiest letter Clemens preserved. It naturally angered Clemens, but his anger abated
after he concluded it may have been written by the man whom he had publicly criti-
cized. Clemens's daughter Susy wrote about the incident:

A little while after the article was published letters began to come in to papa crittisizing it, there were some very pleasant ones but a few very disagreable. One of these, the very worst, mamma got hold of and read, to papa's great regret, it was full of the most disagreble things, and so very enoying to papa that he for a time felt he must do something to show the author of it his great displeasure at being so insulted. But he finally decided not to, because he felt the man had some cause for feeling enoyed at, for papa had spoken of him, (he was the baby's father) rather slightingly in his Christian Union Article. (Clemens, autobiographical dictation of 21 Dec. 1906, in Mark Twain's Autobiographical Writings, ed. R. Kent Rasmussen [New York, 2012], 205)

The enclosure Twain mentions is an unidentified newspaper clipping above which Twain wrote: "If you will keep your eye on the newspapers you will see such instances by the hundreds." The article concerns a girl who reappeared after having disappeared three years earlier after being severely frightened by her teacher's threat of a whipping.

77

78 Main street
Cincinnati O Aug 10th 1885

My Dear "Mark Twain"

I have been compelled on more than one occasion to listen to objections from readers of "The adventures of Huckleberry Finn" to the sketch of the Grangerford and Shepherdson family feud. The mildest form of criticism concludes usually with the statement that to assume the existence of such a state of things in any part of the country is "unnatural, unreasonable ridiculous and absurd." When replying, in some heat I must confess, that this scene though sketched in your matchless style is in as far as the facts go but a leaf from the daily record of our day and times I have been asked with triumphant scorn to produce the data for my assertion which you will readily understand are not always at hand. The enclosed clipping from the Cincinnati Enquirer for Aug. 10th reveals a case exactly in point and is only one of many brought to the notice of the intelligent newspaper reader every year. If it lies in your power either as writer or publisher to bring this knowledge to the attention of the *lunkheads* who disbelieve in the reality of the southern *vendetta,* I pray you do so, and confer an everlasting favor upon

Yours Truly
J. C. Fuller

Clemens's comment: southern feud. | answer

The Grangerford-Shepherdson feud in chapters 17–18 of *Huckleberry Finn* climaxes with the deaths of all the male Grangerfords. Michael Hearn summarizes the historical basis of the feud in *The Annotated "Huckleberry Finn"* (rev. ed., New York, 2001), 189–191n. 17.

John C. Fuller (born c. 1838) was a leather merchant in Cincinnati during the 1880s. His wife is listed as a widow in the 1900 census (USCR). Clemens's reply to his letter has not been found. The clipping to which he alludes is not with his letter; however, on 9 August 1885 the Cincinnati *Enquirer* published "The Kentucky Outlaw: An Interesting Chat with Craig Tolliver, the Terror of Rowan County." Confined in a county jail, Tolliver "suffer[ed] considerable pain from thirty-two buckshot wounds received at the hands of the Martin faction in old Rowan County." Tolliver's interview relates graphic details of the bloody feud between his family and the Rowans.

78

Watseka Ill. Nov 6th 1885.

Samuel L. Clemens Esq.

Dear Sir and Friend;

I have some-what against you! Your books have been always of lively interest to me, and whenever I have read one, have laid it aside with a sigh of relief—because it comes out right. The last volume to receive my attention was "Prince and Pauper" and there is trouble right here. I can not let go of it. I read it and it won't *stay* read. Some how or other, that miserable Tom Canty keeps following me and scratching my imagination until I am forced to go with him again through his troubles. I know it is all a—true story, but it bothers me worse than some little things *I* have told. (I am a minister.)

Can you not devise some remedy for my trouble. Tell me how to get loose, or I may try to become a king myself and just get into no end of trouble.

I am a humble servant in the vineyard, as it were, and I do not think you ought to so unsettle me. At any rate I demand a recipe that will recover me. Do not think I look upon you as an enemy for

I am

Yours,

Edward O. Sharpe

Clemens's comment: Compliments Prince & Pauper

The prince of *The Prince and the Pauper* (1881) who became King Edward VI was a historical figure, but the novel's story is entirely fictitious. Nevertheless, a prefatory passage in the book states: "It may be history, it may be only legend, a tradition. It may have happened, it may not have happened: but it *could* have happened."

Edward O. Sharpe (1862–1942) began working as a Christian minister in Iowa in 1883. Over the next three decades, he had pastorates in Illinois, Minnesota, Texas, and Colorado. The 1920 census lists him as working for a collection agency in Denver,

Colorado, but in 1930 he was listed as a Disciples of Christ clergyman in Denver. According to contemporary news accounts, he was forced out of some of his pastorates when charged with financial wrongdoing (USCR; David McWhirter, "Missionary Tidings," www.mun.ca/rels, accessed 1 Jan. 2011).

79

OFFICE OF A. J. WILLIAMS, M.D.

MCGREGOR, IOWA, Nov. 14 1885

Samuel L. Clemens,

My dear Sir,

I am an admirer of you, and as this admiration is cumulative it has at last got beyond my control, and I am obliged to resort to that solace of all affectionately perturbed spirits, a letter.

The immediate cause of this outbreak is the article which you wrote on that matter of "John Senior."

My wife & I both think that was the best & wisest & most human-hearted thing ever written on that subject, & we want to thank you.

And while my pen is wet, I will, in a professional way, express my gratitude for that quiet humor which has done more good in the world than all the doctors physic. Please keep on making people laugh.

This letter does not require an answer, any more than a cloud requires excuse for raining.

Yours very truly,

A. J. Williams.

Clemens's comment: Compliments for the "John Senior" article

This is one of many letters responding to Clemens's *Christian Union* article (see letters 75 and 76). Dr. A. J. Williams advertised himself as a homeopathic physician during the 1880s (Michelle Pettit, McGregor Public Library, personal communication, 2 Feb. 2011). Clayton County, Iowa, death certificate records include six signed by an A. J. Williams in 1886–1888, but that name does not appear in records for 1880–1885 or 1889–1896. Williams's residence in the county may thus have been brief.

80

THE COLUMBUS EVENING DISPATCH
—AND—
DOLLAR WEEKLY DISPATCH
NO. 26 NORTH HIGH STREET,

COLUMBUS, O, DEC. 5, 1885

Mr. Samuel L. Clemens:

Dear Sir: Permit a humble admirer of your genius to call your attention to the enclosed lines in which the writer has attempted to express the hope that you may grow old slowly.

Yours respectfully
Osman C. Hooper
Ass't Editor

P.S.—I should perhaps have said that I am the author of them and that they first appeared in the *Dispatch,* this evening. ,

O. C. H.

Enclosure

TO MARK TWAIN
ON THE OCCASION OF HIS FIFTIETH BIRTHDAY.

Mark time, Mark! The years are going
And your hair is silvery growing;
Age is flower of Youth full-blown
Yielding pain from effort sown.
    Mark time, Mark!

Mark time, Mark! Your years are fifty,
Humor pleasant, living thrifty;
While your comrades onward go,
Halt in mimic marching, so.
    Mark time, Mark!

Mark time, Mark! For hundreds younger,
Who for wit and humor hunger,
Hurry on through mists of tears
Toward the spot your laughter clears.
    Mark time, Mark!

Mark time, Mark! Then backward striding,
Find amid the young a hiding

From that Foe who, day or dark,
Ever seeks a shining Mark.
Mark time, Mark!

The poem celebrates Clemens's fiftieth birthday on 30 November 1885. Osman Castle Hooper (1858–1941) began his nearly six-decade association with the Columbus, Ohio, *Dispatch* in 1880 as a telegraph editor. He later spent twenty years writing editorials and then became the paper's literary editor in 1917. He continued editing the book page after becoming a professor of journalism at Ohio State University in 1918. He also published histories of Ohio journalism, Ohio State University, and Columbus, Ohio. The Ohio Newspaper Association later named its annual newspaper competition after him (USCR; "Hall of Fame's Founder Is Dead," Cleveland *Plain Dealer*, 12 May 1941; "Osman C. Hooper Newspaper Show: Awards & Judges' Reports," 2010).

81

Bethlehem, Penna
Dec. 9/85

Dear Sir—

Your courtesy in complying so readily with my request calls forth my warmest thanks. "Mark Twain" is become with me as elsewhere, a household word from my wife down to the youngest of our five boys.— 'Innocents Abroad' is the best abused of our books—it threatens to go fast to the dogs in respect of ears, and has suffered not a little from the arbitrary rule of thumb— Last evening, my wife read aloud to the family circle, your interesting contribution to the Dec. *Century*—Like your other writings, it had the merit of gratifying our boy of ten as well as his father—apart from its undertone of genuine humor, we all agreed it would like pure wine, improve with time, because of its vivid representations of a phase in the growth of our civil war, not heretofore recorded in its chronicles.

Sincerely
Wm Howard

Saml. L Clemens Esq
Hartford
Conn

Clemens's comment: Very good

The *Century* article mentioned here is "The Private History of a Campaign That Failed," an embellished account of Clemens's brief service in a Missouri state militia unit at the start of the Civil War that appeared in the December 1885 *Century Magazine*.

William Howard (c. 1834–1902) was a Pennsylvania journalist and politician noted for writing on economic issues. The Greenback Party nominated him for lieutenant governor in 1882 and later for a seat in Congress ("Wm. Howard, Writer, Dead," Philadelphia *Inquirer,* 21 Feb. 1902). No record of his earlier communications with Clemens has been found.

82

On the cars near Erie Pa

Mr. Saml. L. Clemenes
Hartford, Conn.
Dear Sir,

I have just read your paper in the December "Century." I think in such a matter as this I represent the average reader, & so my opinion should have some value to you. I am very sorry you published such a story—It seems to me to be a pity that I have seen the self displayed nakedness of a man whom I have enjoyed & admired to some extent. If you have a boy I hope he has not read this shameful story of cowardice & folly—24 years old!—man enough to have been a river pilot—I was a Captain at 21, after having served from the age of 19—Custer was a Major Genl. at 23, & the gallant captains & Colonels & Brigadiers in both armies, under 23, could be named by hundreds—24 was *pretty old,* in those days—And you, a man of 24, hiding away in terror from rumors forever false a hundred times, fired from the inside of a log hut, upon an unarmed & uniformed man.

The story is revolting & disgusting—and the shamelessness of its voluntary recital, is one of the strangest facts in literature—

Yrs &c
C A Martin

I think the story is a fancy sketch. No such poltroons & fools existed any where—and your own lack of sensibility has let you put yourself into it at the age of 24!

Clemens's comment: anonymous ass.

The author of this criticism of "The Private History of a Campaign That Failed" has not been identified. The name Martin may have been an invention. The letter alludes to the four years preceding the Civil War when Clemens piloted steamboats on the Mississippi. It also alludes to the article's account, probably fanciful, about how the narrator and his companions nervously shot down a horseman who turned out to be an unarmed civilian. During the war, George Armstrong Custer (1839–1876) was breveted a Union Army brigadier at twenty-three and a major general at twenty-six. The letter is postmarked 23 December 1885.

83

Edward W. Lummis,
Worcester College
Oxford.
May 6th 1886

Descend, ye muses nine;
Dictate a lofty strain!
A noble theme is mine:
Mark *Twain*

Phoebus, thy succorer bring,
Nor there, great Jove, refrain
To aid me while I sing
Mark Twain.

O Pegasus, arise
And shake thy shaggy mane!
Exalt unto the skies
Mark Twain.

Strike, strike those sweet trombones!
Blow, blow yon harp again!
And praise in varied tones
Mark Twain

Parched was my heart, & dry,
Parched was my weary brain,
When someone whispered "Try
Mark Twain"

I tried him, ay, & found
Relief from every pain.
Blessed be that simple sound:—
"Mark Twain."

On me, as on the sod
Falls light refreshing rain,
So fell "The Tramp Abroad,"
Mark Twain.

When wits began to roam
What made me clear and sane?
Thy "Innocents at Home,"
Mark Twain.

When lost in crime & sin
What did my heart regain?
Thy "Huckleberry Finn"

Mark Twain.
When I had left my wife,
What called me back again?
Thy "Mississippi Life,"
Mark *Twain*.
Toward suicide I look—
What doth my hand restrain?
"Tom Sawyer" is the book,
Mark Twain.
In sickness, care & want
What doth my soul sustain?
"The Lost White Elephant,"
Mark *Twain*.
All ills that men endure
Each harm & every bane
Some book of thine can cure
Mark *Twain*.
Yet am I racked with doubt
And expectation's pain.
When will the next come out?
Mark *Twain!*
Then kindly send to me
—You will not send in vain—
A copy of it free,
Mark *Twain*.
Or send, (if this request
You cannot entertain)
Your autograph at least,
Mark Twain.

                                                E W Lummis.

Clemens's comment: Poetry

Clemens's reply:

                                        Hartford May 17/86

My Dear Sir:
   If I too were a poet, I would acknowledge your pleasant compliments in verse;
but I am not, & so am forced to say my thanks in the ruder form of prose—
which is like answering the gracious salutation of a bugle with a fog-horn.
                                                Truly Yours
                                                S. L. Clemens
                                                Mark Twain

Mr. Edward W. Lummis

Edward William Lummis was a nineteen-year-old student at Oxford University when he wrote this letter. He later wrote and translated books on theology (English census reports). Clemens himself wrote many, mostly unpublished, poems. Arthur L. Scott's *On the Poetry of Mark Twain* (Urbana, Ill., 1966) contains about seventy examples, but many are considered bogus.

The books to which Lummis's poem alludes include *Innocents at Home*, the title under which the second half of *Roughing It* (1872) was published by Routledge in England; *Life on the Mississippi* (1883); and *The Stolen White Elephant Etc.* (1882), a collection of previously unpublished stories. There is no record of Clemens's giving Lummis a copy of his next book, *Connecticut Yankee* (1889).

84

THE PAUL E. WIRT FOUNTAIN PEN.
ABSOLUTELY DURABLE, PRACTICAL AND RELIABLE.

BLOOMSBURG, PA. Dec. 27th, 1886

Mr Samuel T. Clemens
Hartford Conn.

Dear Sir:
Having heard that you have spoken favorably of our pen, to H. M. Smith & Co our agents in New York I take the liberty of asking you to give us here the benefit of a *copy* of the commendatory letter,—or what would be better a direct line to us. Mr Smith is unable to forward yours, or a copy to us. If you will kindly favor us, we shall make perfectly legitimate use of the same and you will render us very happy. Doubtless you are ceaselessly troubled for autographs, favors in writing &c &c. but I hope you will overlook the average request in that line, and favor us. This is the first time, I assure you, that I have asked you or anyone for anything of the kind, but the temptation is too great and cannot be resisted.

Very Truly & Resfy. Yours,
Paul E. Wirt.

Clemens's comment: Paul E. Wirt

Clemens did almost all his writing by hand and had a special interest in fountain pens. In November 1886, he bought a Wirt pen from Horace M. Smith, a Wirt agent and partner in a firm that manufactured pens and related products (Kevin Mac Donnell, personal communication, 11 July 2011; advertisement in *Illustrated New York* [New York, 1888], 324). After beginning his career as a lawyer, Paul Estherly Wirt (c. 1849–1935) started manufacturing pens in 1885 and eventually held twenty-eight patents. He advertised his pens extensively and aggressively sought endorsements. In 1925, he sold his business ("Paul Wirt, Inventor of Fountain Pen, Dies," Trenton, New Jersey, *Evening Times*, 21 Jan. 1935).

FIGURE 14. Advertisement for the Paul E. Wirt fountain pen.
Collection of the author.

Wirt wrote to Clemens again on 31 December, acknowledging a reply to his first letter that has not been found. On the same date, he sent Clemens a free pen. In 1890, an officer of the rival Sackett Fountain Pen company responded to Clemens's published endorsement of Wirt pens, asking him to try his own product, but Clemens did not reply (John Mandeville to Clemens, 31 Jan. 1890, MTP). While in Germany in late 1891, Clemens wrote to his English publisher: "I have had the misfortune to lose my Wirt fountain pen & am helpless till you send me one. I want a pen that is medium— neither too stiff nor too limber" (Clemens to Chatto & Windus, 9 Oct. 1891, MTP). Seven years later, he wrote an endorsement of Wirt pens the company used in its advertisements (figure 14) (Clemens to Wirt Fountain Pen Co., 11 Oct. 1898, MTP).

85

Mannheim G8 · 5·
Jan. 12ᵗʰ 87.

Dear Sir.

For many weeks we have been owing most of our amusement to your delightful book: A Tramp Abroad. Many an evening we met together: two pupils of sweet seventeen and their aged teacher to read and laugh over your lovely adventure and your experiences in Europe. We were delighted that you did not forget to visit even our most unromantic native town of Mannheim and we followed your travels all through France Germany and Switzerland with unabashed interest and sometimes with uncontrollable laughter and we are proud to say, that, although we are Germans, not one of your jokes was wasted upon us.

But the reason which induced us to venture to write to you is your chapter on the "Awful German Language" in the Appendix to the Tramp abroad. We noticed with interest and joy that the sublimity of our mother-tongue filled your mind with awe and wonder and as we saw that you desired to acquire a real and deep knowledge of that language, we thought you might consider it as a kindness on our part if we tried to further you in that laudable purpose. We therefore venture to send you a few specimens of German construction and grammar which you may not have found in your German books, and which may excite your interest and satisfy your love of knowledge.

Would you mind studying the following sentences:

Bekanntmachung!

Die, die die, die die Grenzsteine beschädigen oder umfahren, zur Anzeige bringen, erhalten 2½ Silbergroschen Belohnung.

Oberamt Buxtehude.

Oh du, der du die das deutsche Volk beglückende Gesetzgebung gegeben hast!

We might perhaps collect a few more samples of the same kind if they were useful to you; we only regret that they come too late to figure in your chapter of the A.G.L.; they might have contributed to give your serious readers a still deeper insight into the beauties and peculiarities of our language.

Will you forgive us the liberty we have been taking in addressing you and ascribe it only to the deep admiration and we may add—affection we have for you.

With profoundest respect we remain Yours faithfully

Auguste Keller G8·5

Lili Kahn

Marie Eberstadt

Clemens's comment: 2 German girls | Answered

The unusual German specimens in this letter are examples of bureaucratic language featuring strings of repeated and alliterative pronouns. The sample beginning *Bekanntmachung!* translates as "Notice! They who report those who damage or knock over the boundary markers will receive a reward of 2½ silver pennies. | Administrative Office, Buxtehude." The second sentence translates as "Oh you who have given the German people the delightful laws."

Lili Kahn (1869–1940) was a member of a large and wealthy Jewish family whose children were privately tutored in the arts. Her father, Bernhard Kahn (1827–1905), was a banker and city council member. Her brothers included Otto Hermann Kahn (1867–1934), who became a prominent New York banker, and the composer Robert Kahn (1865–1951). She herself married another prominent industrialist, Felix Deutsch (1858–1928). After Adolf Hitler's regime took power in Germany in 1933, the Kahn family was dispersed by the Holocaust. Lili died in Belgium in 1940 (M.J. Matz, *The Many Lives of Otto Kahn* [New York, 1984]; T.M. Collins, *Otto Kahn: Art, Money, & Modern Culture* [Chapel Hill, N.C., 2001]; Helmut Weber, *Die Theorie der Qualifikation* [Tübingen, 1986], 15n.6).

Marie Eberstadt (born 1870) was Kahn's first cousin. Auguste Keller has not been identified; he may have been the teacher to whom the letter alludes.

86

3 Circular Road
Withington
Manchester
England.

Dear Mr Mark Twain

My brother and I have read The Adventures of Tom Sawyer, The Adventures of Huck Finn, Life on the Mississippi, and, The Prince and the Pauper, and think them splendid, especially The Prince and the Pauper I think. We have been thinking it would it would be a delicious History of England, if you wrote it, and made a few variations of corse, like you did in the Prince and the Pauper. It would not matter about you making it true if you made it interesting. We should like you to write it so much, please. do

I am your loving reader.

Katie L Corbett.
(aet 9)

Clemens's comment: Little English girl

Katie Corbett was apparently the daughter of working-class parents. An 1881 English census report listed her father as a railroad carriage cleaner and army pensioner. Her father was not listed with the family in the 1891 census, which described her mother as an office cleaner. Her only brother, William, was five years older than she was. Her letter is postmarked 25 May 1887.

87

Los Angeles, Cal.
June 14, 1887.

Mr. S. L. Clemens
Hartford
Conn.

Dear Sir

I take the liberty to address you with regards to "Huckleberry Finn" and ask that you will favor me with an answer.

Has "H—F—" ever been dramatized and if so where can a copy of that version be had if such has been published?

I saw sometime since that you had given up the idea of producing the above mentioned play or rather story, because of your inability to secure one who could properly act the title-role.

I have studied "H.—Finn to some little extent and I think that with a little more and a *few* ideas from some person well acquainted with the author's ideal, I think I could carry the part of "Huckleberry."

Of course, this is the old, old story; an ambitious youth who would an *actor* be; but not out of the usual order of the occurences of these "stage struck boys" I am conceited enough to beleive I am able to act so difficult a part as that of the afore mentioned "boy"

My parents are aware of "little failing" and have submitted to my "fate"; they, I guess having come to the conclusion that I would make a failure at anything else.

Hoping you will pardon the offence of belaboring you with these lines and begging a moments attention for an answer
I am
Yours Respectfully
C. E. Fredericks.
Los Angeles
Care 231 N. Main St. Cal.

Clemens's comment: No answer

> Fredericks has not been identified. The North Main St. address he provided was in the midst of hotels and municipal government office buildings, suggesting he was probably visiting Los Angeles when he wrote. The first major dramatic adaptation of *Huckleberry Finn* reached the stage in 1902.

88

Glenville
Ohio.

My dear Mr Clemens,

Will you be kind enough to settle a family discussion and tell me whether the blunders of children as given in "English as She is Taught" both in your article in the Century Magazine and in the little book published under that title are *bona fide* or not.

It has been asserted that you have announced yourself as responsible for the entire series and that your friend the schoolmistress who submitted her collection to your inspection is a myth.

If it is not asking too much of you will you kindly let me know the truth of the matter and thereby greatly oblige

Yours very sincerely,
Caroline E. Coit.

Sunday, June 19th/87.

Clemens's comment: Logic—if I lied in the article (to this fool), I may still be expected to tell her the truth privately. There is nothing so silly & ignorant & vulgar in "Eng" as is this letter.

> Published in the April 1887 *Century*, "English as She Is Taught" discusses specimens of bizarre misinformation that Brooklyn schoolteacher Caroline LeRow collected from her pupils in a book of the same title.
> Caroline Elizabeth Coit (1860–1934) was an Ohio public school teacher who later won some local renown as a painter (USCR; Obituaries: Cleveland *Plain Dealer,* 9 and 29 Apr. 1934; 1901 and 1920 passport applications. See also letter 94).

89

———

Damascus
Octr 4th/87

To Samuel L Clemens
Hertford
Connecticut

Dear Sir

We have lately returned from a visit to the Pyramids where we have had the great pleasure of hearing from the Bedouin Arabs, who dwell in that vicinity, & conduct visitors to the top of the pyramids, accounts of your marvellous record in climbing the pyramids when you visited them in 1868; indeed we have thought that this fact would be as interesting & astonishing to you as it was to us.

Dear Sir we sincerely congratulate you upon the fact that your unprecedented record of 8 minutes (the time consumed by you in descending from the top of Cheops, sprinting across the intervening plain, to the top of Chephrenes, then returning & again clambering to the top of the Cheops, mirabile dictu all in 8 minutes) still remains unequalled. We must add however that there is some little dispute among the Arabs as to the bona fide character of your record. For some of them, when they informed us of your exploit, stated that you deducted the time consumed each way in sprinting across the intervening space between the two pyramids. One worthy Arab in particular admitted however, "that Mark Twain did indeed do this feat in 8 minutes but it made him sweat awful." It is nevertheless unanimously believed as a sacred tradition among these sons of the desert that you actually did in person perform this feat when you were here with the Pilgrims in '68 & thus they tell all the innocent tourists who now visit this source of your mighty achievement. We need scarcely say that there was no attempt to break the record by

Your obedient servants
Turner Lee
Newcastle Drive
Nottingham
England
& Oliver T. Crane
Morristown
New Jersey
United States of America
Present address | Beyrout Syria

ASCENT OF THE PYRAMID.

FIGURE 15. How the narrator actually climbed the Great Pyramid.
Drawing from *The Innocents Abroad*, 622. Collection of the author.

On 5 October 1867, Clemens visited Egypt during the *Quaker City* tour. Chapter 58 of
The Innocents Abroad (1869) offers an embellished account of his visit, describing
"muscular Egyptians and Arabs" dragging him and his companions to the top of the
great pyramid of Cheops (figure 15). It then describes an Arab descending that pyramid, climbing the pyramid of Cephron, an eighth of a mile away, and returning
within 8 minutes and 49 seconds three times in a row. (That time is credible. During
the late twentieth century, a famous Egyptian tour guide reportedly could perform
the same feat in less than 7 minutes.) The present letter's suggestion that Clemens
himself set the climbing record was evidently intended as a joke.

Oliver Trumbull Crane (1855–1936) was the son of a Presbyterian clergyman who
did missionary work in Turkey, where Crane spent part of his youth. After graduating from Yale in 1879, he studied law and was admitted to the New Jersey bar but soon
abandoned law to ranch in Montana. In 1886, he took up Semitic languages at Princeton. The following year, he went to the Middle East to study in Egypt, Palestine, and
Syria. (His passport application is dated 18 July 1887.) In 1890, he returned to Montana permanently and began a long legal career that included service as state law
librarian (1902–1904) and deputy clerk of the state supreme court (1919–1936) ("Funeral Services for Oliver Crane . . . ," Helena *Daily Independent*, 6 Oct. 1936; F. W.
Williams, *A History of the Class of Seventy-Nine Yale College* [n.p., 1906], 149–153).

Turner Lee (1861–1950) was born into an upper-class family in Nottingham, England. He was a lawyer like Crane, whom he may have met while vacationing in Syria. He later fought in the South African War and in World War I. In 1911, he emigrated to British Columbia and became a rancher ("Fame and 54," www.54thbattalioncef.ca/warpages, accessed 29 Jan. 2011; English census reports).

90

291 Halsey St.
Brooklyn, N.Y.

S. L. Clemens Esq.

Dear Sir,

Chap XX of "Roughing It" ends with a foot-note which reads: "___ but what does the thirteenth chapter of Daniel say? Aha!" I have read the book at least a dozen times but never before thought of looking up that biblical quotation. Last night I did so and behold there was no Chap. XIII of Daniel.

Please explain if you ever do answer such queries, whether it is a typographical error or an obscure joke. It created considerable discussion amongst three friends to whom I was reading, and one of them ascribed it to a desire on your part to make your readers "search the Scriptures." This I doubted and await your answer with anxiety.

Sincerely yours,
Harry Plympton M.D.

Nov. 29. '87

Clemens's comment: Brer W. say to him, "Your friend's solution is correct"

The footnote mentioned in the letter follows a long anecdote in *Roughing It* about Hank Monk driving journalist Horace Greeley on a hair-raising stagecoach ride. The full note at the end of chapter 20 reads: "And what makes that worn anecdote the more aggravating, is, that the adventure it celebrates *never occurred.* If it were a good anecdote, that seeming demerit would be its chiefest virtue, for creative power belongs to greatness; but what ought to be done to a man who would wantonly contrive so flat a one as this? If *I* were to suggest what ought to be done to him, I should be called extravagant—but what does the thirteenth chapter of Daniel say? Aha!"

Most authorized versions of the King James Bible have no chapter 13 in the book of Daniel. However, chapter 12 ends with this verse 13: "But go thou thy way till the end be: for thou shalt rest, and stand in thy lot at the end of the days." To complicate matters further, Clemens's mother owned an 1817 Bible with two additional, and apocryphal, chapters in Daniel; Clemens was familiar with this Bible (Harriet Elinor Smith et al., eds. *Roughing It* [Berkeley, 1993], 612; Gribben, *Mark Twain's Library*, 1:64–65).

Harry Plympton (c. 1857–1908) graduated from Long Island College Hospital in 1880 and soon became temporary superintendent of Brooklyn's Flatbush Hospital.

He specialized in nervous disorders and was later on the Kings County Insane Asylum staff ("Brooklyn," New York *Times,* 31 July 1881; Obituaries: *Medical Record* (New York), 8 Nov. 1908; *Jnl. Amer. Med. Assoc.,* 14 Nov. 1908).

"Brer W.," or "Brer" ("brother"), was Clemens's nickname for Franklin Gray Whitmore (1846–1926), his Hartford neighbor and business agent who helped with his correspondence during the late 1880s. When Clemens was in Europe during the 1890s, Whitmore managed his local affairs; in 1903, he oversaw the sale of Clemens's Hartford house.

91

Bethlehem Pa. Mar. 6. 1888.
81 Church St.

Mr S. Clemens,

Dear Sir,

I presume you receive letters every day from cranks, and persons with largely developed pauper instincts.

Well, I do not think I can be placed in either class, but I am in a strait, and I want help, but I want it on business principles.

I'll make my story as short as I can—"will a round unvarnished tale deliver."

I am a woman, with three children dependent on me for support. I am a graduate of Boston Univ. School of Medicine, and practice here in this fine old borough of Bethlehem.

My daughter is twenty years of age, and has availed herself of every advantage the place affords. She has chosen my profession, but I cannot afford to send her away to study.

My elder son—seventeen years—has educated himself so far, as to meet the requirement for the Classical course in Lehigh University.

My younger son is busy with his books.

If I take them to Ann Arbor, I can complete their educations, and establish a practice.

Now, you wonder what my request is—For $2,600 I can get a comfortable home by paying $1,100 down. This latter sum I want to borrow of you—And what collateral? you ask?

My life insurance, made out for $1,400 payable to you at my death if within five years, thus securing to you, the whole amount and good interest.

I am in good health—forty-six years old, a total abstainer—I come of a long-lived ancestry on my mother's side and short-lived on my father's.

I hope this does not seem too absurd to be considered—It is not an original plan. Senator Dawes thus helped a young woman at Westfield Normal School, and lost not a penny.

My elder son will work at something—he has worked every vacation in the Bethlehem Iron Works—until we can make up the amount to you. Should this meet your approval, I will come to Hartford and make the arrangements. May I have an answer even if you consider me "ein Dummkopf."

Yours Truly
Vashti D. Garwood

Garwood's offer to make Clemens the beneficiary of her life insurance policy was a common begging-letter ploy. As P. T. Barnum observed, however, such offers were worthless unless the applicants guaranteed they would die before the beneficiary did, and Garwood would outlive Clemens by eight years (*The Life of P. T. Barnum* [New York, 1855], 392; see also letter 105).

Vashti Magdalen Detweiler Garwood (1842–1918) was an accomplished person who asked Clemens for a loan at what may have been a low point in her life. A graduate of Boston University's homeopathic medical school, she married Spencer Willard Garwood (1835–1927), a recent University of Michigan Medical School graduate, in 1866. The couple lived in Kansas, where Vashti had four children before separating from her husband in 1880. The year before she wrote to Clemens from Pennsylvania, the University of Michigan faculty directory listed her as an assistant to two professors. She was back in Ann Arbor, Michigan, by 1897, when she was living near the university medical school (*Glen V. Mills' Ann Arbor and Ypsilanti Directory 1897*, 87; "Dr. Garwood Dead," Ann Arbor, Michigan, *Daily Times News*, 8 May 1918).

While in Kansas during the 1870s, Garwood had been involved in the women's temperance movement. In 1910, she and her daughter were among the founding members of the Ann Arbor Equal Suffrage Club ("Equal Suffrage Club Is Formed," Ann Arbor *Daily Times News*, 25 Oct. 1910). She was probably aware that her given name was an icon of the women's rights movement: in the Bible, Vashti was a Persian queen who defied her husband and was replaced by Esther (Est. 1:9–2:17).

Grace Olive Garwood (1867–1946), Garwood's daughter, did study medicine at the University of Michigan but apparently quit after marrying Dr. Frederick Novy in 1891. Three of her five children became doctors. Vashti Garwood's older son, Ralph Garwood (1870–1930), graduated from the University of Michigan in 1892, became superintendent of schools in Puerto Rico in 1905, and later became a University of Puerto Rico dean ("Educator Dies," Springfield, Massachusetts, *Daily Republican*, 6 Feb. 1930). Vashti's younger son was Colver Garwood (born 1873). Garwood's second daughter, Julia (1877–1881), died in childhood (family genealogy pages, Ancestry.com).

Henry Laurens Dawes (1816–1903) represented Massachusetts in the U.S. Senate (1875–1893).

———

92

Liberty Maine July 31 [1888]

Dear Huck

I like your book and you and Tom Sawyer and Jim. I think you are very plucky and know how to get out of scrapes awful well. I should like to know if you have ever heard any thing of the king and the duke since they were riding by (fence) rail, and the men that you and Jim left on the wreck. I wish you would write another book and tell us if Aunt Sally "civilized" you. How old are you? I am thirteen

Please write soon.

I am visiting my aunt and uncle but am going home in a few days so please direct to

Herbert S. Philbrick

Waterville.

Maine.

Care F. B. Philbrick.

In chapter 33 of *Huckleberry Finn*, the scoundrels known as the king and the duke are last seen tarred and feathered, being carried out of town on a rail. They reappeared in an unfinished story, narrated by Huck, that Clemens began in 1897; it was first published as "Tom Sawyer's Conspiracy" in Walter Blair, ed., *Mark Twain's Hannibal, Huck, & Tom* (Berkeley, 1969). In chapter 13 of *Huckleberry Finn*, three murderers stranded on the wrecked steamboat *Walter Scott* apparently drown when the boat breaks up and sinks in a storm. The novel ends with Huck proclaiming, "I reckon I got to light out for the Territory ahead of the rest, because Aunt Sally she's going to adopt me and sivilize me and I can't stand it. I been there before." Huck revisits Sally Phelps in the novella "Tom Sawyer, Detective" (1896). He reveals his age as around thirteen or fourteen in chapter 17 of *Huckleberry Finn*.

This letter is unusual in being addressed directly to Huck Finn. Its author, Herbert Shaw Philbrick (1875–1963), was the son of a machine-shop owner. He himself later became a professor of mechanical engineering at the University of Missouri and at Northwestern University (USCR).

—————

93

Muscatine (Which is situated in Iowa—

Mister Twain

Im a farmer an Iv been a thinkin how as writin' ud be easier work, a seein as how you allus wear good close, an' I dont, and I been a thinkin' if it wouldnt be a good idea fr me to pull up stakes an' write a book

I been a thinkin' I could write a book well 'es not least ways as good as you ever rote—for to tell the truth I dont think them no great shakes, an consider the bibel much better readin for the young, but then it pays.

Now I been a thinkin, an the only thing I couldn't decide about was whether it ud pay better then farmin, an' whether it ud make much diff e rents whether I wrote with my left hand—seein hous Im left handed.

FIGURE 16. Ellis Parker Butler at a later age. Courtesy of the
Library of Congress.

Now I been a thinkin mabby you ud be slick enuff an kind enuf to tell me if
yu thot it wd pay me to quit farmin an go to book makin—and if you thot it wd
make any diff rnts bout writin left handed.

And oblige

Y^r obt servant

E. Butler

P.S. I see where you lived in the paper | I put in a stamp please rite.

The author of this artificially semiliterate letter later became a noted writer in his
own right (figure 16). Ellis Parker Butler (1869–1937) was born and raised in Muscatine, Iowa, from which his letter was postmarked sometime before 31 January 1889.
He started writing fiction for publication at fourteen. Three years later, he left school

to work while continuing to write. In 1897, he relocated to New York, where he edited various magazines and contributed stories, essays, and poems to them.

In 1905, *American Magazine* published a short story that would do for Butler's reputation what the jumping frog story had done for Clemens's four decades earlier. Butler's "Pigs Is Pigs" is a farce about a regulation-bound railroad agent who insists on charging livestock rates for a shipment of pet guinea pigs. When the customer refuses to pay the extra charge, the guinea pigs are sent to a warehouse, where they multiply at a dizzying rate. (The story indirectly inspired the 1967 *Star Trek* episode "The Trouble with Tribbles.") "Pigs Is Pigs" became so popular that it was frequently republished until the title became indelibly associated with Butler's name—to his chagrin. During a long writing career, Butler published hundreds of short stories and dozens of books. By the end of his life, he was judged the most prolific contributor to pulp magazines of the early twentieth century ("Ellis Parker Butler," *Argosy*, 8 Aug. 1931, 148; obituary, Des Moines, Iowa, *Register*, 14 Sept. 1937; Henry B. Chapin, "Lighting Out for the Territory Back East: Ellis Parker Butler, American Humorist," *Books at Iowa* 37 [November 1982]). In a letter to one of his own readers in 1925, Butler named Mark Twain as one of his first loves in literature and praised his skill in developing individual characters (Chapin, ibid.).

94

14 Concord Ave.
Cambridge
Mass.
June 16, '89.

Mr. Clemens,
Dear Sir:—

In the April number of the "Century" for 1887 you had an article entitled "English as She is Taught"

I am the author of the composition therein given called: "Girls," and I should like to know out of mere curiosity, how you happened to get hold of it. The composition was written while I was at Fort McHenry where my father commanded in 1880. He offered a prize to my sister and to me for the best composition. My sister wrote on "Boys," and although she was a year and a hald younger than I, she won the prize, if I remember correctly. But my glory was to come later, as I now see. At that time my eldest sister was at Vassar, and editor of the "Vassar Miscellany"; when came home she found my composition, and seeing its true value, had it printed in that magazine. Unless you took it from there I can't imagine where you procured it.

The composition goes to show clearly the amount of education that an army boy receives even when he is as near civilization as I was at that time. I think I must have been ten or eleven years old when I wrote that article, so perhaps you can imagine how difficult it is for me to enter Harvard this year, for you must know that it is those early years of training that tell. I suppose I have the right to call my self now "A Child of the Century"

You seemed to have written your article to illustrate the poor principle of Public School Education, but I feel called upon to say that my composition, placed as you have it, does a great injustice to these schools, for at that time I had never heard of such schools and my production was that which I am inclined to think any ten or twelve year old child could produce instinctively, providing he or she belonged to the right family. My ideas were those drawn from associations with my sisters, for they were the only girls I knew then, while my spelling, as you saw, was purely phonetic.

Colonel Higginson, whom I have the honor to know personally, wrote an article about me for "Harpers Bazare" in connection with this same subject.

The phrases of that composition have been quoted to me for the last two years, but since you and Colonel Higginson have recognized them, I am, to say the least, proud of them.

On the stength of my first work, I hope that I may feel at liberty to call upon you for a recommendation in English for Harvard College.

Thanking you heartily for the honor which you unintentionally confered upon me I remain, as ever before,

Your sincere admirer

W. DeLancey Howe.

"English as She Is Taught" quotes excerpts from student papers collected by Brooklyn schoolteacher Caroline B. LeRow (see letter 88). This is the passage titled "On Girls":

> Girls are very stuckup and dignefied in their maner and be have your. They think more of dress than anything and like to play with dowls and rags. They cry if they see a cow in a far distance and are afraid of guns. They stay at home all the time and go to church on Sunday. They are al-ways sick. They are always funy and making fun of boy's hands and they say how dirty. They cant play marbels. I pity them poor things. They make fun of boys and then turn round and love them. I dont beleave they ever kiled a cat or anything. They look out every nite and say oh ant the moon lovely. Thir is one thing I have not told and that is they al-ways now their lessons bettern boys. (Century, April 1887, 936)

The correspondent, William DeLancey Howe (1869–1954), was born in Fort Washington, Maryland, and lived in diverse regions–not including Brooklyn—as his family moved among army posts. After graduating from Harvard College in 1893 and from Harvard Law School in 1896, he practiced law in Boston for fifty years ("William D. Howe," Cambridge, Massachusetts, Chronicle, 29 Apr. 1954). His father, Albion Paris Howe (1818–1897), was a West Point graduate and career army officer who served the Union as a brevet major general during the Civil War. His later commands included Fort Washington, Maryland (1868–1872); Alcatraz Island, California (1877–1879); and Fort McHenry, Maryland (1879–1882) (obituary, New York Herald-Tribune,

27 Jan. 1897; Rossiter Johnson, ed., *Twentieth Century Biog. Dict. of Notable Americans* [Boston, 1904], 5: n.p.).

An outspoken advocate of rights for women and African Americans, Thomas Wentworth Higginson (1823–1911) was a Unitarian minister who commanded a Union African American regiment during the Civil War. He later turned his attention to literature and wrote a weekly column for *Harper's Bazar* (later *Harper's Bazaar*).

95

Toronto 28th Aug't 89

Samuel L. Clemens Esqr
Hartford Conn

Dear Sir

I have read your books, They are the vilest trash I ever waded through—I did not think the English language could be writhed into such bosh.

I would just like to place in my album the autograph of the writer who could be guilty of foisting upon a credulous & gullible public such iniquitous twaddle. Kindly do me the favor.

Yours very truly
Fred J. Stewart

Fred J. Stewart (born c. 1849) managed a real estate security company in Toronto and was on the first board of governors of Bishop Ridley College when it was founded in 1889 (Census of Canada, 1891; Paul E. Lewis, archivist, Ridley College, personal communication, 7 Feb. 2011). If he wrote this letter as a joke to provoke a response, he probably failed; his self-addressed stamped envelope remains unused.

96

St Paul Min Nov 24/89

Mark Twain
Hartford Conn.

Dear Sir

I have a Boy four years old and he is full of vim. He wanted me to tell him a story a few days ago and I told him about "A Connecticut Yankee in King Arthur's Court" taken from the Century. He "Caught on" at once and ever since he has been "Hank" The story has to be read and told to him several times a day. He got a piece of clothes line and made a Lasso and using me for a horse he Has a tournament every evening and I wish you could see him drag Sir Sagramour,

Sir Galahad and Sir Launcelot out of their saddles. Then Merlin (his mother) has to steal his Lasso and he gets his gun and shoots Sir Sagramour.

Its kind of tough on me to trot up & down "the lists" for Half an hour at a time but then as ["]Hank" is the most beautifull boy you ever saw I don't mind it For the past two years it has been a fight of about an hour to get him to go to bed Now soon after Dinner he comes to his mother and says "Hank wants his Tights (his night pants) on, and after a Tournament he goes to bed with out a word, all because Hank does that way, and generaly he used to object to saying his prayers But now all we have to say is "Come Hank and say your prayers" and he says "Now I Lay me" In a most touching and reverent manner. We have not been able to get him to go to church for more than a year. He just *would not go* and we have tried to bribe him with every thing under the sun Candy, Fruit, Buggy rides, Cable rides car rides out to see Little Cousins, but *no sir* he would not go.

But this morning I wish you could have seen "Hank" take his Mother to Church. You would have thought that like Tom Sawyer he had "wallowed" in churches all his life. The boy's name is Dean B Gregg, and this is written by his grateful Father

Jesse A Gregg
483 ashland ave
St Paul Minn

Clemens's comment: A pleasant letter | preserve it | SLC

Extracts from *Connecticut Yankee* published in the November 1889 issue of *Century* included all of chapter 39, in which the Yankee (Hank Morgan) takes on heavily armored knights while mounted on a pony—a scene illustrated by two engaging pictures by Daniel Carter Beard.

Jesse Ashton Gregg (1853–1935) was born in what is now West Virginia and grew up in Pittsburgh, Pennsylvania. In 1872, he settled permanently in St. Paul, Minnesota, and was a traveling wholesale hardware dealer (A. N. Marquis, ed., *The Book of Minnesotans* [Chicago, 1907], 196–197; H. A. Castle, *Minnesota: Its Story and Biography* [Chicago, 1915], 2:772–773; USCR). His only child, Dean Bradish Gregg (1885–1975), graduated from Minnesota State University and followed his father into the hardware business. He was the father of the author and playwright Jess Gregg (1919–2011).

In *Tom Sawyer*, Tom loathes going to church. However, after he and Huck Finn witness a murder, they fear their own end is near, and Tom repents of his misdeeds. He vows that if he survives, he will be good and "just waller in Sunday-schools!" (chapter 10).

97

BEAVER WOOLEN MILLS
OFFICE OF WILLIAM ALGIE—ALTON, ONTARIO,
MANUFACTURER OF KNIT GOODS AND WOOLEN YARNS.

ALTON, ONT. Canada, Jany 1890

Samuel L. Clemens
Dear Sir
    Permit a grateful Canadian to express his hearty thanks for the many pleasures your pen has given him during the past 10 or 12 years I have just concluded a pleasant perusal of "The Yankee in King Arthur's Court" and you have earned in it the gratitude of every "lover of liberty" I trust that the time may speedily come, when Chap. XIII will be incorporated into every school book to the end that the "glorious French Revolution" may be understood by the generations to come. Recognizing the broad liberal spirit pervading the whole work I am tempted to ask, why it is that of late years, one of your most telling articles that appeared in "The Memoranda" years ago, has been expunged from authorized publications latterly. I refer to your criticism of Rev. Mr Sabine for his action at the funeral of George Holland. Of course it is none of my business but it was a gem worth preserving.

Yours Faithfully
William Algie

Clemens's comment: Brer, please tell him I have forgotten the article.

Clemens's "Memoranda" article in the February 1871 *Galaxy,* was titled "The Indignity Put Upon the Remains of George Holland by the Rev. Mr. Sabine." It was a response to a 29 December 1870 New York *Times* article about the New York minister William Tufnell Sabine's refusal to conduct a church funeral for the respected comic actor George Holland because he disapproved of theaters. *Connecticut Yankee's* chapter 13, titled "Freemen," addresses the hypocrisy of the term *freemen* in medieval England.

    William Wallace Algie (1850–1914) was a religious freethinker. He owned woollen knitting factories in Alton, Ontario, where in 1888 he founded a library to advance the education of his workers ("The Brydons," brydondale.com/genealogy, and "Alton Mechanics' Institute and Library," www.historicplaces.ca., both accessed 8 Feb. 2011).

    Any reply written by Clemens's business agent, Frank Whitmore ("Brer"), has not been found.

98

HILLSIDE, SAUCELITO,
MARIN CO., CAL.

Jan 12th 1890

S. F. Clemens Esq
Hartford Ct

Dear Sir:

Pardon the privilege a stranger takes in thus writing.

I have just been "revelling" in your inimitable, "King Arthur" and on reaching the 33^d chapter bethought me of how you could, more than a thousand others with philosophy, alter our financial policy with, Satire, or humour

Our "protection" system is to me and thousands of other good people, yourself included I think, Just as grotesque as Knight errantry (in another way of course and considering the enlightenment of an age)

Now, while you are in the vigor of your manhood, and powers why not use the gifts nature has endowed you with to do a great good to your country, and Leave to posterity a fame which ages will not efface.

As Cervantes, destroyed chivalry so can you destroy "protection," or the "thing" that bears that name.

I will send you tomorrow a weak essay of my own perhaps worth reading— perhaps not, at any rate it will have some *new* ideas of Labor

Yours faithfully,
J Richards

Clemens's comment: "Protection." | Will answer

Chapter 33 of *Connecticut Yankee* (1889), titled "Political Economy," contrasts a sixth-century England region living under a "protection system" with one enjoying free trade.

John Richards (1834–1917) was an industrious and inventive man fitting the mold of the fictional Yankee, who "could make anything a body wanted . . . and if there wasn't any quick new-fangled way to make a thing, [he] could invent one." Born in Pennsylvania, Richards later lived in Ohio, where his diverse occupations included millwrighting, machine fitting, tool-works managing, and even two years as a steamboat engineer. During the 1870s, he established branches of a machine-tool company in England and Sweden. In 1880, he founded a tool company in San Francisco. Eight years later, he founded the magazine *Industry.* In later years, his work as a consulting engineer won him a reputation as a man who could solve any mechanical problem. His publications include books on machinery construction and operation. Known as a tireless campaigner again protective tariffs, Richards maintained "that the American mechanic could hold the markets of the world if delivered from the restraints that the tariff imposes" ("Eminent Consulting Engineer Called," *Sausalito News,* 10

Feb. 1917; "Representative American Mechanics," *Machinery*, Engineering Ed., Mar. 1906, 349–350). The copy of the essay Richards mentions is lost, but it was probably his fifty-four-page tract *The Law of Wages* (1890). No reply from Clemens has been found.

Miguel de Cervantes's 1605 novel *Don Quixote of La Mancha* is credited with striking a blow against the romantic pretensions of medieval chivalry. Clemens greatly admired the book, and *Connecticut Yankee*'s attacks on medieval romanticism have been compared to those of *Don Quixote*.

99

Kristian Augusts gade 9, Christiana $^{20}/_1$ 90

Mark Twain, Esq.
America.

Letters like this you are sure to receive so many, that you do not read them, but throw them in the paper-basket. However I resolved upon making a trial, and as you are my favourite author, and I have read all, you have wrote, I hope, you will not take it in bad part, when I beg to ask you for your monogram.

You are not able to imagine the delight, it would give me to have your handwriting, I would frame it, and you would for ever oblige

yours
truly Norwegian admirer
Olaf Halvorsen.
17 years old.

Clemens's comment: Observe, it is U.S. of "*North*" America—an early prompt recognition of the fact that there is now, thank God, another big & great *Republic of the United States* on this continent. | S.L.C. | Feb. 8/90

Olaf Halvorsen appears to have been an aggressive and possibly none-too-discriminating autograph collector. In 1892, for example, he wrote a similarly flattering letter to the English chemist Henry Enfield Roscoe, whose opinion on Norwegian foreign policy he solicited: "I seem to see, how you, frowning over my audacity, throw my letter far away." He signed himself, "Your Devoted Norwegian admirer | Olaf Halvorsen | (19 years old)" (*The Life & Experiences of Sir Henry Enfield Roscoe* [London, 1906], 115–116). Halvorsen also asked the Spanish composer Francisco Asenjo Barbieri for his autograph, pleading, "you are not able to imagine the delight, it would be for me to have your . . . hand writing, and by fulfilling my wish I would be for ever obliged. Yours Truly Norwegian admirer" (Barbieri, *Documentos sobre música española y epistolario* [Madrid, 1988], 655). Other autographs solicited by Halvorsen turn up occasionally in auctions.

Clemens wrote his comment on the envelope Halvorsen had addressed to "Mark Twain, Esq. | Elsewhere in | United States | N. America." Clemens evidently alludes to Mexico, under whose 1857 constitution was a federal republic officially known as the United States of Mexico.

100

State Center, Iowa. March 15, 1890.

Mr. Mark Twain,—

Dear Sir:—

We have been reading your "Life on the Mississippi," and "Huckleberry Finn" in our "Mark Twain Reading Club" and as Secretary of the club, I have been requested to write you, in their behalf, and ask how it is that the chapter taken from "Huck Finn" which appears in "Life on the Mississippi" is not in "Huck Finn." If you will be so kind as to let us know you will confer a great favor upon the Club and

Your Obedient Servant
Albert Johannsen.

Clemens's comment: Brer, please tell him it is too long a story to tell—would require a chapter. | SLC

Chapter 3 of *Life on the Mississippi* (1883) was taken from the unfinished *Huckleberry Finn* (1884). To reduce the novel's length, Clemens's publisher convinced him that the extracted passage contained nothing necessary to the narrative. He was wrong. Johannsen may have observed that the extracted passage explained *why* Huck later knew his raft had drifted past Cairo, Illinois, when he noticed a channel of clear Ohio River water running alongside the Mississippi's muddy water in chapter 16.

Eighteen years old when he wrote this letter, Albert Johannsen (1871–1962) later earned degrees in geology and petrography and became a leading authority on microscopical petrography at the University of Chicago. In still later years, he collected Charles Dickens first editions and Beadle and Adams dime novels—both subjects on which he wrote books. Clemens remained one of his favorite writers, and the name "Mark Twain" found its way into footnotes in Johannsen's 1932 treatise on descriptive petrography ("Memorial of Albert Johannsen," *Amer. Mineralogist* 48 [Mar.–Apr. 1963]: 454–458).

101

Minneapolis Minn
May 26th 1890

Mr Samuel L. Clemens,
Hartford Conn.

Dear Sir:

If you will excuse the "cheek" of a stranger, I would like for you to prove a bet that I made a few minutes ago. I bet B—— that you served in the civil war on the confederate side, B—— says you did not serve at all. The amount bet is forty dollars.

If you will be so kind and to send me an early reply, I will be under many obligations.

Yours Truly
H. D. Christian
404 S. 8th St
Minneapolis
Minn

Clemens's comment: Brer—Tell him I served 2 weeks on the Confederate side. | SLC

Missouri was never a Confederate state, but because Clemens briefly served in a Missouri militia unit formed by the state's secession-minded governor as the Civil War was beginning, he seems later to have believed he had served the Confederacy (see letters 81 and 82).

H. D. Christian has not been further identified. However, a 1900 census report for Minneapolis lists a George H. Christian (c. 1839–1918) at the same street address. A prosperous flour miller, that Christian could have afforded a forty-dollar bet ("Pioneer Miller Has Passed Away," Duluth *News-Tribune,* 20 Jan. 1918).

102

York, Pa.
Oct. 16/90

Mr. Samuel L. Clemens,
Dear Sir:—

Your books are perhaps more widely read than those of any other author. Reform doctrines illustrated by one your inimitable stories would sink deep in the minds of your readers. Will you pardon a suggestion on the part of an entire stranger as to a subject for your pen?

I am a Single Taxer. I was converted by a careful reading of "Progress & Poverty" and I defy any man to read it with a mind open to conviction and with a clear conscience reject its teachings. To my mind it is nothing more nor less than a modern practical application of the Gospel. I not only urge you to study it for your own sake but also to examine the possibilities of the subject for pathos and humor.

I know from your stories and speeches that you are a man with the courage of your convictions and I candidly warn you, dont put yourself under the influence of Mr. George's magic unless you are prepared to see the whole séance.

Very respectfully
Robt. F. Gibson

Clemens's comment: advice gratis!

This letter is one of more than a dozen linking *Connecticut Yankee* with the single tax sent to Clemens in October 1890. The letters are so similar in content, they must have been prompted by someone in the movement. *Progress and Poverty* (1879), by Henry George (1839–1897), was a best-selling book that helped win single-tax ideas a wide following. George argued that imposition of a single tax on land values would eliminate poverty by forcing land owners to use land more productively, thereby raising its value, increasing employment, and boosting wages. *Connecticut Yankee's* illustrator, Daniel Carter Beard (1850–1941), was a single-tax advocate and worked his views into some of the book's illustrations.

A Yale graduate, Robert Fisher Gibson (1866–1957) was a newspaper editor, attorney, and later mayor of York, Pennsylvania. In 1903, he was ordained an Episcopal minister. He was later on the committee that drafted his church's 1928 prayer book (obituary, *The Living Church* 134 [1957]: 38; "Diocese of Harrisburg," *The Church Standard,* 16 Sept. 1905); Bob Gibson, personal communication, 1 August 2012).

1891–1900

June 1891–May 1895	Clemens family closes Hartford house and goes to Europe, from which SLC will return to the United States on business several times; family will never again live in Hartford
December 1891	"Mental Telegraphy" appears in *Harper's Magazine*
January–March 1892	"The American Claimant" is serialized in the New York *Sun*; book publication follows in April
1893	"Extracts from Adam's Diary" appears in *The Niagara Book*; revised story is published in its own book in April 1904
November 1893–April 1894	"Tom Sawyer Abroad" is serialized in *St. Nicholas Magazine*; story is published as a book in April 1894
December 1893–June 1894	"Pudd'nhead Wilson" is serialized in *Century Magazine*; book publication follows in November 1894
April 1894	SLC's publishing firm, Charles L. Webster & Co., goes into bankruptcy, leaving SLC deeply in debt
May 1895	SLC leaves England to begin what will become a round-the-world lecture tour that will enable him to repay his creditors
August 1895–July 1896	Sails from British Columbia with Livy and Clara to New Zealand, Australia, India, and South Africa
May 1896	*Personal Recollections of Joan of Arc* is published
18 August 1896	Susy Clemens dies in Hartford, Connecticut
1897–1900	Clemens family resides in several European countries
November 1897	*Following the Equator* is published
early 1898	SLC pays off the last of his creditors
August 1898	"At the Appetite Cure" appears in *Cosmopolitan*
June 1899	Under Emilio Aguinaldo's leadership, Filipino nationalists begin three-year war against American occupation
September 1899	"Concerning the Jews" appears in *Harper's Magazine*
December 1899	"The Man That Corrupted Hadleyburg" appears in *Harper's Magazine*
15 October 1900	SLC returns to United States after a five-year absence; settles in New York City
30 December 1900	"Salutation Speech from the Nineteenth Century to the Twentieth" appears in the New York *Herald*

103

CANADA
REGISTRATION DISTRICT OF SOUTH ALBERTA,
CALGARY, N.W.T.,

17 Jany 1891

Dear Sir

While on an inspecting Tour at Prince Albert recently I heard a good story regarding yourself. I had just been reading over 'Roughing It' and in speaking about the book to a Hudson's Bay officer He told me the following story.

When the Book first appeared this officer was stationed at Fort Carlton on the North Saskatchewan River in the neighborhood of large bands of Cree Indians and this officer used to amuse himself by reading extracts from 'Roughing It' to the Chiefs explaining the various points thru the aid of an interpreter.

On one occasion, he read very slowly and carefully about the adventures of Mr Bemis as a Buffalo hunter. The Chiefs three in number listened very attentively not manifesting the slightest inclination to be amused. After the story was finished they indulged in repeated grunts, lit their pipe passed it round, and with one accord turned to the head chief Mis-ta-wasis by name, for his opinion, which he did in the following words

"It must have been a wood Buffalo" and the others at once assented and returned to camp in possession of a greater knowledge than they possessed before.

As a great admirer of yours and feeling that you are human and therefore not averse to flattery I felt it my duty to advise you that a mild statement of fact

SUSPENDED OPERATIONS.

FIGURE 17. The "wood buffalo" chasing Bemis up a
tree. Drawing from *Roughing It*, 65. Collection of
the author.

made by you early in your career as a writer has been accepted by men well
acquainted with the habits and peculiarities of the Buffalo.

I remain yrs very Truly

P.M. Barker

Inspector of Titles

Sam¹ L Clemens Esq
Hartford
Con. U.S.

Barker's anecdote concerns a passage in chapter 7 of *Roughing It* (1872): After the narrator's stagecoach breaks down, several passengers join in a buffalo hunt. Their adventure ends in disaster when a wounded buffalo chases a man named Bemis up a tree. An illustration in *Roughing It* shows Bemis firing his pistol at the buffalo as the lumbering animal climbs the tree after him (figure 17). The wood buffalo (or wood bison) the Indians mentioned is a recognized subspecies that once ranged throughout Canada's boreal forest regions. It is possible, however, that Mistawasis's statement could have been alternatively translated as "tree buffalo."

Mistawasis was the first chief of the Mistawasis First Nation, a Cree community in Saskatchewan created in 1876, when he signed Treaty 6 at Ft. Carlton (www.mistawasis.ca/history.html, accessed 10 Feb. 2011). Now a Saskatchewan provincial park, Ft. Carlton was a Hudson's Bay Co. trading post about thirty-eight miles north of Saskatoon.

A native of Ontario, Peter McGill Barker (1843-c. 1910) graduated from the University of Toronto and qualified in law in 1869. A decade later, he was commissioned a captain in a Canadian army battalion. At some later date, he became a federal government inspector of land titles. His son, Quentin J. Barker (c. 1879–1939), immigrated to the United States and served as a U.S. Army doctor (S. H. Barker, personal communication, 1 August 2012; G. M. Rose, ed., *A Cyclopedia of Canadian Biography* [Toronto, 1886], 528; Canadian census of 1891).

104

Barrett House,
co. Broadway × 3ᵈ Str.
New York
14/3 91

Dear Mʳ Clemens,

This moment only I learned your private address, and hasten to tell you how much I appreciated your quoting a passage of one of my books on North America in your most interesting and instructive work "Life on the Mississippi."

This quotation refers to a chapter on "Yellow Jack" in my ["]Mississippi fahrten" published 1881, at Leipzig.

If you would have looked a little further into that book, you would have seen, with how much admiration I speak of you and your knowledge of the great River. I also relate the amusing way how I found out the origin of your "nom de plume" "Mark Twain."

Later travels in the upper waters of the Mississippi and the absence of a complete work on the River in German encouraged me to write one as far as my limited powers enable me to do so, and I have frequently quoted you. I would have preferred to translate your "Life on the M." but our slow and ponderous German public would not have fully done you justice even if my translation would have done so. Their humour is of a different metal—probably in some cases somewhat leaden. I refer to it in the preface of my latest book "Thousand and one day in the occident," of which I enclose a marked Circular.

I have been trying hard to find here in New york, where I have been again for a few weeks, a picture or Photo of "Mark Twain" for some biograph: purposes in Germany, but have failed. Can you put me on the right track?

With the assurance of my great admiration

Very faithfully

Yours

Ernst von Hesse Wartegg.

Ernst Von Hesse Wartegg (1851–1918) was an Austrian writer whose many books included narratives of his worldwide travels. Chapter 29 of *Life on the Mississippi* (1883) quotes about 250 words from his book *Mississippi-Fahrten: Reisebilter aus dem amerikanischen Süden, 1870–1880* (Leipzig, 1881). Clemens inserted the passage while his book was in proofs (H. K. Kruse, *Mark Twain and "Life on the Mississippi* [Amherst, Mass., 1981], 51, 60). It is not known who provided the translation, which can be compared to the same passage in Frederic Trautmann's translation of Hesse-Wartegg's book, *Travels on the Lower Mississippi, 1879–1880* (Columbia, Mo., 1990), 56–57.

105

Galveston Texas

March 29th 1891

S. M. Clemens,

Pardon this liberty and bear with me for the intrusion, and when you have read this which I will try to make as short as possible, and not throw it aside and say the woman is a crank.

I write to ask if I have my life ensured for an amount of money, would you be willing to buy the polecy, for one third or one forth or fifth the amount, pay me the amount agreed on between is now, and at my death for you to receive the full, or remaining amount. You will not have to wait long, for I am now in my sixty fourth year. I have no family. I have nothing; I have never had but little property of any kind, have had to be very diligent in my efforts to make a support, and now that I will soon be growing old and will not be enabled to make that very limited support that I have been enabled to do hereto fore, I have no prospect of receiving any thing by inherritence. So as a last hope I make this strange offer to you. I have been reading your peices ever since you commenced to write and am led to hope you may look on this as it is intended, which is to secure to myself a support for old age. And at the same time you will be fully repayed for the amount advanced and in the end receive a large proffit—I am entirely alone. I have no one to ask for, or expect, any thing from. I had a family at one time. All are dead, which leaves me alone.

Now please answer this as soon as convenient. And I pray that through you, I may be relieved of the sting of poverty.—With hope and respect I am your &c.

Mrs. Ann Williams

Clemens's comment: I think perhaps this better not be answered

An English immigrant, Ann Williams lived until 17 August 1899, when she died in Texarkana, Texas ("Mortuary," Dallas *Morning News,* 18 Aug. 1899). On insurance ploys, see letter 91.

106

Hot Springs, Ark.
May 17" 1891

Samuel L. Clemens,

Dear Sir:—

Without preliminaries or excuses I will at once make the admission that I write to ask a favor & beg you will read my letter before passing judgement on my audacity.—

My little daughter, than whom, you could have no warmer or more ardent admirer, has for years been threatened with a malady that has deprived her of many such amusements & companions as she would have most enjoyed. Her best, most congenial friend during this time, has been Tom Sawyer.

She has entered with him heart & soul, into every experience of his life. So often indeed has the boy been called upon to entertain her that in his present form he can no longer respond; it has occurred to me that possibly you would be willing to give her the pleasure of receiving, directly from you, an autograph copy of the work. I only ask what you alone can give. I will most gladly expect to meet the expense involved.

Could you know the circumstances of the child, I feel assured you would pardon my presumption in making this request. Our present copy of the book will be preserved a lasting testimony to the enjoyment which your wonderful portrayal of childs life, has given to one family of children.

My daughters name is Ernestine. her address. Care Hot Springs Valley Bank.—

Respectfully Yours
Hebe G. Rector.—

Hebe Gower Rector (born 1850) was the daughter-in-law of Henry Massey Rector (1816–1899), who had been governor of Arkansas when the Civil War started. Her husband, Henry Massey Rector Jr. (1845–1905), was a physician, state legislator, local school board member, and president of the Hot Springs Valley Bank. Her second daughter, Ernestine, was about fourteen years old in 1891. She later married a man named Watson Morrison. (USCR; J. H. Shinn, *Pioneers and Makers of Arkansas* [n.p., 1908], 405–406).

107

Goethe Strasse 1, Karlsruhe,
Baden, Germany,
23rd May 1891.

Dear Mark Twain,

Will you obligingly tell me why in German the sun is feminine—*die* Sonne—and the moon masculine—*der* Mond? The Germans themselves can't give me any information on the subject. But they say that you know all about it—that you contributed a valuable appendix—numbered II, I fancy,—to a well-known ethnographical work by one of their most famous authors entitled "Der Landstreicher verreist," and that this appendix deals exhaustively with recondite points of their language. And also I beg to enquire whether the charming features of the lady in the picture "Hello-Central," facing page 478 of your bright and wise book "A Yankee, etc," are imaginary or a portrait? In the latter case I would beg the favour of an introduction. I am referring to the English edition of the book. If the lady is engaged or married it will be a serious matter to me. But you may assure her of my undying admiration meanwhile.

Believe me
Most gratefully yours
Godfrey Egremont

S. L. Clemens Esqe
Hartford,
U.S.A.

Clemens mocked German's seemingly random assignment of noun genders in "The Awful German Language," an appendix in *A Tramp Abroad* (1880)—a book this letter calls *Der Landstreicher verreist* (vagrant traveler). The letter itself was probably a hoax. Its author has not been positively identified but may have been the Godfrey Egremont who was a drama and music critic and secretary of a building society in

" HELLO-CENTRAL!"

FIGURE 18. The Yankee holding Hello-Central in *A Connecticut Yankee in King Arthur's Court*, 525. Collection of the author.

Adelaide, Australia, during the early 1880s. After being convicted of embezzlement, that man fled to Germany but was captured, returned to Australia, and sentenced to prison for six years in 1886. His later history is hazy, but his theater and German connections could be relevant to this letter ("The Charge of Embezzlement against Godfrey Egremont," *South Australian Advertiser*, 28 Apr. 1886; "South Australia," Launceston, Tasmania, *Examiner*, 4 June 1886). That same Egremont may have been the author of *Verse* (New York, 1903), which contains ten poems on Australia. A Gregory Egremont was also the author of *Poems and Songs* (London, 1873). An English government death record for early 1923 lists a seventy-seven-year-old Godfrey Egremont among the people who died that year.

Daniel Carter Beard's illustration of the Yankee holding his baby, Hello-Central, while his wife, Sandy, looks on (figure 18) appeared in chapter 41 of *Connecticut Yankee*. Beard modeled Sandy on the well-known American actress Annie Russell (1864–1936). The Egremont in Australia had a wife and six children; given his theater background, he may have recognized Russell's face in the picture.

108

June 30, 1891

Mr. Sam'l L. Clemens,

Hartford, Conn.

My dear Sir.

I came across a good story about yourself the other day, copied into one of our local papers, and it reminded me of a funny incident that came under our personal notice in Rome, Italy, in Jan'y '75.—I have often told it and as often thought I should enjoy telling it to you—Why not do so now—and in this way?

My husband and I, with a friend, were "doing" the ruins, which we enjoyed immensely,—except that our friend, now an M.C. from Chicago, was occasionally bored by too much talk and too many historical facts from our excellent guide Daniel Schiefi—so much so that he sometimes threatened Daniel with condign punishment if he dared to give him, Col. T—— any more of his facts and figures until he was asked to do so.

One day, being in a friendly mood, the Colonel gave Daniel a section of your delightful "Innocents Abroad" to read—the part containing the account of the trials your party sustained from guides—but Daniel soon politely returned it, saying he was afraid to read much of it because his mind got so much mixed while reading it that he could hardly tell fact from fiction, and he *must* keep facts before him if he expected to be employed as a guide.

However, to let us see that he appreciated what he hd read, and our fine American humor, one day when we were rambling about the "Palace of the Caesars," he suddenly turned to us and with a magnificent sweep of his arm and an insinuating smile, he remarked, "Dese is fine ruins, splendid ruins, all designed by Michael Angelo, as Mr. Marcus Too-ain say in ze Innocents at Home."

Further deponent saith not.

Yours very truly,
Mrs. B. H. Campbell.
Riverside,
Wichita, Kansas.

Clemens received many reports from tourists who used his travel books as guides. This letter concerns passages in *The Innocents Abroad* in which the narrator and his companions complain about the monotony of hearing Italian guides rave how Michelangelo seemingly created everything significant in Italy.

Born Ellen Mills Busselle (1847–1907) in New York City, the present correspondent became Burton H. Campbell's second wife in 1867. After ranching in Illinois during the 1870s, the Campbells moved to Kansas. In 1881, they settled in Wichita, where they later built a twenty-eight-room mansion that became known as Campbell Castle. As one of the wealthiest women in Kansas, Mrs. Campbell held a prominent social position and was a generous philanthropist (obituaries: Wichita *Eagle,* 17 May 1907, and Wichita *Daily Beacon,* 16 May 1907; USCR).

Another native New Yorker, Burton H. Campbell (1829–1908) gradually built up his holdings in western Kansas, where he became a cattle baron. He also had substantial business interests in Wichita. During the mid-1880s, he managed the three-million-acre XIT Ranch (Nat. Register of Historic Places: Nomination Form, "Campbell, B. H. House," 18 Dec. 1972; obituaries: Clark County, Kansas, *Clipper,* 9 Jan. 1908, and *The Unitarian,* Jan. 1908, 74). During Campbell's cattle-driving years, he earned the nickname "Barbecue Campbell." Larry McMurtry made him a character in his 1988 novel *Anything for Billy.*

The member of Congress ("M.C.") from Chicago was probably another former New Yorker, Walter C. Newberry (1835–1912), a Union colonel during the Civil War who represented Chicago in Congress from 1891 to 1893.

109

OFFICE OF A. L. WILSON
ATTORNEY AT LAW

CHERRYVALE, KANSAS, September 5, 1891

Hon. Samuel L. Clemens,
Hartford, Conn.

Dear Sir:

On the 18th of February 1888 my wife and I took the liberty of naming our only boy, who was born on that day, "Mark Twain" and I herewith hand you his photo of recent date.

Yours very truly,
A. L. Wilson

A "Mark Twain Wilson" was, indeed, born on the date this correspondent mentions. The 1910 census lists him, along with two sisters, Blanche and Ethel. Their father, Albert Leslie Wilson (1860–1938), practiced law for more than fifty years. After beginning his career in Cherryvale, Kansas, he relocated to Kansas City, Missouri. In 1933, he returned to Cherryvale (John McGill, *The Beverley Family of Virginia* [Columbia, S.C., 1956], 17; USCR). The photo he sent has not been found.

On 6 December 1905, the senior Wilson wrote again to congratulate Clemens on his seventieth birthday and to report that his son planned to go to New York to pursue an acting career. He added that his son "has always admired you and your writings. . . . He has read all of your books we have been able to obtain for him and I would like to get a complete set of your writings, nicely bound for a present to him. Will you please let me know where they can be obtained and the price?" Clemens's secretary, Isabel V. Lyon, answered his letter. Mark Twain Wilson married in 1914. When he registered for the draft three years later, he described himself as a self-employed attorney in Kansas City, Missouri. (See also letter 191.)

110

MARK TWAIN.

Breathes there a man who's made his Mark
By making light of things 'twere dark;
And Mark my words, 'tis very plain,
This man has split "the blues" in Twain.

Joe Cone.

This poem ain't wuth a cent an' a half,
But surely it's wuth yeour autograf.

J. C.

Postmarked Cambridge, Massachusetts, 14 September 1891, this letter appears to allude to "the blues" in Clemens's humor generally. (Clemens's sketch "A Cure for the Blues" was not published until 1893.) The writer, Joseph Andrews Cone (1869–1918), grew up on a Connecticut farm and apprenticed as a printer at eighteen. In 1889, he began working for a netting and twine company that relocated to Boston the following year. There he became his employer's chief draftsman and also taught mechanical drawing. Meanwhile, he indulged his love of literature by launching his own magazine, *Little Joker and Storyist* (1899), publishing a poetry volume, *Heart and Home Ballads* (1902), and editing a weekly literary magazine (W. W. Cone, comp., *Some Account of the Cone Family in America* [Topeka, Ks., 1903], 263–264; "Mr. 'Joe Cone' a Draftsman and Poet," *The Draftsman* 3 [1904]: 40).

111

411 Union St. Eau Claire Wis.,
7th Dec. 1891.
Dear Sir,—

I am a little girl living in Eau Claire, and admire "Huckleberry Finn" and "Tom Sawyer." Although I am a girl, I would like to play with them and get into such scrapes and would be delighted to find twelve thosand dollars. I didn't like them to take the dead cat, to the graveyard; for I love kitties and wouldn't have one killed for all the warts in Christendom.

I have seen the pictures in your "Sketch Book," I looked at them before I went to bed, I didn't sleep very well or have very sweet dreams, that night.

I have read, and like, some parts of "Innocents Abroad," especialy where the gentlemen were at the hotel in France and tried to express their wishes in French to the waiter who only understood English.

I intend to go to Europe and will go and see the writing of the great "Christifer Columbo" and the mummies if possiable.

It must be fun to write as you do. My grandpa (G. P. R. James) was an author.

I read about you and Elsie Leslie Lyde. She must be nice. I want to be an author and actress, some day.

Please will you write to me or send me your autograph?

Respectively,
Fannie S. James.

The daughter of an English immigrant, Frances (Fannie) S. James (1880–1948) evidently never married, but she had a varied career. After graduating from the University of Wisconsin, she became a journalist in Eau Claire, a medical librarian, and a teacher in several California schools. She eventually returned to Eau Claire and died in her original home ("Miss Frances James Dies Suddenly," Eau Claire *Leader,* 3 Aug. 1948; USCR).

In chapter 34 of *Tom Sawyer* (1876), Tom and Huck find twelve thousand dollars in gold coins. In chapter 9, the boys take a dead cat to a graveyard to cure their warts. Fannie may have been troubled by several pictures of ghosts in *Sketches New & Old* (1875).

The anecdote about the French hotel is in chapter 10 of *The Innocents Abroad* (1869). In chapter 17, the narrator and his companions tell their Genoese guide they have never heard of Christopher Columbus. In chapter 27, they complain that Egyptian mummies in a Roman museum are not fresh.

Fannie's grandfather was the English author George Paine Rainsford James (1799–1860), who wrote more than one hundred books—mostly historical novels. While Clemens was in Germany in 1878, he read James's novel *Heidelberg* (1846), which he called "rot" (*Mark Twain's Notebooks & Journals,* vol. 2, ed. Frederick Anderson et al. [Berkeley, 1975], 126).

Elsie Leslie Lyde (1881–1966) was a famous child actress who starred in a New York production of *The Prince and the Pauper* in 1890. During that period, she spent a great deal of time with Clemens's family.

112

420 East 21st Street, Cheyenne, Wyo. Jan. 19 [1892]

"Mark Twain"

Dear Sir

It is somewhat late in the day, but being much interested in your article on "Mental Telegraphy" I would like to tell you of an occurrence which took place in Wyoming, and which is another proof to add to those you have given.

In November last my husband employed a man named Mescal to do assessment work on some of his mines. After the work was done he left the mines in company with an old miner named Shepherd, for a hunting trip about fifty miles west of Cheyenne, near Laramie City. They had been gone several days, when my husband one day started to return to Cheyenne, from the station near the mines, called Badger, in company with two Germans, Hauphoff and Fredericks. The train being several hours late, Mr Bartlett waited with the two Germans at a hotel in Badger. While the three men were sitting there, Mr Fredericks complained of feeling sleepy, and leaving the other two conversing, retired into another room to take a nap. He was not away very long, but returned, seeming much disturbed, and saying he had not rested well. He said he had had a dreadful dream, and had seen Mescal lying on the ground, and Shepherd sitting by him, who said

"Poor fellow! He has shot himself!"

Mr Bartlett and Mr Hauphoff at once endeavored to dissipate the impression, seeing Fredericks so much cast down, and made light of his dream, and joked him unmercifully, but he was earnest in his declaration that Mescal was dead. Two days after they reached Cheyenne, they received word that Mescal had indeed shot himself, while out hunting in company with Shepherd, near Laramie.

It was an impossibility that Fredericks could have learned of Mescal's death in any other way than by mental telegraphy. A question here presents itself: Why did Fredericks' mind receive the message, when he was neither a relative or particular friend of either Shepherd or Mescal? It must be that some people are more susceptible than others to receive impressions. It is not the first time that such an occurrence has happened to Fredericks.

Begging you to excuse me for intruding myself upon your attention, I remain

Yours very truly

Mary E. Bartlett.

Published in the December 1891 *Harper's Magazine*, "Mental Telegraphy" described the unconscious transmission of thoughts from one person to another over any distance—a phenomenon akin to what later became known as mental telepathy. The essay included anecdotes similar to that described in Bartlett's letter.

Born in Chicago, Mary Jane Eastman Bartlett (c. 1848–1918), spent the 1860s in England, where her father, Zebina Eastman, had been appointed a U.S. consul by Abraham Lincoln. She studied literature and Romance languages there and later did translating work. After moving to Wyoming with her husband in 1878, she was active in public affairs and social reform movements. In 1892, she became the first American woman to organize a women's political club. She was also the first woman nominated to the U.S. Senate by a state legislative caucus. When Wyoming became a state in 1890, she was named the official poet at the formal celebration ("Mrs. Bartlett Will Be Buried Tomorrow," *Wyoming State Tribune-Cheyenne State Leader*, 17 Apr. 1918; anon., *History of Wyoming* [Chicago, 1918], 2:426–427).

Ichabod Sargent Bartlett (1938–1925), a Civil War veteran from Massachusetts, came to Wyoming to work as a military storekeeper. In 1881, he got into mining. Meanwhile, he was drawn into journalism and later became managing editor of the *Cheyenne Leader* (*History of Wyoming*, 2:423–426).

113

32 CHERRY STREET,

WALTHAM, MASS.

Jan. 25/92

To "Mark Twain"

Dear Sir.

I trust I am not taking too much liberty in asking you to kindly name your favorite flower and why?

My object in soliciting this favor is that I may write an article on the favorite flowers of prominent people.

I have received answers from Mrs Harrison, Harriet P. Spofford, Robert J. Burdette, Mary J Holmes, and others. And if you will also kindly grant my request, I shall be truly grateful.

Sincerely,

Lillian Leslie Johnson.

This comparatively trivial query is unusual, but it is possible that Clemens discarded other such letters. The writer, Lillian Leslie Johnson (born c. 1872), later published occasional magazine articles. In 1898, she wrote to an advertising journal about a cookbook she planned to publish and distribute for free (*Printer's Ink*, 16 Mar. 1898, 43). By then, she was married to George Reddington Tower (c. 1861–1938), who was in the paper industry, and was publishing as Lillian Leslie Tower (USCR).

The Mrs. Harrison whom Johnson mentions was probably U.S. president Benjamin Harrison's wife. Harriet P. Spofford and Mary J. Holmes were novelists, and Robert J. Burdette was a midwestern journalist (see letter 54).

114

Blackwater, Mo.
Feb 6/92

To Sam'l L. Clemens, Esq.
Bridgeport, Conn

Dear Sir:—I am reading your story "The American Claimant" as it runs through the "St Louis Republic."

In your last chapter you bring in incidentally a new character—one *Nat Brady*.

Now the character as described makes me think perhaps you had my late father in mind (James W. Brady) Can it be?—or wont you tell me who "Nat Brady" in his timidity and melancholly—in his cowed air—is drawn from. I do not wish to bore you but my own disposition is so morbid, so melancholly—and seemingly so hopelessly and helplessly so, that in my introspection studies Ive wondered if it were not *inherited* and if my father was not about such a boy as you've pictured in "Nat Brady"—for such a one certainly am I. Wont you do me the kindness to reply!

My father died in July, '89—of aortic aneurism. I have your wedding cards and a characteristic letter (relics of "Aunt Betsy Smith" of Hannibal) My sister has your autograph in her collection—and I your picture in mine.

Trusting you will pardon the liberty
I sign myself
Truly yours
Andrew F. Brady Exr

(J. W. B. died)

The American Claimant was serialized in various newspapers, including the St. Louis Republican, during the first three months of 1892. Brady wrote this letter after reaching chapter 12, which introduced Nat Brady, a weak, unemployed tinner who is frequently bullied in a boardinghouse.

A Hannibal, Missouri, resident into the 1870s, Andrew F. Brady was born around 1863—a decade after Clemens left the town. He wanted to know if the melancholic fictional Nat was modeled on his father because he himself was melancholic. However, when he added that his father was unlike Nat, he seemed to contradict the reason for his question. His father, James W. Brady (c. 1825–1889), was one of twelve children of James Brady Sr. (1801–1881), who settled in Hannibal in 1836, a few years before Clemens's family arrived. In 1845, the senior Brady became the town's first mayor. As a boy, Clemens was a close friend of James W.'s much younger brother, Norval "Gull" Brady. James W. himself became a miller and left Hannibal before 1880 (J. H. and R. Hagood, *Hannibal Yesterdays* [Marceline, Mo., 1992], 59–72; USCR).

Elizabeth (Betsy) W. Smith (born 1794/95) was an old Clemens family friend in Hannibal who later lived in Jackson, Missouri. Clemens modeled several minor characters on her (*Mark Twain's Letters* [Berkeley, 1988], 1:94–95n.2).

115

SURROGATE'S COURT,
TIOGA COUNTY, N.Y.
HENRY E. BARRETT, CLERK,

OWEGO, N.Y. April 18 1894

S. L. Clemens,
Players Club,
New York.

Dear Sir:—

It seems that this world would not be satisfying unless one person were allowed to express gratitude and thanks to another. It has struck me as wrong that I should go on and not say to you what I feel.

From my boyhood, when I was kept from play by my interest in "Tom Sawyer" and "Huck Finn," till now, your books and stories have given me more genuine pleasure than those of any other author. I think so often of the *many* pleasant hours you have given me and have made up to me the lack some times of pleasant companions. Mr. Clemens, please accept this in the spirit that it is sent for the intention is good.

My wishes are that you may for many years continue to cheer the sorrowful and make burden bearing easier.

Yours Respectfully,
Henry E. Barrett.

A graduate of Cornell University, Henry E. Barrett (1868–1905) was admitted to the bar in New York in April 1894—a turning point that may have prompted him to write this letter. He practiced law until his early death, which was attributed to the "grip" ("Henry E. Barrett," *Tioga County Record*, 9 Feb. 1905; "Tioga Co. N.Y. Biographies," genealogytrails.com/ny/tioga/biog.html, accessed 20 Feb. 2011).

116

Creswick
October 20th 1895.

Illustrious Sir

You will, I feel sure pardon the liberty I take in addressing you, but I in common with every Australian look upon you as a old friend rather than a stranger; this being so I may with your permission briefly state my wishes.

Enclosed are a few cards engraven upon which is the name of the Mr A. J. Peacock Chief Secretary of Victoria, a native of these parts and one of the "whitest" productions of our island continent. He has represented the Clunes constituency for a number of years within whose area is situated the most wonderful goldfield in Australia.

Many of the pioneer hearts of the early days have fallen upon evil times, and it is proposed giving a big turn out at Allendale (a place probably you have never heard of) in a week or so, with a view of raising money to start a fund for the benefit of the worn out miners in the these parts. "How can you help an object of this kind" will of course occur here, Briefly Sir without the aid of dollars, simply by subscribing your magical autograph or nom de plume on the reverse side of Mr Peacock's card (from whom I readily obtained them) and I will change them into shining gold on the 30th instant.

Every digger who dwells under the blue sky of Australia is familiar with your imperishable works; yea as familiar Sir as the English race are with Dickens, and the very sight of your autograph is a talisman that will open all purse strings. If you are not angry at my request and do not deem me a literary bushranger or an autograph hunter (which I assure you I am not) I may dare to remark that if you consent, the coveted effort of a dip of ink will be intertwined in softest silk by the deft hand of some of my Australian sisters, and enclosed within the leaves of some of your own works, and given as priceless trophies on the date in question.

When you remember your own eventful and early failures in search of gold (or was it mica) in your own land you will I trust forgive this somewhat original request, and grant me the favor of a reply. I know that every moment of your time is precious, especially in Ballarat the scene of all that is worth recording in the history of this country.

Tonight a host of men are journeying across the Dividing range in order to hear the music of your voice and to carry back remembrances of the idol of America and the mirth creator of our own times.

Mr Peacocks brother and myself are also braving the darkness and dangers of the road and would if we dared venture to simply pay our respects to you.

Apologizing for trespassing on you to such an extent, believe me to be one who dwells in a land where blossoms are scentless and birds have no song.

> Yours very Sincerely
> J. Gavan Reilly.
> Receiver & Paymaster
> Creswick
> Vict.

To Saml. L. Clemens
Ballarat

Clemens toured Australia from September 1895 to January 1896. He received this letter while visiting Ballarat, a Victoria mining town, where he lectured twice. John Gavan Reilly (c. 1856–1950) was evidently a civil servant in Creswick, a town about eleven miles north of Ballarat. In later years, he held a series of postmaster positions in other Victoria towns. He was also a local history enthusiast and an amateur poet (Australia Death Index; Australia Electoral Rolls; Tom Griffiths, *Hunters and Collectors: The Antiquarian Imagination in Australia* [New York, 1996], 204). The absence of cards in Reilly's file suggests that Clemens may have complied with his request.

Alexander James Peacock (1861–1933) was a Creswick-born miner and former civil servant. He was chief secretary to the Victoria government from 1894 until 1901, when he became premier under the new state constitution. Chapter 28 of *Roughing It* (1872) tells how Clemens mistook mica for gold while prospecting in Nevada.

117

Vienna, Jan. 16th
1898

Sir!

It would afford me an immense joy to possess your handwriting; you see, I'm not satisfied to have your portrait only, my wishes strive for a higher aim! Would you please have the kindness to write your celebrated name on that photograph and return to me then?!—

Thanking you warmly beforehand, I assure you, that you would make infinitely happy a young and enthusiastic Viennese girl
Elsa Hinterleitner

Clemens received this note while visiting Vienna. The letter is unusual in bearing a photograph of its writer, Elsa Hinterleitner, a Vienna resident about twenty-two years old. Surviving examples of her adolescent drawings (see figure 19) reveal an offbeat sense of humor and enough artistic talent to suggest that she may have pursued a career as an illustrator.

118

1898
Cheshire Feb 7th

Mark Twain:

If I had been granted the privilege of giving any one as much genuine satisfaction as I have derived from the limited number of your works which

FIGURE 19. An 1892 drawing by Elsa Hinterleitner. Collection of the author.

I have been permitted to enjoy, I should like to know it, and in spite of the remonstrances of my family, I am going to thank you *heartily* for the *solid comfort* I have taken in reading "Innocents Abroad" (and *some* of your shorter sketches) With the exception of the Bible and "Uncle Tom's Cabin," I think *very* few articles will—well, *endure*—a second, and especially a *third* reading. About 25 years ago I purchased a copy of "Innocents Abroad" on purpose to loan, (*I* was so delighted with it.) For about 5 years I saw it occasionally (& read it every time I think) Then some one was not as prompt to return it as they should have been, and I lost track of it. I made a great fuss & many inquiries, but could not find it until *last winter!* I ran upon it by accident in a friend's (?) house. I made no apology for walking off with it, farther than, *"Here is my book I have looked for for 20 years!"* I have read it twice since then, and am now going to commence it aloud to my children evenings. Last winter I was idly turning the leaves of a magazine, ("Review of Reviews," I think) and noticed an article "Traveling with a Reformer." I was just about to turn the leaf when I saw some familiar look about one of the two men who were conversing at the top of the page. Another look told me that it *was* my favorite, "Twain," so of course I read it, (as I *never* skip an article of his.) the reading called for two, and that for three, and I finally called a halt at after the *fourth.* I laughed till I was sick (and it wasn't much of a day for laughing either, as I was far from home, and *homesick.*) When I read about your going over to Mrs. Stowe's with collar and tie in hand I laughed till I cried I think. I think you should be thankful to the Lord for giving you the ability to make people laugh, (a good, *wholesome,* hearty laugh) in this world where there are so many tears and so much sorrow and disappointment, so many sad and heavy hearts. Of course I do not know much of your later works as I am unable to subscribe for current literature, and am quite "shut-in" much of the time, but I sincerely hope you are still using your wonderful abilities for the good of your fellow beings. I think I would rather see you than any other person in the world, but of course I never shall.

> Hoping you may long be spared, and be enabled to do much good,
> > I am sincerely, your well-wisher,
> > > (Mrs.) Alvora Miller
> > > Cheshire, Mass

Clemens's comment: Answered | Answered.

A farmwife, Alvora Miller (c. 1850–1930) was widowed a few years after writing this letter but remained in the same county throughout the rest of her life. No reply from Clemens has been found. "Travelling with a Reformer," the sketch to which Miller alludes (figure 20), was published in the December 1893 *Cosmopolitan*. It

TRAVELLING WITH A REFORMER.

BY MARK TWAIN.

FIGURE 20. Samuel Clemens with a "reformer." From "Travelling with a Reformer," *Cosmopolitan*, December 1893. Courtesy of the Mark Twain Papers, Bancroft Library, University of California, Berkeley.

concerns a train passenger who gets his way by subtly conning incompetent railroad employees.

Miller probably read about Harriet Beecher Stowe's encounter with Clemens's collar in a newspaper story widely reprinted in 1894. The incident had occurred twenty years earlier. According to Clemens's own account, after he paid an informal morning visit to his next-door neighbor Stowe, his wife rebuked him for not wearing a cravat and insisted he dress properly and apologize to Stowe. Clemens instead had a servant carry his cravat to Stowe on a platter, along with a note stating he never paid visits "in entirely full dress, lest the effect be too strong upon the person visited; I always went without my cravat; but inasmuch as the person visited might think I had no cravat, it was my custom to send the cravat later, by a trustworthy hand, with a request that after sufficient & satisfying inspection it be returned to me—with a receipt" (Clemens to Mrs. R. M. Yost, 14 Jan. 1887, MTP. See also "He Had Them: A Story of Mark Twain That May or May Not Be True," Bridgeton, New Jersey, *Weekly News*, 11 Apr. 1894; Paine, *Mark Twain: A Biography*, 2:566).

119

THE STAR NEWSPAPER COMPANY LIMITED
TELEPHONE N° 301 HOLBORN.
"THE MORNING LEADER,"
STONECUTTER STREET,

LONDON, E.C. June 12th 1899

Dear Mr Clemens,

Of course it is extremely reprehensible, but I can't help thinking that a dog after a cats tail is a fool to "Mark" in the little matter of jumping at conclusions! I didnt ask you to talk about such a low-down ornery creature as "M.T"!! You shall talk of Authors, Austrians, Arkansaw, anything in the wide-wide & we will taboo Mark Twain. There! Isn't that sweetly generous and I won't ask the size of your socks or how many times a day you don't brush your hair, nor will I request a photo of a corner of your back drawingroom.

I will be good & not worry,—really if you will only reconsider your decision,—I'm sure the man who was so real kind as to *write* & say no, even though he didn't want to, will be too kind to hurt a poor fellow creatures feelings by saying no a second time!

(This pathetic touch ought to fetch you!)

Besides you owe me one for littering up Ludgate Circus with your baggage. Havent I bruised my shins over your trunks outside Cook's? And haven't I—but there, *please* won't you?

Yours still hopefully
Lillie Planner

P .S.

I've got an awful threat up my sleeve—but I will dissemble!

Clemens's comment: Preserve this bitch's letter.

On 1 June 1899, after spending several years on the Continent, Clemens arrived in London, where journalists pressed him for interviews. One was unmarried, thirty-three-year-old Lillie Planner, who wrote for the *Morning Leader,* a radical half-penny paper founded in 1892 that would merge with the *Daily News* in 1912 (English census). Clemens's note makes it clear that Planner annoyed him. On 2 June 1907, when he returned to England to accept an honorary Oxford University degree, Planner wrote to him again. She thanked him for replying to her present letter, written when she was an "ignorant young woman journalist," and renewed her request for an interview. On 18 June, she wrote a third time: "I demand a few words with you. Course, you can write to [the] Editor & get me fired, but I reckon you aint that sort." There is no record of how Clemens responded to these later letters.

The allusion to "littering" is unclear. Ludgate Circus is an intersection where Far-
ringdon/New Bridge and Ludgate Hill/Fleet streets meet, several blocks south of the
Morning Leader's Stonecutter St. address.

120

1900 February 15
Bacau (Romania)

Illustrious Sir,

The Romanian stamp on this letter will cause you profound astonishment.
After you have read this missive you will perhaps again be astonished, knowing
its motive. Who knows that you won't believe that it is the work of a madman
from the other side of the world.

Know this, illustrious sir, that the person taking the liberty of writing to
you enjoys a reputation in his country as other than that of a man deprived of
reason and that it pleases him to believe that this is a reputation he will always
maintain. No, it is not a madman; it is a young man, one who studies literature that gives him the sweetest joy of his life—which over here is not too
happy.

But this is what it's about:

For the long time that I have known your name, I have had a great desire to
own your works. The pieces I have read have been secondhand translations
from the German as few here know English. But I am one of the few people here
who know this language. I learned it myself, some time ago, in order to taste the
beauty of Anglo-Saxon literature in its original form. I believe it superfluous to
say to you that your works, dear Sir, have given me courage to overcome the
difficulties of this study.

Since I have known a little English, my desire to own your works in the
original has been increasing, but as English books are generally expensive and
my means don't permit me to spend much—because I am poor—I had nearly
resigned myself to never owning them.

But the psychology of the man who ardently desires something often invents
the means to achieve it, hence the sudden idea to write directly to you, illustrious Sir.

So if you deign to honor the prayer of a Carpathian mountaineer, he humbly
asks you to send him some of your works (asking for all of them would be
presumptive), and be persuaded that in granting my prayer you will make
happy one who tastes happiness only amidst his books.

Enclosed in this letter, I have the honor to send you, only for your curiosity,
one of our literary journals, in which you will find your "Obsession." This

translation was done by our best poet, Michel Eminescu, who died some years ago.

For a long time I hesitated before writing this letter. But between the fear of appearing ridiculous and the prospect of possible bliss, this last possibility overtook my initial qualms and so I have confided my prayer to the ocean waves, hoping that despite the long and difficult crossing, this letter containing it will reach the illustrious Mark Twain.

Your admirer,

D. D. Patrascan

Bacau

Romania

Europe

A member of a distinguished Romanian political family, Dumitru D. Pătrășcanu (1872–1937) was a satirist and later a university professor. His son Lucretiu Pătrășcanu (1900–1954) would become a founding member and leading theorist of the Romanian Communist Party and hold several ministerial positions after World War II. Because of the younger Pătrășcanu's pro-Romanian positions, Soviet premier Joseph Stalin had him arrested, and he was executed in 1954 (B. A. Cook, ed., *Europe since 1945: An Encyclopedia* [New York, 2001]).

The enclosure Pătrășcanu mentions is missing. It is unclear to what story he alludes, as Clemens never published anything with a title like "Obsession." A journalist and novelist, Mihail Eminescu (1850–1889) was a leading Romanian poet who probably translated the story from a German text. The first Romanian-language book containing Mark Twain stories was published in Bucharest in 1895.

Despite his professed knowledge of English, Pătrășcanu wrote his letter in French, a language over which Clemens had limited mastery. However, Clemens understood French well enough to reply. On 27 April 1900, Pătrășcanu wrote again, saying that the day he received Clemens's reply (not found) was one of the happiest of his life. He sent Clemens a shirt made by his wife "in the national Romanian style."

121

Dont Burn this until you soak it in it will Do

To Mark Twain

Sir

  ˙I have Read with pleasure all your Books and Being a Blunt Western Man from the Cow Boy Country I make My self so D——n Free as to write to My Favorite Author—now to the Point Enclosed find the Cover of a novel— Tracking the Truth—by the By the Author of Barbara This Wedded wife

  Why did not she—for it Must be a Woman—just sign Her name and let it go at that she is too D——n fresh Trying to Make us beleive she Made Herself

Immortal By Writeing a Jim Crow novel so she Has only to Mention it to be
Known it is an Insult to Me at Least and I wish you would give that Kind of
Dyspeptic Writers a Roast in Your *next* Book as You did Harris in Your Tramp
Abroad for fireing Big Words into His Report

I have Served for years in Colorado and Dakota and your Roughing it is Just
Right Huck Finn is Fruit and Tom Sawyer Takes the Pie I have em All—Lets
Have More of them

Waukesha Water is good for Dyspeptics I drink it to Allay the scorching
Effect of Valley Tan

if you Ever lecture where I am Ill Be thar if I get wet

Yours Truly
Few Clothes

Clemens's comment: A sound mind

> The pseudonym "Few Clothes" cannot be confidently linked to any specific person,
> and this letter can only be dated approximately. The writer's comments on "Wauke-
> sha Water" and "Valley Tan" (a cheap whiskey; see chapter 13 of *Roughing It*) suggest
> he may have been at a sanitorium in Waukesha, Wisconsin, which was then noted for
> its healthful water. The allusion to the "Jim Crow novel" hints that the writer may
> have been an African American. A black labor leader named Dan Chain who was
> convicted of obstructing a train in West Virginia in 1912 used "Few Clothes" as an
> alias (William C. Blizzard, *When Miners March* [Oakland, Calif., 2010], 76–78).
>
> The letter, postmarked Waukesha, Wisconsin, 13 November, enclosed the cover of
> *Tracking the Truth,* torn from an undated Illustrated Publishing Co. edition. Appar-
> ently a reprint, it identifies the author only as "the author of *Barbara, His Wedded
> Wife*, etc., etc." Both novels were written by Sophy Beckett. *His Wedded Wife* was first
> published in Munro's Library in 1884. *Tracking the Truth* was evidently first pub-
> lished in an undated edition during the early 1890s. The New York *Herald* of 16 De-
> cember 1893 lists a Sophy Beckett, the widow of Harry Beckett of the late Wallack
> Theater Company, as having recently died at her residence in London, England. The
> same paper's 24 October 1880 obit of Harry Beckett of the Wallack Co. describes
> Beckett (1839–1880) as an English-born actor of "low comedy" who achieved popu-
> larity in the United States but also says he married a Maggie Desmond in 1865.

122

Salem, Mass.,
30 Dec 1900.

Dear Sir:

Will you forgive a stranger for obtruding upon your scant leisure this
expression of gratitude for your *"Salutation"* to the incoming century?

In my opinion it is, so far as I know, the best thing you ever did. Indeed, I
rank it with Lincoln's immortal speech at Gettysburg.

It has done me good. I have stopped taking medicine, now that *somebody* has done *something effectual* to rouse the public from their chronic apathy in this universal reign of terror.

It is a great strain upon one's self-confidence to continue to harbor the conviction that he is right, and all the "powers that be" of Christendom are *wrong* in their fearful onslaughts upon human beings. And if wrong, how appalling the magnitude of the error or *crime!*

You have cheered me. You reassure me against the depressing doubt of my own sanity, and you encourage me to believe there is yet hope that old Waller's sentiment, echoed by Charles Sumner on the title-page of his first great plea for universal peace, may prevail throughout the world:—

"What angel shall descend to reconcile These Christian states, and end their guilty toil?"

I implore you to continue to improve the advantage which the high place you have attained gives you for reaching the public ear and conscience, by stirring up the pharisees until they stop, to *think;* which it would be distrusting the providence of God to doubt must be followed by relenting and repentance.

I end, as I began, with the profound thanks of,

Yours, Cordially,

Abner C. Goodell.

Mr. Samuel L. Clemens,
14 W. Tenth St.,
New York, N.Y.

Clemens's reply:

14 WEST 10TH STREET.

New York, Dec. 31 '00.

Dear Sir:

I think you are right: it *is* a "universal reign of terror." There seems to be a universal reign of error also—& a strange indifference to that formidable fact, in pulpit, press & people. The standard of honor is shrinking pretty fast every where, I think,—among individuals—& has fairly disappeared from Governments. I find but few men who disapprove of our theft of the Phillipines & of our assassination of the liberties of the people of the Archipelago.

I thank you very much for your letter. I shan't receive many of its kind.

Sincerely Yours

SL. Clemens

In response to a Red Cross Society request to write a New Year's greeting from the nineteenth century to the twentieth, Clemens published this brief message in the 30

December 1900 New York *Herald:* "I bring you this stately matron named Christendom, returning bedraggled, besmirched, and dishonored from pirate raids in Kiao-Chow, Manchuria, South Africa, and the Phillipines, with her soul full of meanness, her pocket full of boodle, and her mouth full of pious hypocrisies. Give her soap and a towel, but hide the looking-glass."

Abner Cheney Goodell (1831–1914) was a Massachusetts attorney and historian noted for his library on witchcraft (obituary, Boston *Journal,* 21 July 1914; M. N. Cohen, "Mark Twain and the Philippines: Containing an Unpublished Letter," *Jnl. Cent. Missouri Valley Amer. Studies Assoc.* 1 [fall 1960]: 25–31). The Edmund Waller quotation appeared on the title page of Senator Charles Sumner's *An Address before the American Peace Society . . . 1849* (Boston, 1854).

1901–1910

1901–1903	Clemens family lives in and near New York City
February 1901	"To the Person Sitting in Darkness" appears in *North American Review* (*NAR*)
May 1902	SLC revisits Hannibal, Missouri, for the last time
15 November 1902	"Amended Obituaries," inviting writers to publish obituaries of SLC, appears in *Harper's Weekly*
December 1902	"Was It Heaven? Or Hell?" appears in *Harper's Magazine*
November 1903	SLC takes family to Italy for wife Livy's health
25 December 1903	"A Dog's Tale" appears in *Harper's Magazine*; story is published as a book in September 1904
30 April–5 December 1904	St. Louis, Missouri, hosts world's fair to commemorate centennial of 1803 Louisiana Purchase
5 June 1904	Livy Clemens dies in Florence, Italy; afterward, SLC returns to New York City
March 1905	"The Czar's Soliloquy" appears in *NAR*
5 December 1905	SLC's seventieth birthday banquet at Delmonico's
August–September 1906	"A Horse's Tale" appears in *Harper's Magazine*; story is published as a book in October 1907
September 1906–December 1907	"Chapters from My Autobiography" is serialized in the *NAR* articles are later reprinted in newspapers
June–July 1907	SLC makes last trip to England, to accept honorary degree from University of Oxford
December 1907–January 1908	"Extract from Captain Stormfield's Visit to Heaven" appears in *Harper's Magazine*; story is published as a book in October 1909
June 1908	SLC moves into newly built house in Redding, Connecticut, his last home
December 1908	Publisher Robert J. Collier gives SLC an elephant
24 December 1909	Daughter Jean dies in Redding
January–April 1910	SLC makes last trip to Bermuda and is brought home by his biographer, Albert Bigelow Paine
21 April 1910	Samuel L. Clemens dies in Redding, Connecticut

123

I have heard said many times of late "Mark Twain is losing his power"; and you clearly evidence the fact when, for material, you turn The Holy Scriptures into ridicule.

A Once Great admirer.

In the absence of a postmark, this letter can only be estimated to have been written around 1901—in response to one of Clemens's anti-imperialist essays.

124

501 West 164th St. N.Y. City, Jan. 19, 1901.

Mr. Samuel L. Clemens,
Dear Sir:—
I have been reading your "Yankee in King Arthur's Court," and its adaptability for the purposes of comic opera has greatly impressed me. I have been working it up somewhat and the farther I progress the more certain do I become of its availability for the purpose mentioned. Upon what terms would you be willing

to dispose of the right to dramatize the work? I enclose a stamped envelope and sincerely hope to hear from you. I remain,

Very truly yours,
Edw'd P. Clarke.

Allow me to express my great pleasure to read of the sentiments on equal rights which you uttered at the Hebrew Industrial School for Girls. As a humble believer in the justice and efficacy of equal rights, I rejoice to know that one with so great an influence as yours expresses himself so favorably in no uncertain terms.

E. P. C.

Clemens's comment: Ans Jan 25

This routine proposal to dramatize *Connecticut Yankee* (1889) came to nothing. However, the novel was made into a successful musical comedy by Richard Rodgers and Lorenz Hart in 1927. Of greater interest is the letter's postscript about Clemens's speech at the meeting for the Hebrew Technical School for Girls held at Temple Emanu-El on 20 January 1901. Stating that he had long been "a woman's rights man" in that speech, Clemens endorsed woman suffrage (Paul Fatout, ed., *Mark Twain Speaking* [Iowa City, 1976], 374–376).

A native of Mystic, Connecticut, Edward Perkins Clarke (1872–1934) was a Hartford *Courant* proofreader before moving to New York City, where he continued in the same occupation. He was also active in the Socialist Party. Both his parents were deaf; at party meetings, he occasionally interpreted for deaf attendees, and he published several articles on teaching the deaf (obituary, New York *Times*, 7 Nov. 1934; USCR). Clemens's comment and the absence of Clarke's stamped envelope suggests that Clemens answered his letter.

125

OFFICE OF THE GENERAL AGENT
OF THE HOSPITAL SATURDAY AND SUNDAY ASSOCIATION
OF NEW YORK CITY.
UNITED CHARITIES BUILDING,
FOURTH AVENUE AND 22D STREET.

NEW YORK, Feb 3 1901.

My very dear "Mark Twain"—
It is hard to call you Clemens. As "Mark Twain" you must enter the Valhalla of Immortal Renown. I have just read the editorial in the *Evening Post*—Saturday. I shall hasten to read the full text in the *American Review*.

I hail you as the *Voltaire* of America. It is a noble distinction. God bless you, & weary not in well-doing—in this noblest, sublimest of crusades.

With my whole heart
Yours devotedly,
Frederick F. Cook

This is one of many responses to the February 1901 *North American Review*'s publication of "To the Person Sitting in Darkness," Clemens's biting attack on American imperialism in the Philippines and Christian missionaries in China.

A German immigrant, Frederick Francis Cook (c. 1843–1919) was a newspaper reporter in Chicago from 1862 to 1871; he later published *Bygone Days in Chicago* (1910), a book about that period. By the late 1880s, he was working for New York's charitable Hospital Saturday and Sunday Association (obituary, New York *Times*, 8 June 1919; USCR). There is no record of Clemens's replying to this letter; however, a photograph of him taken around 1907 and inscribed to "J. Fed. Cook" may have been a mislabeled gift to Cook (*Southeby's: The Mark Twain Collection of Nick Karanovich* [New York, 2003], 104–105).

126

WASHINGTON ANTI-IMPERIALIST LEAGUE.

140 B ST. N.E., WASHINGTON, D.C. Feb. 5., 1901.

Samuel L. Clemens, Esq.,

Dear Mark Twain: My household is in a state of extreme jubilation and warm satisfaction, for we have this moment risen from the round table after reading aloud your analysis in the North American of the case of Persons Sitting in Darkness. The four ladies voted to help me thank you for what they think will do an immense amount of good. It has for the moment lifted us out of the state of disgust and despair into which the Master has plunged us. The case has doubtless been put as vigorously before by others, but the splendid satire and blistering irony will give your words a momentum which nothing else could. And hundreds of thousands will read this because you wrote it who could not be got to taste of such truths from any other source. And some of the blamed fools will probably accept your sarcasm for the amiable humor which has always distinguished your work. When a man having the publis ear as you have dares come out with such an unlimited roasting of the powers that be, it gives us great hope. It is late at night but I have just dropped Pettigrew a note and asked him to be sure and include the whole of your article in a speech so as to give it the hospitality of the Congressional Record and the benefit of the franking privilege. I presume he would like to be sure that the proprietors of the North American would not object to this, though, of course, putting it in the Record would be no violation of copyright. Though I am an old-fashioned Republican I have been greatly dispirited since the election. But your defiant trumpet-blast starts the pulses again and sounds like the beginning of a new campaign.

This long letter does not require an answer, but if you come to Washington you must come to see us.

Yours most truly,
W. A. Croffut.

Clemens's reply:

Feb. 8

Good! Make him *read* it to those clams, too. To unload it onto the solemn C. R. is a sacrilegious idea, but sound. I wish it may happen.

Yrs sincerely
S L C

In late December 1900, Clemens sent "Salutation Speech from the Nineteenth Century to the Twentieth" to the New England Anti-Imperialist league before revising it for publication in the New York *Herald* (see letter 122). Afterward, he accepted the league's invitation to be an honorary vice president. In 1899, Croffut organized the Washington branch of the league and became its secretary (Jim Zwick, *Mark Twain's Weapons of Satire* [Syracuse, N.Y., 1992], xxii–xxiii).

Born and educated in Connecticut, William Augustus Croffut (1835–1915) was a widely traveled author and veteran journalist who had interviewed Clemens in Chicago in 1871. During the late 1880s, when he was editor of the *Washington Post,* he received an honorary doctorate from Union College (obituary, New York *Times,* 2 Aug. 1915; C. K. Adams, *The Universal Cyclopedia* [New York, 1900], 252; Gary Scharnhorst, ed., *Mark Twain: The Complete Interviews* [Tuscaloosa, Ala., 2006], 1). Croffut wrote four more letters to Clemens in 1907–1908.

The "Master" to whom Croffut alludes was evidently Republican president William McKinley, who was reelected in November 1900. McKinley's administration prosecuted the war against Philippine nationalists. The South Dakota senator Richard Franklin Pettigrew (1848–1926) had lost his bid for a third term the previous November and had only one month left to serve in Congress. The *Congressional Record* for the second session of the 56th Congress (1901) does not mention Clemens or his essay.

127

THE NATIONAL ARTS CLUB
NEW YORK

Mr S. L. Clemens
Sir.

Please take the advice of one who has known you for quite a quarter of a Century and go back to the Old World. You are not needed here and are unworthy to live under the folds of the American flag. In quite everything you have said and done since your return you have made a consumate ass of yourself. Your Mugwump life has made a pessimist of you in the extreme. You and three hundred pounds of Cleveland ought to go & sit in the shadow of a granite rock & chew the cud of bitterness. You were not made for sunshine & hope.

The Bookman for Jny sized you up rightfully. You may think you are very smart in your speeches, when in fact you are very silly and weak. I am very sorry for your wonderfully charming wife. After you have shuffled off this mortal coil your memory will hardly live a tardy day. Take to the woods and roam in silence.

Rob Roy

Clemens's comment: No ans *and* ~~Sick~~

> The most intriguing thing about this stinging attack, postmarked 9 Feb. 1901, is its uncertain authorship. An obvious pseudonym, "Rob Roy" was the name of a legendary eighteenth-century Scottish outlaw. The fact that the letter is on National Arts Club stationery is suggestive but proves nothing, as nonmembers may have used the stationery. The club was founded in 1898 by New York *Times* literary and art critic Charles de Kay (1848–1935), but his handwriting looks nothing like Rob Roy's. Another possible candidate is Harry Thurston Peck (1856–1914), the editor of the *Bookman* who probably wrote the unsigned critique the letter mentions. Titled "As to Mark Twain," that article called Clemens "first and last and all the time, so far as he is anything, a humorist and nothing more. . . . A hundred years from now it is very likely that *The Jumping Frog* alone will be remembered." Peck's later suicide suggests mental instability, but his handwriting also does not resemble Rob Roy's.

128

Peoria, Ill., Feb. 23, 1901.

Samuel Clemens,
Hartford, Conn.

My Dear Sir:—

I have just read in "The Public" certain extracts from your article "The Person Sitting In Darkness" written by you for the February North American Review. I think I can realize something of the criticism that may come to you directly or indirectly as a result of your article.

Ever since boy-hood—when your writings captivated me—I have regarded you as my favorite humorist. And my regard for you has grown steadily as I have become more familiar with your works. If anything that I may say may be of any encouragement to you or serve to counteract in any degree any of the jibes or criticisms, I will gladly say that your article touched my heart deeply and it has raised you in my estimation even higher than ever before. Men with sufficient moral courage to speak their convictions are not so numerous. Your article has all the marks of genius and, aside from its humor, is a scathing arraignment of sham and hypocrisy.

The reading of your works has been a source of great delite and profit to me. Among others, I have read Tom Sawyer, Huck Finn, Innocents Abroad, Roughing It, Connecticut Yankee, Prince and Pauper, American Claimant, Puddnhead Wilson, and a number of shorter productions.

As one who believes in liberty and in the principles of the Declaration of Independence, and as a Single Taxer, I take the liberty of expressing to you, in this feeble way, my appreciation of you and your work and to commend your recent article in particular.

Yours Truly.
Clayton Ewing
408 Bradley Ave., Peoria, Ill.

Clemens's comment: Very handsome

Clayton James Ewing was younger than his letter may suggest. Barely twenty-four when he wrote it, he was working as a railroad clerk and living with his widowed mother and three sisters. In 1910 he worked for a railroad in Indiana. In 1918, shortly before World War I ended, he went to France as a secretary of the National War council of the YMCA to serve troops of the American Expeditionary Force. Two years later, he was back living with his mother and sisters in Peoria, doing bookkeeping work for an insurance company. He never lost his enthusiasm for the single-tax movement. In 1920, he ran as an elector for the Single-Tax Party's presidential ticket. In 1924, he ran for trustee of the University of Illinois on the Commonwealth Land Party ticket. By the 1930s, he was the head of the Chicago chapter of the Henry George Foundation and traveled and spoke about tax reform (1918 passport application; USCR; Peoria *Morning Star,* 28 Oct. 1920; Rockford, Illinois, *Daily Register Gazette,* 29 Oct. 1924; New Orleans *Times-Picayune,* 27 Jan. 1932).

129

Putnam, Conn.,
Feb. 27th, 1901.

Samuel L. Clemens, Esq.
Hartford, Conn.

My dear Mark Twain:

I am very glad you wrote and published that article in N.A. Review. It's the truth: and truth hurts. The carping censorious editors pecking at you are like a flock of jackdaws pecking at the great American eagle. A man of your comprehensive views need have no fears. Stand by the courage of your convictions.

Yours, admiringly,
Gilbert A. Tracy

Clemens's reply:

Gilbert A. Tracy Esq.,
Dear Sir:
Although you, in charity and kindness for a busy man, have forborne to require an answer, I cannot deny myself the pleasure of saying, out of my heart, I thank you.

Sincerely yours,
SL Clemens

An eastern Connecticut farmer and former teacher and high school principal, Gilbert A. Tracy (1836–1918) was also an amateur historian and lifelong Abraham Lincoln enthusiast. During the mid-1860s he clerked in the War Department in Washington, D.C., where he frequently saw Lincoln. In later years, he collected Lincoln materials, communicated with fellow enthusiasts, and published occasional articles on Lincoln. His most important work was *Uncollected Letters of Abraham Lincoln* (1917) (USCR; F.R. Gay, "Splendid Collection of 'Lincolnana' at Watkinson Library," Hartford *Courant*, 2 Mar. 1919).

130

CRIPPLE CREEK CLUB

CRIPPLE CREEK, COLO. March 3, 1901.

S. L. Clemens Esq
Dear Sir:
    I have just read your article in the North American Review on the Filipino proposition. There is nothing to laugh at in what you say, but in my judgment it is the most compact, truthful and withering criticism of the McKinley policy that I have read. You have the facts all the facts. Long life to you and *stay with them.*

    I served as a private soldier in the Colorado Regiment and was on the Island of Luzon from July 18, 1898 until July 16, 1899. We thought we went there to liberate the Filipinos even as other American soldiers went to Cuba to help free the Cubans. But the Americans who crossed the Pacific "to liberate" remained there to enslave.

"The pity of it all!
I congratulate you on your overwhelming, truthful exposition of the great crime.

Yours Sincerely,
N. E. Guyot.

Clemens's comments: Ans | from a soldier—first rate.

> Born in Jamestown, New York, to French immigrant parents, Napoleon Eugene Guyot (1860–1933) was a bookkeeper in Massachusetts until around 1885, when he went to Colorado and did accounting work for a smelting company. In May 1898, shortly after the Spanish-American War began, he enlisted in the First Colorado Volunteer Regiment and was sent to the Philippines, where he audited public accounts in Manila. In November, after fighting with Spain had ceased, Guyot telegraphed Colorado's governor in the name of the volunteers, asking that the men be recalled because of poor rations and sickness. His message was widely published. After he was discharged in San Francisco in September 1899, he caused an even bigger stir by publicly charging large-scale corruption in the army's Philippine auditing department. He then returned to Colorado, where he prospered as a mining engineer. In early 1911, while the Mexican Revolution was developing, his name appeared briefly in news stories about a proposed American filibustering expedition into Baja California, but no evidence has been found to prove Guyot himself was involved. A year later he was involved in major mining strikes in Colorado. By 1930, he was living in Los Angeles, where he later died in a veterans' hospital. Clemens's reply to his letter has not been found (M. I. Swift, *Imperialism and Liberty* [Los Angeles, 1899], 286–287, 315–317; "Charges of Corruption at Manila," *Literary Digest*, 16 Oct. 1899, 453; G. R. Hunt, *Colorado's Volunteer Infantry in the Philippine Wars, 1898–1899* [Albuquerque, N. Mex. 2006], 106–107; L. L. Blaisdell, *The Desert Revolution: Baja California, 1911* [Madison, Wis., 1962], 58–59; Susan K. Harris, *God's Arbiters: Americans and the Philippines, 1898–1902* [New York, 2011]).

131

Turnersville Texas
March 5th 1901.

Dear Sir:—
Praise to the Eternal! A voice has been found. Praise! that a man whose honesty no man doubts; who possesses the love and admiration of his fellow countrymen; who has a stood face to face with Truth, and heard her words, has dared to repeat the message in tones which encircle the earth, and which will go ringing down through the ages.
Praise the Eternal, for Mark Twain.

FIGURE 21. Edwin Brenholtz. Courtesy of the Brenholtz family.

In my own way, I have endeavored to repeat *Her* words; but this voice is weak, and could not get much of a hearing; and now my utterances are value-less: to-day they would be but a weak imitation of yours.

Well, what matter?

The message has been delivered. That was the important matter.

With sincere love and respect
Edwin A. Brenholtz.

To
Mark Twain. The Voice.
New York City
N.Y.

Clemens's comment: Ans

Clemens's reply:

New York, March 18, 1901.

Dear Sir:

Although you, in charity and kindness for a busy man have forborne to require an answer, I cannot deny myself the pleasure of saying, out of my heart, I thank you.

Sincerely yours,
S. L. Clemens

Mr. Edwin A. Brenholts
Turnersville, Texas.

> Edwin Arnold Brenholtz (1859–1953) (figure 21) worked as a civil engineer for Pennsylvania mines and railroads until his health prompted him to move to Texas, where he took up farming when he was twenty-nine. He also began writing poetry and prose and corresponded extensively with public figures. He contributed to socialist publications and wrote books, including *Fate: The Story of a Study of a Human Life* (1902), *In the Last Degree* (1904), *Recording Angel: A Novel* (1905), and *Voice of Equality* (1905). According to his great granddaughter, a socialist press refused to publish his last novel, *The No Respector*, because he refused to change the ending in which his protagonist destroys a super weapon instead of handing it over to the socialists (Anne Pinkey, personal communication, 3 August 2012; "Edwin Arnold Brenholtz," www.angelfire.com/retro/mysterypics/eab.htm, accessed 28 Feb. 2011).

132

Darlington Ind. March 26 1901

S. L. Clements; Hartford, Con.

Dear Sir:

I have just finished reading your production, "To the person sitting in darkness," and must say that it is an astonishing *production*, to come from one who claims to be sensible. Truly I had always thought you to be a christian! Please excuse seeming impertinence but for the sake of some of us poor Hoosiers who have been kept busy making apologies for you of late tell us. Were you ever ajudged insane? Be honest, truly how much money does the Devil give you for araigning Christianity and missionary causes? Do you feel something like an ass that has just finished a "great big puffin" bray? Is there any sign as yet of your hoof being cloven?

Your friends are anxious to know these things.

A. S. Buchanan.

An alumnus of the Princeton Seminary, Augustus Sherman Buchanan (1863–1942) served as a Presbyterian minister for many years in Indiana and Illinois. At the time he wrote to Clemens, he was a pastor in Darlington, Indiana (USCR; *Princeton Seminary Bull.* 5, no. 1 [May 1911]: 64). Paine's *Mark Twain: A Biography* (1912) quotes several lines of Buchanan's letter, identifying its writer only as a "critic with a sense of humor" (p. 1134).

133

Your (former) countrymen were sorry for your troubles and were glad when you got out of them. But ninety eight out of a hundred now feel you are unworthy & if you knew how they feel you would go (guilty) abroad & stay You are not worthy of citizenship in a land which you so outrageously slander & villify— while you have nothing but praise & comfort for its enemies—shame on you—

—many students—

Postmarked New York, 26 March 1901, and addressed to Mark Twain's 14 West 10th Street residence, this anonymous postcard was written by one hand. The "troubles" to which it alludes were Clemens's well-publicized struggle to pay off creditors of his bankrupted publishing firm during the 1890s. After succeeding, he made a triumphal return to the United States in October 1900, ending a five-year absence. The students evidently objected to "To the Person Sitting in Darkness," which implicitly praised the nationalists whom the United States was fighting in the Philippines.

Another postcard signed "Students" and postmarked 30 March 1901 appears to be written in the same hand: "You ought to go to Philippines and take Aguinaldo's place You deserve more punishment than he! You are a more intelligent but more culpable rebel and Coward[.]" Emilio Aguinaldo (1869–1964) was the Filipino nationalist leader.

134

18, QUEEN'S GATE PLACE,
LONDON, S.W.

April 17th 1901

Samuel Clemens Esq.
c/o North American Review
New York City

Dear Sir:

I have read with a great deal of interest what you have written regarding the missionary question in China and I give you my candid opinion that what you have done is of very great value to the civilization of the world.

There is no man living whose words carry greater weight than your own, as no one's writings are so eagerly sought after by all classes.

I have heard that the missionary takings in America have fallen off immensely on account of the truth that has been brought to light by the late trouble in China. It is said that the lectures and writings of Vivekananda in the States caused the missionary takings to fall off over a million dollars a year and I feel sure that your own writings will cause a still further falling off.

Without any doubt the missionary propaganda in China is the cause of all the present trouble in China.

I have made a study of this question for years and have collected an immense amount of data which is at your disposal if you should wish to use it.

I am sending to you enclosed a letter which was written by Mr. Ivan Chen the secretary of His Excellency, Sir Chihchen Lofengluh, Chinese minister, in reply to a ridiculous attack that was made by Julian Ralph on the superstition of the Chinese. Mr. Ivan Chen has written another article but he could find no newspaper that would accept it.

He has received a large number of congratulatory letters from all over the world and a few abusive ones—

Yours very truly

Hiram S. Maxim

S.M.

This is the first of four preserved letters Sir Hiram Stevens Maxim (1840–1916) wrote to Clemens shortly after Clemens published "To the Person Sitting in Darkness." Clemens's reply has not been found, but Maxim acknowledged it in his own letter of 19 June 1901, which expands on his criticisms of missionaries.

An American-born British subject, Maxim was an eminent inventor best known for developing the first fully automatic and portable machine gun during the 1880s. The Maxim gun, as it was known, helped extend European imperialism over non-Western societies and advanced copies of its design would contribute greatly to the slaughter of World War I. Paradoxically, Maxim was long concerned about the harm done to China by Western missionaries. He explained his antipathy toward them in *Li Hung Chang's Scrap-Book* (1913), a collection of extracts from published sources interspersed with his own lengthy commentaries. Maxim stated that his book's goal was "to save human life and prevent human suffering" by combatting folly (p. xxii). A chapter titled "Missionaries in Other Lands" quotes Clemens on the negative impact of missionaries in the Hawaiian Islands (p. 350). A chapter on Joan of Arc assails Christian belief in devils and quotes Clemens's *Personal Recollections of Joan of Arc* (1896) as a source (pp. 103–104).

Swami Vivekananda (1863–1902) was an Indian scholar who represented Hinduism at Chicago's 1893 World Parliament of Religions and helped introduce Hindu systems of belief in America. Li Hung Chang (1823–1923) was a leading Chinese statesman and diplomat whom Maxim befriended. Chih Chen Lo Feng-luh (1850–1903) served as secretary to Li Hung Chang during his 1896 tour of the United States and was later China's minister to Great Britain. In September 1900, the American journalist Julian Ralph (1853–1903) wrote a scathing article about Chinese beliefs for the London *Daily Mail*.

135

[New York City]
April 25, 1901.

Mr. Samuel Clemens,

Dear Sir:—

None have enjoyed your witty writings more than I, or laughed more heartily. And if no harm is done it is a good thing to make people laugh. But you have looted pure and noble Christian character. What reparation can you make? Our Savior says, of the treatment given his little ones, "Inasmuch as ye did it unto one of the *least* of these my brethren, ye did it unto me." You join those hooting at your Savior on the cross, when you set the rabble hooting at those who have taken their lives in their hands to carry out his parting command, "Go ye into all the world, and preach the gospel to every creature."

I know well what heroic souls they are, for I am
A sister of one of the "little ones."

Clemens's comment: Use this as a mis^h text.

This attack on "To the Person Sitting in Darkness" was postmarked Westfield, New Jersey. Its anonymous writer hints that she was a missionary, which is why Clemens wrote "mish text." The biblical passages it quotes are from Matt. 25:40 and Mark 16:15.

136

New York City,
Nov. 21, 1901.

Dear Mr. Mark Twain:—

I am a little girl six years old. I have read your stories ever since they first came out.

I have a cat named Kitty, and a dog named Pup.

I like to guess puzzles. Did you write a story for the Herald Com-pe-ti-tion? I hope you will answer my letter.

Yours truly,
Augusta Kortrecht.

Clemens's comment: Lame attempt of a middle-aged liar to pull an autograph.

Clemens's suspicion was probably correct. The letter is written in the mature hand of an adult. Its likely author was the writer of children's verses and stories whose name was really Augusta Kortrecht. Born in Tennessee around 1871, Kortrecht was orphaned at an early age and raised by a widowed aunt in Memphis. At some point, she spent two years in a German school. From around 1901 through the mid-1910s, she published numerous stories and verses in magazines and two books, *Dixie Rose* (1910), about a southern school girl, and *Dixie Rose in Bloom* (1912), in which the girl attends a German school. A possible reflection of both her background and how she approached Clemens is the theme of relationships between young children and parents that pervades her writings. She later married a man named Preston but was divorced by 1920. By that time, her interests had shifted to child welfare and she did social work in Boston into the 1930s (USCR; "Writers of the Day," The Writer [June 1919]: 89–90). Augusta's older brother, Alexander Humphreys Kortrecht (born 1859), married Mary Wilson Polk, a grandniece of the former U.S. president James Polk in 1884 (J. T. Moore & A. P. Foster, *Tennessee: The Volunteer State* [Nashville, 1923], 4:68).

137

301 SOUTH MAIN STREET
HARRISONBURG, VIRGINIA

My Dear Mr. Clemens:

I want to thank you for the autograph. The advice is so good. "When people are looking" is so comforting for I hear the "We ought never to do wrong" all the time. I have read your books many times. Of course Tom and Huck are my favorites. I think they are both fine but I believe Huck is the best. Tom went to so much trouble just to give a dramatic effect. Huck was more human. They both led charming lives. I wish you would write some more books like these and have some girls in them. Just so they would not spoil the adventures of the boys.

No matter how many times I read your books I always laugh. I positively "make the welkin ring."

Your friend.

Enid Sipe

Enid Sipe (1893–1964) probably wrote this undated letter after 1901: it is in the cursive script of a child at least eight years old. One of three daughters of a lawyer, she traveled to Europe with her family in 1905 and later attended Virginia's Sweet Briar College, a women's school begun in 1900. By 1920, she was married to George W. Brent (1891–1963), a career U.S. Army officer with whom she had three children (USCR; Carol Brent, personal communication, 28 July 2012; passenger manifest, SS La Lorraine, New York, 2 July 1905; Sweet Briar College yearbook, 1911). The context of the letter is unclear. Sipe may have written to Clemens to thank him for an autographed photo obtained for her by a mutual friend.

Sipe's last sentence is adapted from a line in chapter 5 of *Tom Sawyer Abroad* (1894) in which Tom says, "when a person made a big speech the newspapers said the shouts of the people made the welkin ring." The phrase goes back several hundred years.

138

30 Weld Hall
Harvard University
Cambridge Mass.
January 7, 1902.

Dear Mr Clemmens,
Dear Sir,

However I have not the pleasure of your personal aquaintance, on account my being a stranger students of English, my deep respect to you tempts me to send you some of my unfinished poems for your kind critics.

Would your goodness toward Japanese not condemn this my intrusion to your leisure?

Very sincerely Yours
Hydesaburo Ohashi.

Enclosure

THE MISTY MOUNTAIN MOON.

Around the slant brows of the misty peak,
Toward the rustic arbor on the rocky ledge
Adele and Jack, with Jet, a spaniel black
Athwart the green, along the maple hedge,
Strolled both, arm in arm, like lovers young
Into the hovering deepmost mountain mist.
The crescent moon was casting its dim light
Upon the sleeping valleys, calm and whist
And mildly shed its misty rays on high.
No twinkling stars burned in the clouded sky,
But some faint lights shone in the sylvan vale,
With here and there a mirror facéd lake.
They sat there leaning on the arbor rail;
It was his farewell night.—Tomorrow dawn
His duty, for sweet peace and for the sake
Of concord, to the war would find him gone.

· ·

The slight sounds of a tender whispering
Were heard, anon the silence, vast and deep,
And then came kisses warm and passionate,
Whilst Jet barked madly at the rocky steep.

Hydesaburo Ohashi.

Clemens's comment: The Jap's poems

This is the first of three preserved letters Hydesaburo Ohashi (1877–1918) wrote to Clemens. It also enclosed a second poem, "Maude and O-Hana," about an American girl and Japanese girls walking together. Ohashi sent a third poem, "Music," to Clemens on 7 January. However, it was the "Moon" poem that intrigued Clemens. On 12 January 1902, he wrote to W. D. Howells, "Don't you want to discover a Japanese poet & introduce him to the public?" He went on to praise Ohashi's poem, concluding, "I cannot claim to know poetry when I see it, but instinct moves me to think that the talent must be in this Jap." (*Mark Twain–Howells Letters,* ed. H. N. Smith and W. M. Gibson [Cambridge, Mass., 1960], 2:739. The editors mistakenly state that Ohashi's "poetry is not extant."). Around the same time, Clemens wrote to Ohashi himself. That letter has not been found, but Ohashi's letter of 14 February thanks him for his kindness: "I expected to receive from you not such praise to which my work is not fit but your criticism on my unpolished lines or mistakes, or my other poor points!—because I am a bit of a yellow-beaked bird whose caroling needs a more instruction from the mother bird!"

Reputedly a member of the Japanese nobility, Ohashi came to the United States in 1889. After attending high school in Brookline, Massachusetts, he studied at Harvard College in 1899–1900 and 1901–1902. Afterward, he failed at an importing business but later turned his inventions in typewriter ribbons and carbon paper into the successful H. Ohashi & Co. enterprise. After he died in 1918, his two former American wives fought over his estate. According to a warm obituary written by a Harvard classmate, Ohashi saw business only as a means to fostering his larger interest in internationalism. He "was a profound student of Oriental and Occidental literatures and philosophies" who "meant to write a great book" about his philosophy of "Positive Knowledge" (George Allan England, "Hydesaburo Ohashi," *Harvard College Class of 1903: Quindecennial Report, June, 1920* [Norwood, Mass. 1920], 221–222; "Japanese Wed 2d American on 'Gentleman's Agreement,'" New York *Tribune,* 8 Dec. 1920).

139

My dear "Mark Twain":—

In your *"Roughing It"* you tell a yarn about somebodys old black ram in the course of which you relate a touching anecdote of a fellow who got mixed up into a vat of carpet dye & was woven into a piece of Brussels carpet & you proceed to relate how the sorrowing kinsfolk held solemn obsequies over these same yards of carpet. This stirring tale has often moved me to emotion, though, to speak frankly, I had *"me doots"*

Now comes your triumphant vindication! I call your attention to the enclosed clipped from todays N.Y. *"Times"*

Yours sincerely & admiringly

Geo T Davidson

St Lukes Hospital N.Y. Mch 2 1902

Enclosure

BURIAL SERVICE OVER A RAIL.

FROM NOTES AND QUERIES.

The brother of a friend of mine was some few years since a curate in one of the iron-working towns of Lancashire. One day a man in the parish of which he had charge fell into a furnace of molten metal, and of course vanished forever. The comrades of the poor fellow were greatly concerned, and did not rest till the curate had consented to bury with religious rites one of the rails into which the iron was run. The rail selected was inclosed in a wooden box, borne to the graveyard, and laid solemnly in the ground, though, I understand, it was not taken into the church.

Chapter 53 of *Roughing It* (1872) contains the famous "Story of the Old Ram." It includes an anecdote about a man falling into a machine that wove him into fourteen yards of carpet, in which he was buried. His widow would not "let them roll him up, but planted him just so—full length. The church was middling small where they preached the funeral, and they had to let one end of the coffin stick out of the window. They didn't bury him—they planted one end, and let him stand up, same as a monument."

Davidson has not been further identified. However, the 21 April 1899 New York *Times* has an article on the arrest for larceny of a George T. Davidson who had chaired the House Committee of the Democratic Club.

———

140

4021 Locust St.

Philadelphia

24, May, 1902

Dear Mr Clemens:

I thank you very much for your prompt reply, also for your opinion of my work.

I am glad you thought there was talent in my poems, but I was very much surprised, and disappointed to hear you say, you could be of no use to me, because "my work did not possess that higher quality, which is known as genius, and makes a poet's success." I am well aware that genius, which is given to but few in each century, can only achieve a permanent place in Literature, but I think you will admit that talent can be made to pay, as our ever increasing number of "Periodicals," with their hosts of contributors prove.

It was the hope of making my talent remunerative that led me to ask the helping hand of you.

I believe I explained when I wrote you, that I write short stories as well as poems, but as I cannot afford to have them type-written, I have small chance of having them read. Editors are so busy they will not take the trouble to read a written manuscript, unless one has made a name, or has influence

Having learned this by experience, and knowing that you must have a large acquaintance among those interested in our leading magazines I thought perhaps if I told you of my hard struggle, and *you saw any talent in my work you might be willing to speak a word for me*. But if I have erred in my judgement, I can only regret it, as it has entailed trouble upon you and been a keen disappointment to me.

Sincerely yours.

Mary A. Geisse

Clemens's comment: I tried to make this fool understand (without saying the naked brutal words) that she has neither talent *nor* genius—with this damned result. [and] *Ans.*

> Following an earlier exchange that has not been found, this letter expresses the disappointment of Mary Alberteen Geisse (1866–1935) over Clemens's comments about a manuscript she had sent him. Clemens's caustic comment here expresses his exasperation over demands from aspiring writers seeking his help. Nonetheless, Geisse persevered and published a small volume titled *Poems* in 1904 under the pseudonym "Felix Connop," with her real name under the book's copyright notice. The volume contains two verse prefaces. One is a facsimile of a handwritten poem, "Shadows," dated 1 June 1901—one week after her second letter to Clemens. The other, "Author's Preface," might be read as a slap at Clemens:

> > Let the critics have their fling,
> > Since it pleases me to sing.
> > I shall blithely go my way
> > Heedless of the things they say,
> > Quite content if word of mine
> > Makes one truth more brightly shine,
> > Or can send a genial glow
> > Through the heart of frend or foe.
> > For I hold the proverb true,
> > Be its wisdom old or new,
> > That "A simple verse may teach
> > Him whom sermons cannot reach."

The 1900 and 1910 U.S. censuses list Geisse as an "artist" living with her mother and sisters. The 1920 census lists her as a resident in the Philadelphia Hospital for the Insane.

141

Elizabeth N J July 16 1902

Mr Samuel L Clemens
Tarrytown N Y

Dear Sir:—In the light of your recently quoted remark that Sunday School Libraries only circulated "Good-Goody" books I thought you might be interested in the fact that the Sunday School Library of the Central Baptist Church of this city of which I am librarian is perhaps the first S.S. Library in the country that has on its shelves a *Complete* set of your works.

Not uniformly bound, purchased at various times, but *all* there[.] "Joan of Arc" was first the others followed as soon as obtainable and this collection of books represents my personal taste in literature so that we Have full sets of Dickens, Scott, Bulwer, Cooper, Conan Doyle, Hugo, Reade et als besides any new novels thought worthy of circulation

I have weeded out most of the trash I fell heir to and now have 1500 vols and add about 200 a year.

I write the foregoing because I have a great affection for your writings: every scrap of an address or essay or lecture of yours is eagerly read by me and will be as long as you may be pleased to write or speak in public.

With Best Wishes for a Long Afternoon of Life,
I remain
Yours Respectfully
L Fred Silvers
1087 Lafayette Street

Clemens's reply:

[31 July 1902, York Harbor, Maine]

Dear Mr Silvers:

It does indeed interest me—and greatly pleases me, too. Also it squares an old account, heals an old sore, banishes an old grievance: the turning of Huck Finn out of the Concord (Mass) circulating library 17 years ago because he was immoral & said he would stand by Jim & go to hell if he must. I think your selection of authors is a healthy advance upon the old-time S.S. library menu.

Sincerely Yours
SL. Clemens

P. S. But to be strictly honest with you, I very greatly value those old goody goody books, too they made clean & honest children

> The recent "remark" to which Silvers alludes has not been identified; however, Clemens was known to disdain "goody-goody" books. An autobiographical dictation he would record in March 1906 recalled the Sunday school books he read as a boy: "They were pretty dreary books, for there was not a bad boy in the entire bookcase. They were *all* good boys and good girls and drearily uninteresting, but they were better society than none, and I was glad to have their company and disapprove of it" ("Chapters from My Autobiography" [chapter 23], *North American Review,* Oct. 1907, 165).
>
> Louis Fredrick Silvers (1869–1955) was a grocery clerk when he wrote this letter. By 1910, he owned a grocery store. A decade later, he was sexton of his Baptist church. Shortly before writing to Clemens, he answered a New York *Times* challenge to suggest humorous books appropriate for reading aloud to weary listeners. Silvers's first choice was Opie Read's *Old Ebenezer* (1897). His second choice was Mark Twain's account of his trip to Bermuda (presumably the 1877 sketch "Some Rambling Notes on an Idle Excursion"). He added: "Mark Twain's 'Connecticut Yankee' and 'The American Claimant' are also good, but of all his works, 'The Adventures of Tom Sawyer' is best" (USCR; "From Readers: Pleasant Reading," New York *Times,* 24 May 1902).

142

JAMES R. SWAIN, COUNTY ATTORNEY
GREELEY COUNTY.

GREELEY, NEBRASKA, Oct. 7, 1902.

Mr. Mark Twain:
Riverside, New York.

Dear Mr. Twain:—

I've been going to write to you for a long time, ever since I saw that piece in the paper about Huck Finn being a bad book.

I am a little girl twelve years old. I have read Huck Finn, about fifty times. Papa calls it my Bible, I think it is the best book ever written, and I don't think it would hurt any little boy or girl to read it. I think it would do lots of them a lot of good. I don't think that preacher knew what he was talking about.

I think the folks know it all by heart, I have told them so much about it, especially all of Jim's sign's. Poor Huck, he did get into more trouble, and get out of it so slick.

When I was down to Omaha, this Summer papa and I looked every book store in the whole city, it seemed to me, to find Tom Sawer, but we couldn't find it, and I was just ready to cry when we got home. I supposed that we could find it at the first store we went to; an then we didn't find it at all.

I think Huck is just fine and I wish there was more like it.

> Your true friend
> Gertrude Swain.

Clemens's comment: Write this child a note, & add her letter to the introduction of the new Huck.

Clemens's reply:

New York City. Oct. 16/02

My dear Child:

.I would rather have your judgment of the moral quality of the Huck Finn book, after your fifty readings of it, than that of fifty clergymen after reading it once apiece. I should have confidence in your moral visions, but not so much in theirs, because it is limited in the matter of distance, & is pretty often out of focus. [But these are secrets, & mustn't go any further; I only know them because I used to study for the ministry myself.]

> Truly yours
> Mark Twain

The Sunday, 24 August 1902, issue of the Omaha *World-Telegram* reported that the juvenile department of the Omaha library had barred *Huckleberry Finn*, as "criticisms of the book have been made in the pulpit and press." The following Sunday, the newspaper reported it had received a letter from Clemens on the matter. Dated 23 August, his letter contained these remarks:

> I am tearfully afraid this noise is doing much harm. It has started a number of hitherto spotless people to reading Huck Finn, out of a natural human curiosity to learn what this is all about—people who had not heard of him before; people whose morals will go to wreck and ruin now.
>
> The publishers are glad, but it makes me want to borrow a handkerchief and cry. I should be sorry to think it was the publishers themselves that got up this entire little flutter to enable them to unload a book that was taking too much room in their cellars, but you never can tell what a publisher will do. I have been one myself.
>
> MARK TWAIN

On 14 September 1902, the *World-Herald* published an unsigned editorial, "Reading for the Boys," blasting the library's censorship. "What are we coming to anyway," it asked,

> When namby-pamby public library boards exclude from the juvenile shelves that great boy's book, "Huckleberry Finn," while they inconsistently dish up the worst kind of fiction for adults. . . . The wholesome wit of the stories of "Tom Sawyer" and

"Huck Finn" not only would not hurt the boy but would refresh the mind of the
adult reader if his thinking compartments be not too much surcharged with the
morbid, unnatural vagaries of many of the modern writers of fiction. . . . Put the
boy to reading nothing but the literature styled 'good-goody' and he will probably,
some day, break over into the worst fields of the yellow back, if he reads at all.

Gertrude Ellen Swain (1890–1974) was the daughter of James R. Swain (1863–1929), a
prominent Greeley, Nebraska, attorney who served twelve years as county attorney,
two terms as Greeley's mayor, and later as president of his county bar association. In
1916, Gertrude married into another prominent Greeley legal family when she wed
Thomas Wunibald Lanigan (1888–1964). An active Democratic Party worker, Lanigan later ran for several public offices and was a special assistant to the attorney
general of the United States in Washington, D.C., during the 1930s. Gertrude also
had two sons who became lawyers. She retained lifelong interests in gardening, literature, and art; was active in the women's suffrage movement; and became an accomplished painter. According to her oldest granddaughter, she remained a lifelong
devotee of Mark Twain, whose letter she was proud of owning. She enjoyed reading
from Mark Twain's books to her grandchildren, adding running commentaries on
the lessons about social awareness and civic duty they contained (Gail Bannon, personal communication, 6 August 2012; USCR; "Nebraska Politics," *World-Herald*, 20
July 1916; "Round about Nebraska: Tom Lanigan's Work," *World-Herald*, 9 Dec. 1935).

143

LAW OFFICE
EDWIN BAYLIES,
107 MADISON ST.,
JOHNSTOWN, N.Y.

Cork Center, November 25th, 1902.

Mark Twain, Esq.,
New York,

Dear Sir:

We enclose herewith an obituary notice which we have long had in stock and
have impatiently awaited an opportunity to publish in our weekly edition of the
Cork Center Gazette, but have been prevented from giving to the public
through a neglect on your part to take such action as would make the article
available. We notice your advertisement in Harper's Weekly of November 15th,
and hasten to enroll ourselves as competitors for the prize you offer for the best
obituary upon your demise. We have made several changes in the original draft
in order to comply with the condition that the article shall be suitable to read in
public. The original draft contained certain allusions to yourself that were
deemed better omitted if the notice is to be read before a mixed audience. But
we trust that the desire expressed by you in the postscript to the effect that the

letter to the editor of *Harper's Weekly*, printed on November 15, 1902.

Amended Obituaries

To the Editor:

Sir,—I am approaching seventy; it is in sight; it is only three years away. Necessarily, I must go soon. It is but matter-of-course wisdom, then, that I should begin to set my worldly house in order now, so that it may be done calmly and with thoroughness, in place of waiting until the last day, when, as we have often seen, the attempt—to set both houses in order at the same time has been marred by the necessity for haste and by the confusion and waste of time arising from the inability of the notary and the ecclesiastic to work together harmoniously, taking turn about and giving each other friendly assistance—not perhaps in fielding, which could hardly be expected, but at least in the minor offices of keeping game and umpiring; by consequence of which conflict of interests and absence of harmonious action a draw has frequently resulted where this ill-fortune could not have happened if the houses had been set in order one at a time and hurry avoided by beginning in season, and giving to each the amount of time fairly and justly proper to it.

In setting my earthly house in order I find it of moment that I should attend in person to one or two matters which men in my position have long had the habit of leaving wholly to others, with consequences often most regrettable. I wish to speak of only one of these matters at this time: Obituaries. Of necessity, an Obituary is a thing which cannot be so judiciously edited by any hand as by that of the subject of it. In such a work it is not the Facts that are of chief importance, but the light which the obituarist shall throw upon them, the meanings which he shall dress them in, the conclusions which he shall draw from them, and the judgments which he shall deliver upon them. The Verdicts, you understand; that is the danger-line.

In considering this matter, in view of my approaching change, it has seemed to me wise to take such measures as may be feasible, to

acquire, by courtesy of the press, access to my standing obituaries, with the privilege—if this is not asking too much—of editing, not their Facts, but their Verdicts. This, not for pres-

ent profit, further than as concerns my family, but as a favorable influence usable on the Other Side, where there are some who are not friendly to me.

With this explanation of my motives, I will now ask you of your courtesy to make an appeal for me to the public press. It is my desire that such journals and periodicals as have obituaries of me lying in their pigeon-holes, with a view to sudden use some day, will not wait longer, but will publish them now, and kindly send me a marked copy. My address is simply New York city—I have no other that is permanent and not transient.

I will correct them—not the Facts, but the Verdicts—striking out clauses as could have a deleterious influence on the Other Side, and replacing them with clauses of a more judicious character. I should, of course, expect to pay double rates for both the omissions and the substitutions; and I should also expect to pay quadruple rates for all obituaries which proved to be rightly and wisely worded in the originals, thus requiring no emendations at all.

It is my desire to leave these Amended Obituaries neatly bound behind me as a perennial consolation and entertainment to my family, and as an heirloom which shall have a mournful but definite commercial value for my remote posterity.

I beg, sir, that you will insert this Advertisement (1t-eow, agate, inside), and send the bill to

Yours very respectfully,
MARK TWAIN.

P. S.—For the best Obituary—one suitable for me to read in public, and calculated to inspire regret—I desire to offer a Prize, consisting of a Portrait of me done entirely by myself in pen and ink without previous instruction. The ink warranted to be the kind used by the very best artists.

FIGURE 22. Mark Twain's letter to the editor of *Harper's Weekly*, 15 November 1902. Collection of the author.

obituary shall be calculated to inspire regret was not intended as a condition, as it ought not to be assumed that your offer is made in bad faith. We have gone to the limit in making the obituary as favorable to you as the facts would permit.

Should we succeed in securing the prize offered we would suggest that in the portrait forwarded to us, as a concession to conventionalism in art, although perhaps at the sacrifice of the realistic, you endeavor to eliminate the corkscrew expression of your eyes noticeable in the sample accompanying the advertisement, and that you also add a mouth should there be sufficient room for that feature in the drawing. We have noticed that in the portraits of our great men of modern times the mouth is made as prominent as in the original.

Faithfully Yours,
Z. Pfennig,
Obituary Editor Cork Center Gazette.

P.S. We do not publish your obituary now and send you a marked copy as requested for the reason that if not successful in the prize contest the obituary will differ from the one herewith submitted in essential particulars. Z. P.

OBITUARY

Mark Twain, AT LAST, is dead. These simple words will be read with but one feeling by all our subscribers from Baffin's Bay to the Gulf of Mexico, and from the Atlantic to the Pacific. In comparison with this announcement the views of Mr. Mitchell on the ethics of the coal strike sink into insignificance. To this traveler who has just passed over the Divide into the Great Beyond the question of coal supply is no longer open. He is apparently at rest. "After life's fitful fever he sleeps well," a privilege memory denied him for many years. We bespeak for him on the other side a tolerance not accorded him here.

The subject of this notice was born near a small hamlet on the trail to Thunder Mountain in the State of Idaho, soon after the appearance of the great comet which preceded the war of 1812. It was commonly predicted at the time that the comet would be followed by disaster. Mr. Twain's boyhood days were passed upon a raft in the Mississippi River where he acquired a liberal education and a knowledge of navigation. While engaged in this pursuit he was a constant reader of the editorials in this paper and was inspired by them to adopt literature as a profession. Many of his best efforts have appeared anonymously in these columns, and will be soon offered in book form as premiums to new subscribers who pay in advance our regular price of two dollars if paid in money, or three dollars if paid in produce.

In addition to his contributions to this paper Mr. Twain found time to write several books, notably, "Roughing it," "Paradise Lost," "Innocents Abroad," "The Vicar of Wakefield," "Huckleberry Finn," "Barriers Burned Away," and a poem entitled "Beautiful snow." From a cipher recently discovered in the latter work it is suspected that Mr' Twain wrote the Mormon Bible and a work on games commonly accredited to one Hoyle. But undoubtedly the best and most finished production of this author was his Scrap Book. We have sat for hours with our eye glued to the pages of that book and wondered at the hold its columns had upon us.

As a writer Mark Twain was a success. And yet he knew nothing of the Scotch dialect, and could not report a base ball game or a prize fight in the ordinary style of a sporting editor. He was remarkably sincere in all his statements and painfully acurate in all his descriptions. Naturally serious and inclined to melancholy his writings partake of these characteristics to a marked degree. Some have classed him with Baxter, others with Bunyan, and still others with Watts. We class him with Jeremiah. Upon the whole we almost regret his death.

The 15 November 1902 issue of *Harper's Weekly* published an open letter from Clemens titled "Amended Obituaries" (figure 22). Because he was approaching seventy, he said he wanted to set his worldly house in order and appealed to journals and periodicals to publish whatever standing obituaries of him they had pigeonholed and then send copies to him for correction. His postscript added: "For the best Obituary— one suitable for me to read in public, and calculated to inspire regret—I desire to offer a Prize, consisting of a Portrait of me done entirely by myself in pen and ink without previous instruction. The ink warranted to be the kind used by the very best artists."

This widely reprinted appeal elicited many letters from readers offering original obituary notices. Pfennig's submission is perhaps the most imaginative. "Z. Pfennig" is clearly a pseudonym for the attorney Edwin Baylies (1840–1925). "Cork Center" is the name of a creek running through Johnstown, New York (Baylies's home), and the Cork Center *Gazette* never existed. A native of Clinton, New York, Baylies studied law at his hometown's Hamilton College before spending most of the 1860s in California, where he taught school and mined. Upon returning to New York, he passed the bar and settled in Watertown. After making Johnstown his final home, he wrote law books for a local publisher and later for his own firm, and earned a national reputation as an authority in that field. Meanwhile, he practiced law, served as city attorney and postmaster, and became admired for his brilliant wit ("Edward Baylies Dies Suddenly," New York *Morning Herald*, 19 May 1925; "Tribute to Edwin Baylies," *Morning Herald*, 20 May 1925).

A clever mixture of fact and fiction designed to "inspire regret," Baylies' bogus obituary is filled with allusions to real people and events that had nothing to do with Clemens. Baylies wrote during the midst of a great coal strike and dropped in a mention of John Mitchell, president of the United Mine Workers. Clemens, of course, was born in Missouri, not Idaho. A great comet did pass over the earth in 1811, and some people thought it had portended the War of 1812 and other events, but Halley's Comet was the one in transit when Clemens was born in 1835. Clemens wrote several of the books Pfennig attributes him, but *Paradise Lost* (1667) was written by John Milton, *The Vicar of Wakefield* (1803) by Oliver Goldsmith, *Barriers Burned Away* (1872) by Edward Payson Roe, and "Beautiful Snow" by Joseph Warren Watson. Baylies probably mentioned the Book of Mormon because Clemens mocked it in *Roughing It*. Edmond Hoyle was an eighteenth-century English authority on games. The "Scrap Book" comment alludes to Clemens's invention, the self-pasting scrapbook, which had glue strips printed on its pages. (See also letter 28.)

The figures to whom Baylies compares Clemens seem almost random. "Baxter" may be an allusion to the early eighteenth-century Scottish metaphysician Andrew Baxter, who wrote about the human soul. "Bunyan" is certainly John Bunyan, the seventeenth-century author of *Pilgrim's Progress* (1678, 1684), from which Clemens took the subtitle of *The Innocents Abroad, Or, The New Pilgrim's Progress*. "Watts" is probably George Frederic Watts, a contemporary English Symbolist painter. "Jeremiah" must be the "Weeping Prophet" of the Old Testament.

144

7, LEINSTER MANSIONS,
LANGLAND GARDENS,
HAMPSTEAD, N.W.

20 xii 02.

Samuel L. Clemens, Esq.
Hartford, Conn., U.S.A.

Dear Sir,

I have just (5 [minutes ago]) finished one of the best short stories I have ever read. I refer to you story in the December *Harper's*. I want to thank you for writing so pathetic, so perfectly true, a story, AND to ask you, when it comes to be reprinted, to omit the question with which the story concludes and, in its omission, to drop the title.

You know what was the answer, and so does every one who has read the story, and, in knowing it, they share the joy of the two heroic souls who *heard* it.

Yours sincerely,

W ᵐ Digby.

Clemens's reply:

RIVERDALE ON THE HUDSON

(N.Y. City) Jan. 14.

Dear Sir:

Yes, I know—as do you, and many others—but there are thousands upon thousands who believe they know that the answer was the other one. Thousands?—indeed there are several millions of them. And they would be prompt to say, too, that in excusing the lying done in that tale I brought a judgment upon myself. The story was published as of Xmas Day. On that day my wife had been lying feeble & helpless in bed nearly 5 months, & it had been 3 months since I or any one except a daughter, the doctor, & a trained nurse had seen her face; on that Xmas Day my other daughter was lying near to death in a remote part of the house, ^(pneumonia)^ & the diligent lying of the tale was going on! The mother does not suspect that for three weeks there has been another trained nurse in the house. She thinks Jean (the sick daughter) is having fine times outside with the neighboring young people, skating, skeeing & tobogganing—the other daughter gives her a full account of it every day. For the last ten days I have been allowed to see my wife ten minutes every day. Yesterday she spoke of a play, & said "Send Miss Lyon with Jean to the matinèe to-morrow." I came very near saying "Why, Jean can hardly sit up in bed, yet"—but I caught myself in time & gave the promise.

Sincerely Yours

SL. Clemens

"Was It Heaven? or Hell?" in the Christmas issue of *Harper's Magazine* is a sentimental story about the moral dilemma elderly sisters face while tending their dying niece and the latter's dying daughter. Though rigid in their belief that *any* kind of lie is a mortal sin, they hide the true condition of each from the other. The story ends with the lying aunts awaiting the judgment of an angel of the lord. Digby's letter objects to the story's title and closing line: "Was it Heaven, or was it Hell?"

A.B. Paine devoted an entire chapter of *Mark Twain: A Biography* (1912) to this story, pointing out that Clemens received many letters from readers about it. He also elaborated on parallels between the family dynamics of the story and recent developments in Clemens's own family (see chapter 226; see also J.D. Wilson, *A Reader's Guide to the Short Stories of Mark Twain* [Boston, 1987], 275–278). Most letters from readers praised the story, but one published in *Harper's Magazine* in May 1903 objected to its "misleading moral." The magazine's editor, Henry Mills Alden, devoted five columns of his "Editor's Study" to the letter.

Clemens appears not to have known that William Digby (1849–1904) was a British journalist and author of several books on the condition of Indians living under British colonial rule. His own book, *Following the Equator* (1897), discusses that subject at length, but Digby's last book on India, *"Prosperous" British India* (1901) does not mention it. Digby was known as a champion of Indian rights. After he died in 1904, Mohandas K. Gandhi praised him in an obituary in his South African newspaper, *Indian Opinion* (Gandhi, *Collected Works*, 6th ed. [Delhi, India, 2000], 4:105).

145

PTB

753 LINCOLN PARK BOULEVARD

Chicago, Ill.
December 23—

Mr. Clemens
Elmira
N.Y.

My dear Mr. Clemens,

When I was four years old I spelled out "Tom Sawyer" to myself, defending my copy from all would-be readers until I had finished it. Since that first reading (and I should not dare say this unless it were truth) there has been no joy in my life that you have not made richer, no sorrow that your work has not show me how to bear—*best*. May I send to you the thanks of an American woman. May I say to you that I am very proud to be of this race that you have made almost worthy of your citizenship?

With all that Christmas means, I am
Margaret Potter Black.
(Mrs John D.)

Clemens's comment: Preserve this.

Possibly a delayed response to "To the Person Sitting in Darkness," this letter may have been written in late 1902. Margaret Horton Potter Black (1881–1911) was the daughter of the powerful Illinois steel tycoon Orrin W. Potter (1837–1907). She earned notoriety in 1899 when it was revealed that *Social Lion,* an intimate novel about Chicago society she had published under the pseudonym Robert Dolly Williams, was written by the teenage daughter of a prominent Chicago family. The book was considered so shocking her father tried to suppress it. Afterward, she published nine more novels under the name Margaret Horton Potter. Clemens owned three of the titles published after 1901, but no evidence he read any of them has been found. (Gribben, *Mark Twain's Library*, 147). Harper & Brothers published several Potter books, and she was a guest at the birthday banquet Harper held for Clemens in 1905.

On January 1, 1902, Potter married the attorney John D. Black. In March 1910, a judicial hearing ruled her mentally incompetent. Two months later, another hearing declared her insane and sent her to a sanitarium. Her husband sued her for divorce in October, on the grounds of habitual drunkenness. In December 1911, several months after being released from a sanitarium, Potter was found dead from an overdose of morphine tablets ("Woman Novelist Insane," New York *Times*, 6 May 1910; "Would Divorce Novelist," New York *Times*, 6 Oct. 1910; "Young Author Takes Overdose of Morphine," Springfield, Massachusetts, *Republican*, 23 Dec. 1911).

146

FRANK L. EATON,
OXFORD, MICH.
ATTORNEY AND COUNSELLOR AT LAW.

Ypsilanti, Mich., Jan. 3rd, 1903

Mr dear Mr. Clemens:—

I have just finished reading that portion of your "Life on the Mississippi" describing your crossing that Island 66. Each time I read this, I gather greater force from the lesson, which it teaches, of the value of unshaken confidence in what one knows.

I have been the proud possessor of a set of your works for more than a year, and I think that the lesson to be learned from that one particular chapter is worth the full value of the books, and I know of nothing that I have read in recent years, which has done me as much good, or has been as helpful to me at various times, as that particular instance. I have, therefore, taken the liberty of writing you and tell you how much I appreciate it, and of my earnest wish that the youth of the entire land might read the story and grasp its full meaning.

I have the honor to be,
Your sincere admirer,
F. L. Eaton

To:
Mr. Samuel L. Clemens,
Rivervale, N.Y.
P

Chapter 13 of *Life of Mississippi* recalls a trick played by master pilot Horace Bixby on his cub pilot to test his confidence in his newly learned knowledge of the river. As the cub steers his steamboat into the safely deep crossing at island 66, the nervous behavior of other crew members so shakes his confidence he thinks he is about to run the boat aground and panics. Afterward, Bixby drives home the lesson that one should never lose confidence in what one *knows* to be true.

The writer of this letter has proven elusive. A 1903 Ypsilanti city directory lists a railroad freight and passenger agent named Frank L. Eaton; that job title seems unlikely for a qualified attorney, however.

147

ON ESCAPING FROM INDIANS.

I wish to compile a Hand-book of Method on this subject. Can you help me by sending me brief notes descriptive of your favorite method of Escaping from Indians and of Escaping Capture by them when in danger thereof? I ask information on the two points because I shall divide the book into two parts, to-wit,

First, On Escaping Capture by Indians;

Second, on Escaping from Indians after Capture.

I enclose a blank which will enable you to answer my questions with little trouble.

Yours respectfully,
J. C. Dana.

Newark, N.J. April, 1903

"CAVE RAMUSCULUM MORTUUM."
—CHINGACHOOK..

Enclosure

To John Cotton Dana,
Public Library, Newark, N.J.

My favorite method of escaping from
Indians is that described in _ _ _ _ _ _ _ _ _ _ _ _
by _ _ _ _ _ _ _ _ _ _ _ _ _ _ _ _ _ _ _ on page _ _
My favorite method of escaping capture by
the Indians when in danger of capture is that
described in _
by _ _ _ _ _ _ _ _ _ _ _ _ _ _ _ _ _ _ on page _ _
_ _ _ _

If you prefer to do so, describe below your
favorite methods without reference to book or
author; or give the methods you have yourself

successfully tested or would like to test. J.C.D.

Name_ _ _ _ _ _ _ _ _ _ _ _ _ _

Address. _ _ _ _ _ _ _ _ _ _ _

Clemens's comment: What a proposition!

Clemens may have thought this typed letter's author was a crank, but John Cotton Dana (1856–1929) was actually a distinguished and innovative librarian and museum director. A Dartmouth-trained attorney with a diverse background, he directed the public libraries of Denver, Colorado (1889–1895); Springfield, Massachusetts (1898–1902); and Newark, New Jersey (1903–1929); founded the Newark Museum (1909); and served as president of the American Library Association (1895–1896). He also published scores of articles and books. A book about escaping from Indians was apparently not among them, however. The printed letter he sent to Clemens he also sent to others, and he apparently received many replies. The 26 May 1903 Newark *Evening News* reported on his survey and quoted him on why he had undertaken it. Explaining that he had grown up "playing Indian," he said, "I devoured good Indian stories and planned, as many others have planned before and since, just how I would elude the wily savages. My circular is simply to get views on this interesting subject. I am getting views all right. That some of them reflect on my mental condition doesn't worry me. I am having plenty of fun, I can tell you. As to the 'Handbook,' I may speak more definitely when my replies are all in" (quoted in Jane Durnell, "The Cardelius Syndrome," *Imprint: Oregon* 3, no. 1 [spring 1976]: 18, 20–21).

Dana's letter, postmarked 28 May 1903, Newark, New Jersey, reflected his iconoclastic attitude toward accepted views on education, libraries, and, especially, reading. His irreverence can be seen in his letter's bogus Latin quote from Chingachgook, the Mohican hero of James Fenimore Cooper's Leatherstocking novels. Translated roughly as "beware of broken twigs," the phrase may have been inspired more by Clemens's savage 1896 essay "Fenimore Cooper's Literary Offenses" than by Cooper's actual writings ("John Cotton Dana: Newark's First Citizen," www.libraries.rutgers .edu; B.E. Ford, "A Champion of Individual Liberty: John Cotton Dana" [2006], www.npl.org, both accessed 18 Oct. 2011).

148

Allegheny, Pa., Oct 5, [1903]

Mr Samuel L. Clemens,
New York,

My dear sir:—

I write this letter simply for the purpose of expressing my admiration and gratitude for the enjoyment I have had from Huckleberry Finn, A Connecticut

Yankee, and all your other works, and for the satirical way you have dealt with the Catholic Religion.

Hoping that you may often yet use your pen against Catholicism, and wishing you a long life and every possible happiness, I remain,

Yours respectfully,

The "Boss"

Clemens's comment: Compliment without charges | Keep it

Some of Clemens's strongest attacks on Roman Catholicism appear in *Connecticut Yankee,* whose title character was known as the "Boss." Clemens liked this anonymously written letter because he could not be expected to answer it. (See also letter 176.)

149

12, DENNINGTON PARK ROAD,
W. HAMPSTEAD, N.W.

11th Sept. 1904.

Dear Sir—

You have, of course, & justly many letters from admiring readers—I feel I too must add to them, altho I have never yet written to an author that I have not met. But I feel I especially owe you a tribute as it is probable you saved my reason.

I lost my fiancé—also my dearest friend, & a not inconsiderable fortune within a month. I have not the stocism of many & so broke down—your book "Extracts from Adams Diary["]—brought forth my first laugh—for which I most truly thank you.

May I without intrusion sympathise with you in the lose of your wife?—I have been a great admirer of your writings since the days I read your books on the sly at School!

With very many thanks to you that you are so gifted as to be able to write to enliven the hearts of the depressed.

Your very sincere Admirer

N. M. Rosenberg.

Extracts from Adam's Diary is a whimsical account of Adam's growing infatuation with Eve in the Garden of Eden. First published with a slightly different text in 1893, it was issued as an illustrated book in April 1904.

The English census of 1901 lists Nellie Rosenberg as a thirty-two-year-old "Lady Housekeeper" at the London address in this letter. According to a government baptism register, she was born Nellie Mary Rosenberg in Camberwell in 1867. Her remark about losing her fiancé and a "fortune" suggests that the fiancé may have been her twelve-year-older employer, Woolf Phillips, a stock broker.

150

HOBBS BROS.,
CARRIAGE BUILDERS.
GEOG. W. HOBBS.
CHAS. H. HOBBS.

NINEVEH, N.Y., Oct 8th 1904.

Mr. Samuel L Clemmens
Elmira N.Y.

My Dear Mr Clemmens,

Please allow me to extend to you my heartfelt sympathy for the bereavement which you have experienced in the loss of your life partner.

Having passed through this sad experience of parting with the wife of my youth during the past summer I feel excused in writing a fellow sufferer without formal introduction.

As a reader I have known you for years, and as President of our Public Library have advocated your Books as helping to drive away sorrow and to make the world brighter.

Hence it seems doubly sad that one who has done so much to lighten Lifes burdens, should be called upon to suffer such deep sorrow and at this time of life.

In the midst of my own suffering I truly pity you.

Kindly Yours
Geo. W. Hobbs

Clemens's comment: Put in tin box. | SLC

Many condolence letters Clemens received after his wife, Livy, died in Italy on 5 June 1904 were from people who had recently suffered personal losses. George W. Hobbs (born 1843) had been married to his wife, Ellen, for thirty-nine years when she died in 1904. Three years later, he married a much younger woman. A lifelong resident of Colesville, New York, he was the son of a carriage maker and longtime justice of the peace. Hobbs himself studied law for two years only to quit that field to concentrate on carriage making. Through at least 1910, he and his younger brother, Charles H. Hobbs, operated their own carriage factory in nearby Nineveh (USCR; W. S. Lawyer, *Binghamton: Its Settlement, Growth, and Development* [Boston, 1900], 974). Hobbs's letterhead is truncated here.

151

Chicago, Ill.
Feb. 12, 1904. [1905]

Samuel L. Clemens (Mark Twain)
Care of Harper & Bro. Publishers
New York

Dear Sir:,

I thought I would drop you a few lines telling you an odd adventure my uncle and two other men and myself had in "Tom Sawyers" cave in Hannibal Mo.

My uncle took me with him in a house-boat from St Paul to St Louis to see the fair and we stopped at Hannibal, where we expected mail and purchased a few of your pictures at the post-office and then went to the cave.

We tied up the boat, took a lantern and forgot our coats, for which we were sorry afterwards. The main gate to the cave was locked, and as it was then two o'clock we sent a boy to Hannibal for the key, but the man said he gave it some-body. Then we went about fifty feet to the left of the main entrance, and climbed the hill about fifty feet to a small entrance to the cave which was nailed in with boards. After much squeezing we broke in there, and the board snapped shut after us, but we did not mind that then. We each gathered and armful of sticks and at ever turn we made we would cross two sticks to show us our way out.

We had been going downhill nearly all the time when my uncle took a flash-light picture of us, on a ledge where there was four different paths When we came down we could not find the sticks, and we traveld in there for four hrs, and all were cold and scared. They had been scaring me but never said any more when the could not find the sticks.

We at last stumbled out at the main entrance were Indian Jo died, and as that was locked, we all got together and broke it down—all glad to get out This happened Aug. 10, 1904, but I did not know where to write to till now.

yours truly
your friend
Willie Shine.
824 Englewood Ave
Chicago Ill.

Clemens's reply per Isabel V. Lyon with his addendum:

New York.
Feb. 16, 1905.

Dear Master Willie:

Mr. Clemens has been ill for a long time, and so wishes me to write for him and tell you that he has greatly enjoyed reading your letter. He wishes me

FIGURE 23. Willie Shine painting the houseboat on the river.
Courtesy of the Hayes/Shine family.

to say that he knows from experience that you had an adventure in the cave,
and that it might have had a tragic ending.

Very truly yours,
(Miss) I. V. Lyon,
secy.

Indeed that is very true.

Mark Twain

Hannibal's famous cave is a limestone formation about two miles south of the town.
With an estimated 260 passageways extending over 6.5 miles, it is a dark labyrinth in
which one could easily get lost. Clemens played in the cave as a boy and well knew
how dangerous it could be. In *Tom Sawyer* (1876), Tom and Becky Thatcher spend
three days lost in a fictional version of the cave. After they escape through an opening
far from the main entrance, Judge Thatcher has the main entrance sealed with an
iron door. Later, the miscreant Injun Joe is found dead behind the new door.

A lifelong resident of Chicago, William Thomas Shine (1889–1980) was a school-
boy when he boated down the Mississippi River to the St. Louis world's fair. He actually traveled with four men: his maternal uncle, James E. McDade (1872–1953); H. Jo-

seph Moynihan; Daniel F. O'Hearn; and Thomas C. M. Jameson. McDade was a Chicago school principal in 1904; the other men were Chicago schoolteachers, all of whom eventually became principals themselves. An eccentric bachelor, McDade later served as superintendent of Chicago's elementary schools. Chicago's K–12 Mc-Dade Elementary Classical School is named after him.

McDade organized the month-long expedition down the river and left a thirty-four-page typescript log that provides lively details of the building of the houseboat (figure 23) in St. Paul, Minnesota, and its day-to-day progress down the river. The travelers lived on the boat while spending a week at the St. Louis fair and afterward sold it for seventy dollars and returned home by train. McDade's vivid account of their adventure in the cave reveals that their plight was even more perilous than Willie's letter suggests. Their ordeal ended when they used their bodies as a battering ram to break open the cave's main entrance from inside, "at the very spot were Injun Joe was found dead." When they finally got out, the travelers "grabbed our stuff, made for the houseboat, and pushed off" (McDade, "Adventures with a Houseboat on the Mississippi: St. Paul to St. Louis," 34). A contest-winning essay titled "How I Spent My Vacation," signed by Willie Shine, appeared in the April 1905 issue of *Our Young People*. It does not mention the cave episode but adds colorful anecdotes about the houseboat voyage. The brief essay's mature style suggests that McDade may have had a hand in writing it.

Willie himself lived another seventy-five years, married, had three children, and worked as a traveling salesman (USCR; "680 Mile Houseboat Trip Down Old Man River in 1904 Is Told in Log," Lake City, Minnesota, *Graphic*, 20 July 1950). According to one of his sons, "Dad often spoke of his childhood trip down the Mississippi and the adventure 'in the Mark Twain Cave.'" Also, Willie's "Uncle Jim" was a frequent houseguest who "would regale us with his and dad's versions of 'The Great Adventure on the Mississippi'" (Gerald J. Shine, letter to R. Kent Rasmussen, 25 July 2012).

152

HOTEL CARLTON
84TH STREET NEAR BROADWAY,
NEW YORK.

ANDREW J. KERWIN, JR. PROP.

NEW YORK, Apr 1st 1905

Mr S. L. Clemmons
Dear Sir.

I would not give ten cents for the autograph of Moses, Jesus or Christopher Columbus, so do not acknowledge receipt. I respect them all, but I admire the weather beaten warrior who keeps his brain young and now as ever rides to the front and delivers a thundering, and what will help to be an effective blow for liberty. I have just read your article in the North American Review on the

Russian Czar (I call the whole Bureaucratic gang a Banditti alias government.) Same old Mark Twain I said to myself "he is a grand old fellow I have read between the lines of the writings of all his life a something that makes for liberty. He feels it, he understands it, he promotes it."

I once had the pleasure of a Conversation with you on the Boston train just before you left for Australia—to resolve with you is to accomplish. Some writings of a man stick out more than other parts for instance that bold crack at the "old masters" It is over twenty years since I read it, but its young in my memory. You made me laugh as I went by the Tyrolean Alps last year. I thought that Sanitarium for those that cannot get up an appetite must be in the neighborhood. Those eggs! I doubt whether a man ought to be forgiven for springing a thing like that on the public, but we will forgive you, dont do it again.

I see by the cablegrams that your article on the Banditti was criticised, but you anticipated the criticism in your article. It is always a wonder to me how many people can shed crocodile's tears, or as you say they are honest but do not look deeply into things. It takes ingrained liberty to feel for liberty. You are so dyed in the wool with the principle of liberty that you have to help spread it. More power to your elbow.

Yours Truly
Luis Jackson

Clemens's "The Czar's Soliloquy" (*North American Review*, Mar. 1905) is a response to Czar Nicholas II's order to fire on striking Russian workers in St. Petersburg on 22 January 1905. It has the czar contemplating his naked body in a mirror as he reflects on his recent crimes. "Old masters" is probably an allusion to *The Innocents Abroad* (1869), which repeatedly mocks great European works of art. The letter's reference to a "sanitarium" alludes to Clemens's sketch "At the Appetite Cure" (*Cosmopolitan*, Aug. 1898), describing a Bohemian (not Tyrolean) health resort called Hochberghaus, where people went to have their appetites restored. The unnamed "article on the Banditti" was probably "To the Person Sitting in Darkness" (see letters 125, 132, 135, and 145), which calls imperialist forces "bandits."

Luis Jackson (1856–1927) was born in Liverpool, England, where he apprenticed in the freight-forwarding business. In 1884, he immigrated to the United States and undertook railroad work in Chicago. While serving as industrial commissioner for the Chicago, Milwaukee & St. Paul Railroad (1891–1903) and the Erie Railroad (1903–1914), he campaigned to integrate American railroad services and traveled throughout the world studying railroads in other countries, including Russia—whose czarist government he spoke out against. His publications include a pamphlet titled *Russia Dominates the World* (3d ed., Montclair, N.J., 1915); it mentions that "Mark Twain, a typical American, a lover of his fellow men, when he attacked Czarism, did so without gloves" (p. 11; obituary, *Erie Railroad Magazine*, July 1927; "Comes to the Erie," New York *Evening Tribune*, 31 Mar. 1903; U.S. and English census reports).

153

Denver
Colorado
April 1ˢᵗ 1905.

Mr. Samuel Clemens,

Dear Mr. Mark Twain

I am a High School girl and I write to thank you for the hilarious joy your books afford me.

I have been known to make people run from their houses to stand out side my window and listen with horror to shriek after shriek and giggle after giggle when I read about the man that got carried through the carpet machine and his widow bought his pattern.

They are a never ending source of pleasure to me and I want you to know that I am one more in the vast multitude who appreciate your books and if you have a wee spare moment please write me a little note that I can keep among my treasures.

Your admiring friend
Marion Thurston Tibbitts
925 Lafayette St.
Denver
Colorado

The old ram's tale in chapter 53 of *Roughing It* relates how a carpet factory worker was "nipped by the machinery" and woven into fourteen yards of carpet, which his widow bought and had buried after a church funeral.

Marion Thurston Tibbitts (born 1889) was the daughter of Charles Nelson Tibbitts (born 1852), a mechanical engineer from Ohio, and Merial Lucinda Park Tibbitts (1859–1945), a University of Wisconsin graduate and former Colorado high school teacher and assistant principal. Marion herself was a preparatory student at the University of Denver in 1906–1907 and was a "vocal instructor at home" in 1910 (USCR; E. H. Park, *The Park Record* [Denver, 1902], 77–78; *Univ. of Denver & Colorado Seminary Catalog* [1906–1907], 100). (See also letter 139.)

154

156 Wortley R^d
London Ont
Canada
Sept 4 1905

Dear Mr Cleomens

Dear Sir: I feel that I have no right to intrude myself into your life, but ever since the days when I read "Tom Sawyer" ["]Inocence Abroad," ["]Roughing it," New Pilgrams Progress and A Yankee at King Arthurs Court down to the present time, when I am following the Equator with you I have wanted to thank you for the pleasure and instruction you have given me.

I really think the knowledge to be gained from the above works is invaluable to one who has not had the advantages of treavel

The sincere admiration of one unknown individual cannot be of very much importance to you whome the whole reading world admires. But if my best wishes for a long life (many years of life yet) and continued prosperity can convey only a small part of the pleasure to you that you have rendered to me I shall feel repaid—I dont take off my hat to Kings or Emperors or even Governors General but I like a man who can see the truth (and tell it.) I raise my hat to you sir. And remain dear Sir Yours truely

Len G. Westland

Clemens's comment (in Isabel V. Lyon's hand): ans.

Clemens's reply:

Dear Mr Westland,

And I, also, take off my hat to you; and with many thanks to you for what you have said,—

I am
Yours Truly
Mark Twain

A lifelong resident of Ontario, Leonard George Westland (1862–1934) was an interior decorator. Like Clemens's daughter Jean, he was afflicted with epilepsy. His 1905 residence, the Westland Building, housed an antique store in 2011 (Ontario death; certificate; 1919 Ontario census report).

155

Oct. 26th 1905.

Samuel L. Clemens.

Dear Mark Twain,

I crossed over to this country more than twelve years ago, with an Italian boy of sixteen, who had walked from Rome to Paris, where we met.

His delight and my delight too, was to read together a French translation of Huckleberry Finn. Our knowledge of America was confined to "Huck Finn," and on arriving in Boston Harbor, the boy said to me "Qui est ce George Vashington dont on parle tant"? I told him the little I knew. To day the boy is a well educated man, speaking three languages, the Father of two gifted children and earning $25 weekly in a N.Y. engraving house. A thorough American in the sense of the Americanism Mark Twain stands for—freedom from tradition, independent judgment, humor & wholesomeness. Little Huck started us; and I sign (for my boy friend as well as myself) gratefully,

One of your innumerable
unknown friends.

The only clue to the identity of this letter's authorship is that it may have been written by a French immigrant living in New York City. The only French edition of *Huckleberry Finn* published before 1905 was issued by Hennuyer of Paris in 1886.

156

"THE DARK PLACES OF THE EARTH ARE FULL OF
THE HABITATIONS OF CRUELTY."

THE ANIMAL RESCUE LEAGUE,
TELEPHONE, 51 CARVER STREET, BOSTON, MASS.
OXFORD 244.

November 8, 1905

Mr. Samuel Clemens,
Boston, Mass.

Dear Sir:—

Having seen through the medium of the newspapers that you are in this city, I venture to ask you if you will confer on me the great pleasure and honor of a visit to this Home for homeless, suffering and undesired dogs and cats which I established nearly seven years ago. It is not far from Beacon Street, neither is it in a disagreeable part of the city and if you would give a little hour out of your

Boston visit to look over this place I think you would not be sorry, and I know you would give me a pleasure I should never forget.

Naturally you will think I want money from you, or an entertainment, but I beg you to believe that I would be more glad to see you here than any other writer in the world,—to have you lay your hand on little blind Fairy's head, a deserted Pomeranian, and speak a word of good cheer to other dogs and cats that are waiting here for homes to be offered them, and give me the privilege of speaking face to face with one whose books and stories I have not only read and admired since they first appeared in print, but have never ceased to read and admire.

I wanted to write to you when that wonderfully beautiful and pathetic story—The Tale of a Dog—appeared,—the best plea against vivisection I ever read, but I did not. However, I did what perhaps was better, I bought and caused others to buy a considerable number of the story in its book form.

Will you try to call here some day between ten and four? I will gladly send a carriage for you if you would like me to do so.

Sincerely yours,
Anna Harris Smith.

Clemens's comment: Will dictate answer. | SLC

When Clemens visited Boston in early November 1905, several reporters interviewed him. Among the stories they published is an illustrated four-column article in the 6 November issue of the Boston *Journal*.

Anna Harris Smith (1843–1937), this letter's author, was a passionate advocate of animal rights. A member of a wealthy family, she married Huntington Smith, the editor of the Boston *Beacon*, for which she also worked before founding Boston's Animal Rescue League in 1899. The Clemens story to which she alludes is *A Dog's Tale*, which was first published in the 1903 Christmas number of *Harper's Magazine* and issued as a book in September 1904. It concerns a dog who saves her master's baby from a fire, only to see her own puppy callously killed in a scientific experiment. Written to support Jean Clemens's antivivisectionist views, the sentimental story became a favorite among animal rights advocates.

Clemens's reply to Smith has not been found, but it appears he did not accept her invitation to visit her animal shelter. She wrote to him again on 6 November 1907, thanking him for having autographed books donated for sale at a shelter benefit two years earlier. She added that the same donor was willing to buy twenty-five copies of *A Dog's Tale* or *A Horse's Tale* if Clemens would sign them for the next benefit. Smith also expressed her wish that Clemens would do a public reading for the benefit of the shelter. Notes on this letter indicate Clemens's willingness to sign the books (J.W. Leonard, ed., *Woman's Who's Who of America . . . 1914–1915* [reprint, New York, 1976], 754; A.M. Sammarco, "Anna Clapp Harris Smith," in *Dorchester: A Compendium* [Charleston, S.C., 2011], 76–77; "Boston's Haven of Rest for Poor, Abused and Neglected Animals," Boston *Journal*, 15 Feb. 1903).

157

JOSEPH DICK.

Honored Sir,

Although you probably should prefer my silent gratitude, the restraint imposed upon me by the impossibility of thanking sweet Dickens, my other benefactor, is so chafing, that I cannot deny myself the compensating pleasure of thanking you for the inexhaustible pleasure coming to me from the reading of your works.—As a mark of my gratitude I wish to tell you that both, my father, who is in the wilds of Hungary and who read your sketches in German, and myself, consider your best work "The Experience of the McWilliams family with membranous Croup." My father, who had had similar experiences, shrieked with delight on reading it. And although he considers defacing or injuring a book a high crime, he actually cut that sketch from the book and read it to everybody he knew. The last sentence of it particularly delighted him.

A cat may look at a king and a bore may write to a humorist and satyrist. That and my sincere admiration are my only excuses for troubling you.

May all the good humor and happiness that you shed upon the world light up and warm your life to the end.

Most respectfully yours
Joseph Dick.

Toledo, O. Novemb. 9th 1905.

1306 Broadway

"Experience of the McWilliamses with Membranous Croup" (1875) was the first of three frame stories about the fictitious McWilliams family that Clemens based loosely on his own family. His daughter Clara (1874–1962) suffered from croup as an infant. The story's last sentence is bracketed: "[Very few married men have such an experience as McWilliams's, and so the author of this book thought that maybe the novelty of it would give it a passing interest to the reader.]"

Joseph Dick was born in Hungary in 1868. After being educated in a Vienna gymnasium and serving in the Austrian army, he immigrated to the United States in 1892 and naturalized as a U.S. citizen in 1897. During his first sixteen years in the country, he lived in Toledo, Ohio, where he worked as a musician and taught French in a public high school. He later relocated to New York City, where he appears to have worked at a variety of jobs through at least 1930 (USCR; Toledo Central High School yearbook for 1904; 1913 and 1914 passport applications; *Polk's Toledo City Directory* for 1897, 1898, and 1906).

158

THE BRESLIN
NEW YORK.

30 Mayfield Road
Cleveland Nov. 26th

Mr. Samuel Langhorne Clemens:
N.Y. City.

My Dear Mark Twain:
Of all the lions in my den, you are the largest, since your picture (by Spiridon, not by Sarony) measures about 25 × 20, exclusive of its four inch fame.

It hangs there in token of my admiration of you as a publicist, as a writer of dramatic romance and as a humorist.

Much as I admire you as a writer, I admire you more as a man who has achieved the pinnacle of success without having his democracy perverted in the least degree—as one who has preserved his ideals.

I have long wanted to tell you so, but have hesitated to intrude. Now I sieze the opportunity presented by your attaining the Scriptural age. Under another cover I send you a memento, with inscription.

Now that I *have* intruded, I feel inclined to go to the limit and to remark that I also shall have a Seventieth birthday in a little more than thirty years.

If you have read my book by that time and feel inclined to retaliate with any one of your new, old or middle-aged books suitably inscribed, I'll promise to read it—again.

With my warmest esteem and deepest admiration.
Cordially yours
Edmund Vance Cooke.

Cleveland O.
30 Mayfield Road
Nov. 28th 05

The book Cooke sent to Clemens was *Chronicles of the Little Tot* (1905), containing this inscription:

SAMUEL LANGHORNE CLEMENS AT SEVENTY
TO
MARK TWAIN AT THE SAME AGE.

Whene'er I read your works, I find
A curious brain, a deeper mind,
An actor in the double rôle,
A blithesome heart, an earnest soul;

And yet, when I unweave the mesh,
I find these Twain are of one flesh.

So, now, when seventy years of youth

Make yours The Golden Age in truth,
I put this tribute in the book
Of your admirer, Edmund Cooke,
Who loves Mark Clemens' sun-bright brain,
Who loves the soul-deep Samuel Twain.

Cleveland, Nov. 30th, 1905.

Clemens's seventieth birthday on 30 November 1905 elicited many congratulatory letters, partly because the "threescore years and ten" mentioned in Psalms 90:10 was considered a person's scriptural age. Edmund Vance Cooke (1866–1932) himself would not quite reach that age. Known as the "poet laureate of childhood," he had worked in an Ontario sewing-machine factory for fourteen years before supporting himself as a writer and lecturer. During the 1920s, he read his poems on a Chicago radio station. The pictures to which he alludes were portraits by the Canadian-born New York photographer Napoleon Sarony and an 1898 painting by the Italian portrait artist Ignace Spiridon ("Selected Poetry of Edmund Vance Cooke," *Representative Poetry Online*, rpo.library.utoronto.ca/poet/74.html, accessed 20 Oct. 2011).

159

Dec. 5, 1905. Fern Hill
Montclair N.J.

Dear Mr. Twain:—

This is your birthday and I want to say how glad I am that you are seventy years old.

Wheeler and I (he is my brother forteen years old) read your stories lots. Wheeler is just getting over an operation for appendicitis, and so his nurse read your funny things to him, but it hurt him to laugh hard.

I am ten years old, and I take music lessons.

We have two turtles, two pupies, and one dog, two angora kittens, about twenty doves and twenty-four gold-fish.

Your stories are good to read when we are sick. Wheeler would cry out "read! read! read!" when he was sick. I think Wheeler is a good deal like Tom Sawyer, only he isn't into as much mischief, but he knows how to get me to do his work for him allright.

Do you know that one of my ancestors, Rev. Samuel Whiting, married a daughter of Lord St. John in your book of "Prince and Pauper," so I am related to Edward Tudor, I suppose, if he were alive now I might be made a Knight. But still I just as leave be an American and be President.

Father reads his old diary to us every Sunday evening, (after the Bible reading.) He was twelve years old and on his birthday said this.—"My presents were one comb, one Jewsharp, a scarf, two dozen cards, *very well satisfied*."

I hope you will be able to put "*very well satisfied*" after your birthday list.

We shall be happy to have you come out . . . and see us and our dogs someday.

Sincerely your friend
Charles Whiting Baker Jr.

> Accompanied by a hand-drawn silhouette of a turkey captioned "for Mr. Mark Twain's Birthday Dinner!," this letter was written on the day when Harper & Brothers hosted Clemens's birthday banquet at New York's Delmonico's Restaurant. The correspondent, Charles Whiting Baker Jr. (1895–1918) was the son of Charles Whiting Baker Sr. (1864–1941), a civil engineer, chief editor of the *Engineering News*, and author of several books on economic issues. Charles Jr. later studied at the University of Vermont and died during World War I while serving as a sergeant in the U.S. Army's air service. His brother, Jefferson Wheeler Baker (1891–1960), had a long career as an investment counselor. Charles's remark about Wheeler's getting him to do his work is an homage to Tom Sawyer's persuading friends to whitewash a fence for him. The boys' family was proud to trace its Baker and Whiting ancestry back to the early colonial era. It is possible they were descended from the Lord St. John (c. 1483–1572) of *The Prince and the Pauper*; however, St. John was not related to Edward Tudor (USCR; *The National Cyclopedia of American Biography* [New York, 1918], 16:103; "Vermont News" [obituary], St. Johnsbury, Vermont, *Evening News*, 15 Oct. 1918).

160

CHAMBERS
UNITED STATES COURT OF CLAIMS
WASHINGTON, D.C.

December 14, 1905.

My dear Mr. Clements:

Ever since I have been old enough to regret, I have regretted that you deserted the lecture platform before I was old enough, or was living in a place where I could hear you. After years of reflecting on your writings, I have decided to write you a letter, and tell you that my life has been made happier, and I have come to look at things in a sunnier light, than I would had I never been raised on a diet of Mark Twain.

I have read all of your books I have been able to get hold of, I believe all, and am boy enough yet to say that I think the Adventures of Huckleberry Finn is my favorite, with Tom Sawyer a close second. I think every child in the land should have those books offered to it as soon as it begins to take pleasure in reading, and I am sure from my own experience that much happiness would result.

I will not take more of your time, if, indeed you read this letter. I have had it in me to write you something of my admiration, and feel better that it is out. I never wrote a letter like this before, and never will again, in all probability. That, you will probably say, is the best thing in the letter.

Wising you many a happy return of your birthday, and a circle of congenial friends during the rest of your life, I remain,

Respectfully yours,
John D. Rhodes.

Clemens's reply [printed card with signed note in Clemens's hand]:

To you, & to all my other known & unknown friends who have lightened the weight of my seventieth birthday with kind words & good wishes I offer my most grateful thanks, & beg leave to sign myself

dear Mr. Rhodes,
Your & their obliged friend
Mark Twain.

New York, Dec. 6, 1905.

Alas, they have shut Huck & Tom out from the youths' department of the Brooklyn Blind Asylum library!

Truly Yours
SLC

An expert stenographer, John David Rhodes (1880–1970) was a federal court clerk at the time he wrote to Clemens. On 10 May 1907, he went to Annapolis, Maryland, to report on a dinner speech Clemens delivered at the State House. He became the first official reporter for the new U.S. Chamber of Commerce in 1912 and began a forty-five-year career as an official debates reporter in the U.S. Senate in 1919 (USCR; S.P. Caplan, "John D. Rhodes, 90, Senate Official Reporters of Debates," Washington *Post*, 31 August 1970; R.C. Byrd, *The Senate, 1789–1989* [Washington, D.C., 1991], 2:316).

The library incident Clemens mentions occurred in November 1905, when the superintendent of the children's department of a Brooklyn public library moved copies of *Tom Sawyer* and *Huckleberry Finn* to the adult department. The incident had nothing to do with a "blind Asylum," but Clemens was pleased with the publicity it generated (Paine, *Mark Twain: A Biography*, 1280–1282).

161

THE CRAIG RIDGWAY & SON COMPANY
STEAM HYDRAULIC MACHINERY
COATESVILLE, PA.

Dec. 26, 1905

My dear Mr. "Mark Twain":—

Of course you are pestered to death but for many years I have been a great admirer of yours and in consequence I was presented yesterday with a handsome edition of your works by Harpers.

I would just dearly love to have your autograph to paste in the favorite volume which to me is your "Roughing It."

The reason this particular volume is my favorite, is because 30 years ago when I was at school I smuggled it into the sacred precincts of the great study room of the Quaker College, where all was supposed to be Peace, Quiet, and Hard Study. With my Latin grammar before me I had "Roughing It" sliding in and out under the lifting cover of the desk. I was reading about the fellow who had the pepper pot pistol and put up the deuce of spades and killed the mule. He did not want the mule but the owner came out with a shot gun and persuaded him to buy it. And then I haw, hawed right out in meetin'—and I can see the consternation yet of the gentle quakers. I dont now remember how many millions of words I had to write for days afterwards, but I remember I worked overtime at it—and have never forgotten since that I lived on this mundane sphere when I read a fascinating book.

So as I know you are a good natured man, under the exhilaration of the Christmas season I have screwed my courage up to ask you for the Autograph—but I will not think any the less of you if you if you do not give it, since a well known and popular writer like you, who has so gone into the very hearts of all the people must have your mail fairly burdened with such fool requests. But then it dont hurt to try and besides I am always lucky! I also have a little philosophy which while perhaps not so good as yours it often answers. Here is one expression of it, maybe you have not gotten it in your scrap book.

> The lightning bug is brilliant
>   But he hasn't any mind
> He stumbles through existence
>   With his head light on behind.
>
> But the measuring worm is different
>   When he starts out for pelf
> He reaches to the limit
>   And then he Humps himself!

And that is how I am trying to get the Autograph!

Yours with regards
Wᵐ H. Ridgway

Clemens's reply in Isabel V. Lyon's hand:

Dec. 31. 1905 = "None Genuine without this signature on the bottle:

Truly Yours
Mark. Twain."

Wm H. Ridgway

Coatesville Pa.

The anecdote about a man shooting a mule appears in chapter 2 of *Roughing It.* The letter also paraphrases a line from chapter 9 of *Connecticut Yankee,* in which Sir Dinadan tells a story about a lecturer whose best jokes draw no laughs from his audience. Afterward, "some gray simpletons . . . said it had been the funniest thing they had ever heard, and 'it was all they could do to keep from laughin' right out in meetin.'"

The Quaker College mentioned by William Hance Ridgway (1856–1945) was Pennsylvania's Swarthmore College, from which he took a bachelor's degree in 1875 and qualified in civil engineering in 1879. He then had a long career in the steel foundry business. An active community leader, he established Coatesville's charitable U. and I. Club for boys in 1897 and spent many years as superintendent of a Presbyterian church school in Coatesville. Known as the "Ironmaster," he wrote a weekly "Sunday School Lesson" column in the Lexington *Herald* in 1908 and later published several books on Sunday school teaching.

The original author of Ridgway's lightning bug poem is unknown, but the verse circulated at least as early as the 1890s. Clemens's reply was not original, either. He borrowed the phrase "None genuine without this signature on the bottle" from patent medicine advertisements (USCR; *Register of Swarthmore College . . . 1862–1920* [Swarthmore, Pa., 1920], 42, 131, 179; "Coatesville U. and I. Club Does Wonderful Work for Charity," Philadelphia *Inquirer,* 24 July 1902).

162

Waco, Texas
Jan. 25, 1906

Mr. Samuel L. Clemens,
My dear Mr. Clemens,—

No doubt you receive so many letters from admirers all over the globe that you don't have time to read them all. But maybe you'll make an exception in this case, anyhow.

I am a teacher of English in Baylor University and I make a practice of reading every scrap from or about you. You have an unlimited number of friends down here, unknown to you, but to whom you are indeed well-known, in print if not in the flesh. The other day, in a class that is doing advanced work in composition with a view to journalism, I assigned as a subject for an impromptu theme an appreciation of some living writer. The themes were to be written in twenty minutes, then read aloud in class. When the papers were turned in, I found, by actual count, that exactly one-third of the members of the class had written of you.

We are also preparing to make a study of your work in another course, "Typical Living Writers," and are looking forward with much pleasure to it.

I want to thank you, personally and in behalf of these young men and women here who think so much of you, for the pleasure you have given to us, with the rest of the world, through your writings. God bless you!

Yours most sincerely,
Dorothy Scarborough
Baylor University

An instructor at Baylor since 1898, Dorothy Scarborough (1878–1935) was to become an important folklorist and regional writer. After relocating to New York City in 1916, she earned a doctorate in literature at Columbia University, where she taught for the rest of her life. Her dissertation, "The Supernatural in Modern Fiction" (1917), has some discussion of *Connecticut Yankee, The Mysterious Stranger,* and other Clemens works. Scarborough also published a half dozen novels and several volumes of short stories and poems, mostly with Texas settings. Her best-known novel, *The Wind* (1925), was made into a silent film starring Lilian Gish in 1928 ("Dorothy Scarborough," *Dictionary of American Biography,* Gale Biography in Context online; and "Scarborough, Emily Dorothy," *Texas State Historical Association* online—both accessed 22 Oct. 2011).

163

March 22nd 1906

342 WEST EIGHTY-FIFTH STREET N.Y.

Mr "Mark Twain"

My Dear Sir—Many times each week I receive the flattering compliment of being mistaken for your distinguished self. As I pass on the street, people say, "there goes Mark Twain"! I get it on every hand. Recently at Palm Beach, many hotel guests thrust this honor upon me, and sent their children for my autograph. When I declare most solemnly that you and I are *twain,* people still hang around with a sort of foolish, incredulous smile, waiting for me to say something funny.

I am but a modest man, occupying that "post of honor" the private and unembellished station, and this crowning with anothers laurels is somewhat embarrassing—I am wondering if this similarity of appearance has worried *you*. If so, I pray you to consider that I did not select my forbears, or use my influence with them as to how I should be fashioned: and must therefore disclaim responsibility in the matter.

I have admired your productions & hailed your growing fame, since away up in the Sierras, ever so many years ago. I used to read over and over again your letters from the Sandwich Islands, in the Sacramento "Bee"—I most sincerely hope that many happy and useful years are still in store for you.

With much Respect, yours Truly,
F. B. Goddard
342 W. 85th St. N.Y.

P.S. That you may judge about the alleged likeness, I send photo of myself, taken recently, by a friend on the Nassau stmr—also a late clipp'g from the Jacksonville "Times-Union"—

Frederick Bartlett Goddard (1834–1910) was apparently living in California in 1866, when Clemens wrote travel letters about Hawaii for the Sacramento *Union*. In 1869, he published *Where to Emigrate and Why: Homes and Fortunes in the Boundless West and the Sunny South*, which discusses California at length. He later became a New York stockbroker. In 1903, he listed his occupation as "Merchantile Agency" on a passport application. His other publications include *The Art of Selling* (1889) and *Giving and Getting Credit* (1895) (USCR; "Arrival of the Sacramento—List of Passengers..." Sacramento *Daily Union*, 27 June 1865; "Died," New York *Times*, 13 Aug. 1910).

<hr>

164

Rockville Md.
March 31st 1906

Dear Mr. Twain,

I know you will be surprised to hear from a little Maryland girl that you have never seen.

I wish I could know you, for I have enjoyed your books so much and I want to write and tell you how much I have enjoyed them.

I think it was so funny for those people of Boston to make a law that no children under a certain age should read your books, for I read them long ago and I think all children would enjoy them as much as I did if they could only read them.

FIGURE 24. Frederick Bartlett Goddard. Courtesy of the Mark Twain Papers, Bancroft Library, University of California, Berkeley.

I wish they would publish your letter to them for I want to see it so bad and I would love to save it.

I am eleven years old and I live on a farm near Rockville. Once this winter we had a boy to work for us named John, we lent him "Tom Sawyer" to read and one night he let his clothes out of the window and left in the night. The last we heard from him he was out in Ohio, and father says if he had lent him "Tom Sawyer abroad" to read he would not have stopped on this side of the ocean.

With love from your little friend, & hoping to hear from you soon

Elizabeth Owen Knight

Elizabeth Owen Knight (1894–1981) grew up on a Maryland farm near Washington, D.C. She later worked at Washington's Walter Reed Hospital. During the 1920s, she married Jacob S. Kasanin (1897–1946), a Russian immigrant who became a distinguished researcher in psychiatry and coined the name "schizoaffective psychosis" for a specific psychotic condition (USCR; Emanuel Windholz, "Jacob S. Kasanin—1897–1946," *Psychoanalytic Quarterly* 16 [1947]: 94–95).

165

Sound Beach, Conn.
August 25, 1906.

Dear "Mark Twain"—

Please dont write any more such heart-breaking stories. I have just been reading Soldier Boy's story in Harpers, I dont think I would have read it had I known what was to come to Soldier Boy.

You used to write so differently. The note of pathos, of tragedy, of helpless pain creeps in now, more and more insistent. I fancy life must have taken on its more somber colors for you, and what you feel is reflected in what you write

You belong to all of us—we of America—and we all love you and are proud of you, but you make our hearts ache sometimes.

When your story of the poor dog was published in Harpers I read it and I cant tell you what I felt. I have never re-read it and I try not to remember it, but I cant help it, and now this story of Soldier Boy. It sinks into my heart, I feel like stretching out my hand to you and saying "I, too, feel these things, the dumb helpless pain of all the poor animals, and my soul protests against it, mightily but impotently, like yours."

I hope there is a heaven for animals somewhere, where they wont have to be with men, and you hope so too, dont you?

Dont think I am hysterical, notoriety-seeking, or a crank. I am neither, only just poor and common-place—and—no longer young, but I *feel* all these things.

I beg to subscribe myself,
Most respectfully yours,
(Mrs) Lillian R. Beardsley.

To
Mr. Samuel L. Clemens.
By, Harper & Bros.

New York City.

Clemens's reply:

Dublin.
Aug. 28. 1906.

Dear Madam:

I know it is a pity to wring the poor human heart, & it grieves me, to do it; but it is the only way to move some people to reflect. The "Horse's Tale" has a righteous purpose. It was not written for publication here, but in Spain. I was asked to write it to assist a band of generous ladies & gentlemen of Spain who have set themselves the gracious task of persuading the children of Spain to renounce & forsake the cruel bullfight. This in the hope that those children will carry on the work when they grow up. It is a great & fine cause, & if this story, distributed abroad in Spain in translation can in any degree aid it, I shall not be sorry that I complied with the request with which I was honored.

Sincerely Yours
(sd) S. L. Clemens.

To Mrs. Lillian R. Beardsley.
Sound Beach.
Conn.

To support a campaign against Spanish bullfighting, Clemens wrote "A Horse's Tale" for the August and September 1906 issues of *Harper's Magazine* (Paine, *Mark Twain: A Biography*, 1245–1247). The sentimental tale traces the history of Soldier Boy, a former U.S. cavalry horse, and his young orphan owner, Cathy Alison. After both go to Spain, Soldier Boy is stolen. When Cathy later sees the horse gored in a bullfight, she rushes into the ring, where she, too, is gored.

Born Lillian B. Robertson (1867–1925) in Coventry, Connecticut, the writer of this letter later married Arthur M. Beardsley (born 1868), a custom house clerk. The couple apparently had no children (USCR; Findagrave.com, accessed 9 Dec. 2011).

166

Hyattsville Md.
17 October 1906.

Dear Mr. Clemens:

It is probably that you have seldom had the honor of having your writings read from a Roman Catholic Pulpit,—but last Sunday the honor was accorded you.

So deeply was I impressed by the reading of the last chapter of your autobiography in the N.A. Review that I determined for the edification of my congregation to read that portion of it relating to your beloved daughter Susan.

One by one I read her puzzling questions:—

1 What is it all for?
2 The Indian Incident
3 What is "little things"
4 Adequate Punishment.

These Questions speak volumes concerning the reflective powers of your child. I briefly commented on each of them to a spell-bound congregation and they have probably done some thinking since

Without question this is the first bit of writing that I have ever had the pleasure of reading from your fun.

May God bless you, and may your beloved daughter Susan have received in this in the land of Vision answers to her questions by a light across which there are no shadows and by which *in this world* the Catholic Church answers questions of children of her age, and men of yours.

With best wishes, I am,
Sincerely
J. P. Tower
St. Jerome's Rectory.

The "Chapters from My Autobiography" installment in the 5 October 1906 *North American Review* tells the moving story of twenty-four-year-old Susy Clemens's death in 1896 and recalls incidents from her childhood in which she grappled with philosophical questions.

In a follow-up letter of 23 October 1906, Tower thanked Clemens for replying and asked him if he wished to see what he had said about Susy in his sermon. Clemens's reply has not been found

A native of Massachusetts, James P. Tower (1865–1934) was ordained a Roman Catholic priest in Baltimore in 1892 and took charge of the St. Jerome Parish in Hyattsville, Maryland, in 1896. Sometime after 1909, he started teaching at St. Charles College, a seminary in Baltimore, where he spent the remainder of his life (USCR; "Church Free of Debt," Baltimore *American*, 20 Jan. 1903).

167

1626 John st
Baltimore Md
Oct. 17, 1906

Dear Mark Twain:

Writing this letter is one of the pleasantest duties I have to perform before leaving for "Hell or Hadleyburg"—which the doctor tells me must be soon now.

In fact I'm living beyond my time,—because he said Oct 15 was my last day "on live"—The only reason I didn't die on that date was that I wanted to read your latest story in Harpers. Some people see Naples and die,—I prefer to read Mark Twain & die. I've never seen Naples,—and dont expect to. I've read almost everything youve written,—and when I finish your whole output I'll give up seeing Naples and die happily without that privilege.

But—

I want to thank you for all the pleasure your books have given me during many years of confinement to my room. Life would frequently have been dull indeed had it not been for the companionship of Huck Finn, Col. Sellers, et al.

When I get to Hell the greatest torture that I will have will be the possible knowledge that you shall have written something else I shall not be permitted to read.

Yours gratefully
Benj Ochiltree.

The author of this letter has not been identified. No Ochiltree is listed in Baltimore city directories for 1906 and 1907. R.L. Polk's 1916 directory for Manhattan and the Bronx lists a Benj Ochiltree, an agent for the American Refrigerator Transit Co.

The phrase "see Naples and die" goes back at least as far as the eighteenth century. In chapter 30 of *The Innocents Abroad*, Clemens wrote, "'See naples and die.' Well, I do not know that one would necessarily die after merely seeing it, but to attempt to live there might turn out a little differently."

168

18 Chatham Square
New York City
Oct 19. 1906

Dear Mr Clements,

As an Irish admirer of yours who has travelled 4000 miles mainly to see you, may I request the privilege of calling on you to pay my respects.

Indeed I might claim this as a right. Here is the proof: Twenty four years ago a little Irish boy lay dying in a Liverpool hospital. The nurse spoke to him very kindly—a bad sign—& asked if there was anything he would like, which was even worse. In hospitals politeness is saved only for those who will soon be beyond the need of it. He wearily asked for a book to read, & they gave him "Babylon" by Grant Allen. There was a quaint American interest in the book which made the boy discover America for the first time. Before that it had been only a place on a map. Then he became interested, threw the first book away, & demanded one about America—& they gave him Huckleberry Finn. He read it, & laughed, & laughed, & laughed, until he fell into the first sound sleep he had had for a fortnight. When he awoke twenty six years later—it was only hours, but it seemed years since he had read the book—he hollered for it again, & got it, & had some breakfast, the first for a week, The nurse was rude to him but he didn't mind—he had Huckleberry under his pillow. This is why he didn't pay much attention to the doctor's remark that it was a miraculous recovery, & Nature still had a fat purseful of miracles left. The boy only grinned, & knew better: it was Mark Twain.

Since then he has passed through the gallery of Tom Sawyer's friends, has travelled all over the world with various Innocents, & Tramps, & occasionally tramped with himself as the chief Innocent. But he always swore that some day he would shake Mark Twain by the hand in order that he might tell his children's children of it some day, & after that, get past St Peter with Mark's grip as a passport.

The 'some day' has now come, &, if that little boy (a bit changed but, after all, I hope not very much) cannot see the man who evolved Huckleberry, Jim, & that one-laigged nigger o' Mister Bradish, well, he will go away sorrowfully believing that Mr Samuel S. Clements is not half so fine a being as Mark Twain.

> Believe me, dear Mr Clements,
> Yours sincerely
> Chris Healy

An 1885 novel by the Canadian-born Grant Allen, *Babylon* is about a New York farm boy and an English peasant boy who win fame as artists in Rome. The "one-laigged nigger" and Mister Bradish are mentioned in chapter 8 of *Huckleberry Finn*.

On 31 August 1906, the British journalist Christopher A. Healy (c. 1873–1935) arrived in New York from Liverpool—a distance of about 3,300 miles. He was making his first visit to the United States, intending to tour American cities. The New York address from which he wrote was the site of a Salvation Army Working Men's Hotel. His 1904 book about European politics and travel, *Confessions of a Journalist,* has a chapter titled "The Twopenny Doss: A Night in a Salvation Army Shelter" (pp. 363–370). Despite Healy's admiration for Clemens's travel books, his book's only allusion to Clemens is a description of the humorist Alphonse Allais as "the French Mark Twain" (p. 265). A note written by Isabele V. Lyon indicates Clemens intended to reply to Healy's letter, but any reply he sent has not been found (passenger manifest, SS *Carmania,* Ancestry.com, accessed 24 Oct. 2011; L. D. Miller, *New York Charities Directory* [21st ed., New York, 1912], 187).

169

> 109 Bastable Block,
> Syracuse, N.Y., November 15, 1906.

Samuel L. Clemens, Esq.,
New York City,

My dear Sir;

Having occasion to try to improve my mind, I called recently at the Carnegee library in this city and asked for "A Tramp Abroad." The young woman who presides over the distribution of the books at said library said;—"You already have one book of fiction, you cant take out two." But I argued, you surely dont call "A Tramp Abroad" fiction; it is travel or history, rather." "Its fiction," she remarked, decisively.

I hope you will tell Mr Carnegee that if he allows your works on travel to be called fiction you will take them out of his libraries altogether.

Yours truly,

John A. Lockwood.

Classifying *A Tramp Abroad* (1880) as fiction has some validity. Clemens built its narrative around his 1878–1879 European travels but invented many of its characters and incidents.

Clemens was a personal friend of the wealthy industrialist Andrew Carnegie (1835–1919). After Carnegie sold his business interests in 1901, he spent the rest of his life dispersing his fortune to philanthropic causes, including thousands of libraries that were named after him.

Born in Germany to traveling American parents, John Alexander Lockwood (1856–1941) joined the U.S. Army in 1880. He served in western cavalry units, taught military courses at what is now Michigan State University, and fought against so-called insurgents in the Philippines. In 1900, he retired from the regular army as a colonel but continued his military career by organizing and teaching military programs at several colleges and universities. In 1903 he published a handbook for military cadets at colleges (Ralph Berstein, "Col. John Alexander Lockwood, U.S.A. . . ." *Hahnemannian Monthly*, Feb. 1919, 65–71; W. J. Beal, *History of the Michigan Agricultural College* [East Lansing, 1915], 78, 271, 422–423).

Lockwood's father, also named John Alexander Lockwood (1811–1900), was a U.S. Navy surgeon who befriended Herman Melville in Egypt in 1856. He figures prominently in accounts of Melville's travels in the Mediterranean (see, e.g., Hershel Parker, *Herman Melville, 1851–1891* [Baltimore, 2002], 310–311, 321–322, 336).

170

Buenos Ayres Nov 22^{d} 1906

Mr Mark Twain
New York

Dear Sir

I kindly take the liberty to ask you the favor of an autograph upon the inclosed postcard.

It is not possible that the signature of the States' prime humorist, and all o'er known writer, should be the only one that fail in our „Golden Album," that will be exposed in the first months of next year in the Autographic Show of our town, and in which are represented the principalest autographs of the State—

rulers and Scientific, Literary Celebrities. M^r Th. Roosevelt also granted us with his aimed signature

In the hope, it may please you to agree with our demand I remain, dear Sir,

thankful,

COMMISSION DU "GRAND ALBUM D'OR"

LA PRÉSIDENTE

Your obedient Servant

Miss Carmen Ramos.

This letter, composed in English, is a rare example of a message to Clemens from a Latin American. The volume of correspondence he received from foreigners was partly a function of the availability of his books in other countries. Virtually no South American editions of his books were published before the 1930s, and few editions were published in Spain and Portugal before the 1920s. Neither Carmen Ramos nor her "Golden Album" has been further identified.

171

821 W. Grace St.

Richmond V^a. Dec 13. 1906

Dear Mark Twain:

Ever since I read, in my childhood, my first story from your pen, it has been the great desire of my life to meet Mark Twain.

Now, I am a woman of five and thirty, and the years are flying, and the goal of my desire seems to recede as I approach. Yet, strange to say—strange, because nearly all childish desires change in the lapse of years—the desire is still as strong within me as ever it was.

Once I saw you. I was only a child—but I marked that day with a white stone. You were driving, and it was all I could do to keep myself from running after your carriage and crying, "Please, Mr. Mark Twain, stay long enough to speak to a little girl who thinks you are the greatest man on earth."

I am sure I should not have so much self control now. But youth is so hopeful of opportunities.—You must be overwhelmed with such communications as this—and yet. The longing is still great within me to run after your carriage and cry "Stop long enough to speak to a little girl who still thinks you the greatest man on earth."

Cally Ryland.

Clemens's reply per Isabel V. Lyon:

21 FIFTH AVENUE

2 December 19' 06

Dear Miss Ryland:

I am thankful to say that such letters as yours do come—as you have divined—with a happy frequency. They refresh my life, they give it value; like yours, they are always welcome, and I am always grateful for them.

Sincerely Yours
[signed:] SL. Clemens

The only child of a Confederate war veteran and bookshop owner, Cally Thomas Ryland (1868–1947) was inclined to misstate her age. It is clear that her mother died a week after she was born in 1868. Ryland appears to have been a lifelong resident of Richmond, Virginia—a place Clemens seems not to have visited during Ryland's youth, so it is difficult to estimate when she may have seen him. After her father died in 1903, Ryland became society editor for the Richmond *News Leader.* In 1904, she published a novel, *The Taming of Betty.* Her other publications include *Aunt Jemimy's Maxims* (1907), a collection of African American maxims in heavy dialect (USCR; Walter Ryland, "Cally Thomas Ryland," and rootsweb.com/ancestry.com, "Re: Cally Ryland, 18??–1947," boards.ancestry.com/surnames.ryland, both accessed 24 Oct. 2011).

———

172

C. B. FLEET,
DRUGGIST AND MANUFACTURING CHEMIST,
700 MAIN STREET.

LYNCHBURG, VA. Dec 14th 1906

Mr Saml. L. Clemmens, or
  Mr Mark Twain,
Dear Sir,

I trust you will excuse the liberty I take in inflicting on you this letter. I have wanted to write to you for a long time to tell of a little occurrence here, several years back, but I was afraid you would think I was lying. It is true, however, every word of it.

In one of your writings, you tell of going to lecture somewhere and the chairman of the Lecture committee, wishing to make himself agreeable, told you how much he enjoyed reading your "Heathen Chinee." I believe you, in reply, agreed with him that you had never written anything better! Well, I can 'go you better' on that.

We have in our town a certain Mr. H.—a good fellow not overloaded with brains nor surfeited with 'book-learnin', but who associates with people of education and refinement. He shoots off his mouth mighty easy and without embarrassment.

A year or two before Jno. T. Raymond's death he came here and played Col. Sellers. I was fortunate enough to see him in this play and was so delighted with the play and his performance that I wanted to talk about it with every one who came into my place of business. This Mr H. drifted in and I said "H. did you go to see Raymond last night?"

"Raymond? Raymond?" he queried "what about him?"

"He was at the Opera House and played"—

"Oh yes," he broke in, "yes he played the 'Gilt Aidge.' No, I didn't go. Fact is when you've seen one of Shakespeare's plays, you've seen pretty much all of 'em!"

I was speechless.

Now, Mr Clemmens, where is Bret Harte and his little "Heathen Chinee"? To be classed with the great Bard of Avon! What more can you ask?

Excuse me for taking this much of your time. Every word of it is true.

Yours truly
C. B. Fleet

Bret Harte, not Clemens, wrote "The Heathen Chinee." A New York *Times* article of 12 December 1905 reporting on Clemens's seventieth birthday banquet related George Washington Cable's anecdote about a man who met Clemens and told him he had read all his works, but the only one he could recall at that moment was the "Heathen chinee." The actor John T. Raymond (1836–1887) spent twelve years touring the United States while performing as Colonel Sellers in a dramatic adaptation of *The Gilded Age* (1874).

After serving the Confederacy in the Civil War, Charles Browne Fleet (1843–1916) began a long career as an innovative pharmacist in Lynchburg, Virginia. During the 1880s, he invented the product that became ChapStick. He sold the rights to that product for only five dollars in 1912, but by then he had launched the C. B. Fleet pharmaceutical company, which would flourish as a major producer of laxatives, enemas, and related products into the twenty-first century (obituary, *Southern Pharmaceutical Jnl.* [June 1916]: 1218; C. B. Fleet Co. time line, www.cbfleet.com/about-history.php, accessed 24 Oct. 2011; C. B. Fleet, "The Fredericksburg Artillery Boys," Richmond, Virginia, *Times-Dispatch*, 8 Jan. 1905).

173

52 Greetby Hill
Ormskirk
29.12.06. Lancashire
England.

Mʳ S. L. Clemens,
Dear Sir

I wonder if you would care to hear how much my husband & self appreciate your books. We have been married 4 years & I have bought him one of your works each birthday & at Christmas. He is never tired of reading them & they keep him at home many a time when he would be out at night He reads them aloud to me & I enjoy the reading as much as himself. The reason I am writing is to beg a favour of you. Would you be kind enough to give me your phota so that I can give my husband a surprise on his next birthday? We have one hung up that I cut from a paper but I should dearly prize a real phota I dont seem able to come across one here & we arent so well off else I might if I was rich. My husband earns £1/- per week as a booking clerk on the railway. We have a little boy six months & his father says when he is older he will tell him about poor little Huck & Tom Sawyer. Perhaps you will be too great a man to answer this & grant my request as we are only humble cottagers. I trust Ive done no harm writing. I have just been reading some extracts in our paper copied from your articles in the "North American Review" I am sorry you lost your daughter Susy you seem to have had a lot of trouble in your life but you always come up smiling. This seems a long letter but I will have to pay 2½ to post so I will get my money's worth. The only thing is I am sorry you arent an Englishman & more especially a Lancashire man, perhaps you will put this in the fire I hope I have a phota from you

I beg to remain
Yours respectfully
Edith Draper

To "Mark Twain"
Mʳ S. L. Clemens.

We thought of calling our baby after you but we had to give him a family name. A happy New Year

Clemens's reply:

Jan. 15 '07.

I will comply with pleasure, dear Mrs Edith. My secretary will choose a photo which will go handily in the mail & I will autograph it.

Indeed I shouldn't regret it if I were an Englishman—& particularly a Lancashire man.

Sincerely Yours

S L . Clemens

[enclosure, written on a photograph of Clemens on a rocking chair:]

To
Mrs. Edith Draper

with the best wishes of
Mark Twain
New York

Jan. 17/07.

No further information about the Drapers has been found. At the time Draper wrote, Chatto & Windus's cheap editions of Mark Twain titles sold for two shillings (approximately fifty U.S. cents), an amount equivalent to more than half her husband's daily salary.

174

[1907?]

My dear Mr. Clemens:—

Do you want to help me out of a great difficulty?

I have a wager with a friend, and its a very nice wager—for the person who wins. Naturally I'd like to be it.

I've taken the liberty of writing to you because you can help me more than anyone else.

The wager is this,—I say that you are the wittiest person of the age, and my friend says he knows of some one who is just as witty (not meaning himself—)

Now please, dear Mr. Clemens will you let me have your opinion? I shall be waiting anxiously, and the prize is *lovely,* and I am

Yours in true admiration,
(Miss) Margaret Heller.

Saturday—

Clemens's comment in Isabel V. Lyon's hand: I know perfectly well that she is on the winning side. I have been noticing for 70 years & I know she is on the winning side. She must get that bet doubled before the other party know she has got inside information

The author of this undated letter was probably the Margaret Heller who resided at 133 East 77th Street in New York City in 1910. A widowed mother of three born in c. 1881, that Heller immigrated to the United States from Hungary in 1907. By around 1912, she was married to another Hungarian immigrant, a barber named Joseph Vajda (1879–1965). The couple later lived in Michigan and Florida (USCR).

175

U.S.S. Georgia, Navy yard, Boston
Sunday, Feb. 10–1907

My dear Mr Clemens:

Will you excuse a personal letter which has no other excuse for itself than that it is you who have made me want to write it. I have resisted the temptation for twenty years, hoping to be introduced to you someday, but if you are going to wear white flannels around in winter, I fear I will not meet you.

Twenty-five years ago my brothers and I used to read Tom Sawyer aloud; the listeners correcting, from memory, any slip of the tongue on the part of the reader.

I have read "Ferguson" at Gibraltar; the "son of far away Moses," at Smyrna, and have followed the Equator with you. My wife and I have read Tom Sawyer and Huckleberry Finn,—and Joan of Arc;—and our small boy is waiting impatiently until he is old enough to hear Tom Sawyer read aloud and understand it. Crossing the Mississippi I see little of the bridges and cities, but catch a glimpse of the old river life at the steamboat wharves.

I have known you for so long, and you have brought into my life so much happiness and mirth, unmixed with bitterness, that I hope I may thank you for it all without seeming to intrude. "Concerning the Jews," you have come nearer to the mark than anyone else: I am a Jew, and know. But in Tom Sawyer and Joan of Arc, the heart of a boy and the heart of a girl, you have taught me what no one else has me. You have shown me the way to help children—and men—in the daily walks of life; you have made me judge their actions more charitably, more understandingly; and you have taught me the power of kindliness and sincerity.

Still hoping that I may meet you some day, I remain—

Very sincerely
Stanford E. Moses

A Georgia native, Lt. Commander Stanford E. Moses (1872–1950) graduated from the U.S. Naval Academy in 1892 and enjoyed a distinguished naval career. He wrote this letter from the recently commissioned battleship *Georgia*. He may have had his chance to see Clemens the following June, when the *Georgia* was part of President Theodore Roosevelt's "Great White Fleet," which visited the Jamestown Exposition, where Clemens was a special guest. Afterward, the fleet circumnavigated the globe to demonstrate American naval might. Moses later held many important commands, most notably in 1925, when he directed the air squadrons attempting the first flight from California to Hawaii (USCR; *Register of the Commissioned and Warrant Offices of the Navy . . .* [Washington, D.C., 1906], 183, 192, 200; "Moses Heads West Coast-Hawaii Flight," Dallas *Morning News*, 30 June 1925).

Clemens first wore a white suit publicly in winter in December 1906, when he testified before a congressional committee; his suit attracted wide attention. Moses's facetious objection to Clemens's wearing white in winter probably stemmed from the Navy's rigid tradition of wearing white uniforms only during the summer.

176

West Lynn, Mass. April 17, 1907.

"Mark Twain"
New York.

Dear Sir:—
'Apropos of your very entertaining little book on "English as she is Taught"— the following *true* story fits in well—A teacher asked her class of boys to tell the difference between herself and a clock. A bright little urchin in the rear row raised his hand and said—"You have a face and the clock has a face, and you have got hands and the clock has got hands, and—and (reflecting) the clock has got a pendooleum and you aint."

Yours very truly,
J. A. Mc M.

Clemens's comment: Preserve this. Frame it. It is the second time in 40 years that a stranger has done me a courtesy & charged me nothing for it. Such a thing is usually accompanied by the man's address, so that I can pay him a hundred dollars' worth of Thank-you for 2 cents' worth of a complimentary attention. SLC

On "English as She Is Taught," see letters 88 and 94. It may be appropriate that searches of Lynn, Massachusetts, census records and city directories have not identified a likely author of this letter, as Clemens regarded the impossibility of replying to it as its chief merit.

177

A man of mark, Mark you.
Named Mark, Mark that *Two*. (Twain)
He's but the mark, mark it!
Mark is here, with all his wit.

Welcome

On 18 June 1907, Clemens arrived in England to accept an honorary degree from Oxford University. This anonymous postcard, postmarked two days later in London, was one of many messages of welcome he received. It was addressed simply to "Mr Clemens | ("Mark Twain") | London." Clemens sailed home on 13 July.

178

3723 W. 41 St.,
Cleveland, O.,
Sept. 29, 1907.

Dear Sir,
I am a boy who is collecting cigar-bands. I have six-hundred different including one hundred-and-fifty different ones with faces on them. In the Chicago Sunday Tribune to-day, I saw that you smoke a great many cigars "without life belts around them," but I also saw that you had many boxes of imported cigars around the house. Imported cigars usually have bands around them. Could you send me some of the bands? I do not mind if they are alike as I think bands from New York would be rare and easy to trade with the other collectors around here.

Yours expectantly.
Edward Anthony.

Clemens's dictated comment: Mr. C[lemens asks me to] write for him and say that he has given all the cigar bands from his imported cigars to a little friend who asked for them; and he regrets that he has none.

Clemens was well known to be a heavy smoker of cigars but he preferred domestic tobacco. A. B. Paine, who knew him intimately during his last years, tells how he once declined an offered gift of special imported cigars, saying he never smoked the expensive Havana cigars he already had (Paine, *Mark Twain: A Biography*, 1303).
   A descendant of seventeenth-century New England's Roger Williams, Anne Hutchinson, and Mary Dyer, Edward Mason Anthony (1894–1954) was born and raised in Cleveland, where he became a clerk for the New York Central Railroad. In

1937, he relocated to Detroit. Throughout his life, he wrote about his family history. He also had an appreciation for poetry. Samples of his own childhood verses appeared in the Sunday children's pages of several issues of the Cleveland *Leader* in 1904. Anthony kept his cigar band collection pasted in two or three notebooks, which his namesake son sold during the late 1970s. A grandson, who also bears his name, later took up pasting cigar bands in a notebook himself (Edward Mason Anthony IV, personal communication, 3 Sept. 2012; USCR).

179

REED & PRINCE MFG. CO.,
DUNCAN AVENUE.
WORCESTER, MASS.

October 28th, 1907.

Samuel Clemens, Esq.,
Hartford, Conn.

Dear Sir:—

In your book "Following the Equator" you tell about Cecil Rhodes making his start on his successful career through finding a newspaper in the stomach of a shark containing news of war between France and England. I wonder if this is a true bit of history, or a brilliant example of Twainism, as I am unable to verify it in any life of Cecil Rhodes?

I am enclosing as a small token of my esteem a steel engraving of our first President, and an addressed envelop in which I trust I may have the pleasure of receiving your kind reply. I am

Yours very sincerely,
W. Emory Wardwell
W.E.W./V.

Clemens's comment in Isabel V. Lyon's hand: Tell him that it will not be found in any biography of Cecil Rhodes, because Rhodes was of a jealous nature— Merely a romance which I made up for my own amusement

Clemens visited South Africa in 1896, when the region—then divided among British colonies and Afrikaner (Boer) republics—was in political turmoil. Cecil Rhodes (1853–1902), the prime minister of the Cape Colony, had recently backed an abortive raid led by Leander Starr Jameson to overthrow President Paul Kruger's government in the Transvaal. Fascinated by Rhodes's political audacity and success in amalgamating the diamond industry and extending the British Empire into present Zimbabwe and Zambia, Clemens wrote at length about him in *Following the Equator* (1897). Chapter 13 contains an entirely fictitious account of Rhodes launching his business career in Australia on the eve of the Franco-Prussian War of 1870–1871. It has Rhodes learning of the declaration of war in a ten-day-old London newspaper extracted from a shark and using that information to persuade a Sydney wool-broker to buy up Australia's entire "woolcrop" in anticipation of Europe's coming need for military uniforms. Aside from the fact that Rhodes never visited Australia, the tale is inherently implausible because of the impossibility of a shark's swimming from England to Australia in ten days.

Born in Massachusetts, William Emory Wardwell (1883–1956) had a successful business career himself. After working for Worcester's Reed & Prince Manufacturing Co., he was a salesman for a steel and wire company and later the manager of a Providence, Rhode Island, investment company. In 1924, he patented an invention for "improvements in a top-roll construction for spinning frames." He married but never had children (USCR; Charles Nutt, *History of Worcester and Its People* [New York, 1919], 349).

180

Dear Mark Twain—

Years ago when a slip of a girl, I made a funny slip of the tongue over your name.

It was when you were giving a joint reading here, with Geo W. Cable

As I was hurrying along to your reading with my dear old grand-daddy we were overtaken by a man friend who wanted to know, where we were bound, all so fast I explained—"We're going to hear Cain and Able read." Over the laugh this raised I disclaimed the suposed witticism by declaring it to be a mere slip of the tongue Thereupon my grand dad complained—"What makes you so d——d over honest, why not take the credit?"

So there was more laughter and we reached the church where you were waiting in a most merry mood and joined the "brilliant audience."

It chanced to be my only evening in the company of the delightful foils— Twain and Cable—alias Cain and Able.

Linnie M. Bourne

Mrs. L. M. Bourne

2027 Hillyer Place N.W.

Washington D.C

3rd Nov 1907

Isabel V. Lyon's comment: Answd Nov. 11 '07

Melinda McKelden "Linnie" Bourne (1857–1937) was more mature at the time of the incident than her letter suggests. She probably attended the last reading of Clemens and George Washington Cable's long "Twins of Genius" tour, at a Washington, D.C., Congregational church on February 28, 1885—a date two weeks after her twenty-eighth birthday. Born Melinda Young in the District of Columbia, she married

Thomas C. Bourne (1845–1891), an English immigrant who became a government clerk, in 1881. His death a decade later left her a widow the remainder of her life. By 1891, her family was already living at 2027 Hillyer Place. Census reports for 1900, 1910, and 1920 show her and her son, Thomas R. Bourne (1890–1922), at the same address with her mother, Catherine McKelden Young (1834–1924). Linnie was evidently never employed and may have lived on an inheritance. The grandfather whom Linnie mentions was probably Catherine's father, John Cox McKelden (1809–1886), an Irish immigrant who became a successful banker in Washington, D.C. ("John C. McKelden's Will," Washington *Critic-Record*, 2 Sept. 1886). On 28 January 1922, Linnie's son died in Washington's Knickerbocker Theater roof collapse, which killed nearly one hundred people (Richmond *Times-Dispatch*, 30 Jan. 1922).

181

165 Madison Avenue,
New York City.
November 30th, 1907.

My dear Mr. Clemens:

I have seen in the New York Tribune this morning that to-day is your birthday—and it is mine too!

I am writing to wish you many happy returns of the day and to tell you that I think Tom Sawyer is the nicest boy I have ever known.

Sincerely yours,
Florence Benson

(Written in my best handwriting)
Mr. Samuel L. Clemens,
21 Fifth Avenue,
New York City.

Clemens's reply:

21 FIFTH AVENUE

Dec. 1/07.

Dear Florence:

Thank you for your nice note.

[*Private.*] I have always concealed it before, but now I am *compelled* to confess that *I* am Tom Sawyer!

Sincerely Your friend
S L . Clemens

Florence Benson turned fourteen the day she wrote this letter. Information about her later life has proved elusive, but her 1922 passport application confirms she shared Clemens's birthday. In that year, she was still living in Manhattan, unmarried and employed as a secretary. Passenger lists on Ancestry.com record Benson's trips to Europe in 1914, 1922, and 1925. The Concord Free Public Library of Massachusetts, from which Benson's letter comes, also has an undated typescript of a memo she composed about the letter. It explains how she came to write to Clemèns and expresses her thoughts about his reply: "It may be my imagination but I feel that he was telling the truth . . . when he said it was the first time he had ever 'confessed' it and that he thought it an amusing way to send the fact out into the world by way of an unknown little girl."

182

My Dear Mr. Clemens,

I wish to thank you for your "Autobiography" published in the "Press." The first Sunday I cut the first chapter, using your portrait (cover of magazine,) for the first cover, and every sunday after cutting from paper and pinning it together. Your own was interesting but dear little Susie's, was to me the best of all. I could hardly wait for the next Sunday's Press to come.—And all your own words and feelings concerning her I can sympathize with, as we had only parted from our own beautiful daughter Ruth, a short time before.—If we had taken her dear body back to our old home, they would both be lying under the snow in "Woodlawn."—But I felt that I wanted her near me.—She was taking a nurses training in "St. Johns" in Brooklyn. A *born nurse* the doctors all said, that I think must have come from her father's side, with so many doctors.—This same daughter was so proud, when in High School, called up to write a sketch about yourself your books &c, to add that your summers were spent in Elmira and that she had often seen you riding home in the afternoon behind a beautiful pair of black horses, that almost seemed to be *flying.*—Before your Autobiography was published, I met that summer a lady from Denver who was a great admirer of your books, I told her all I knew about you, Quarry Farm, the stone watering throughs, then she said but he says he isn't going to published his "life" until he *dies, I wish he would publish it"*!!

Then we laughed! There was only one way to have it—. Then in the fall it came.—While in Elmira three years ago, a young colored woman came into my friends' house selling, kitchen articles. She accidentally informed us who she was, then I told her that I had seen her fathers picture, (John Lewis) in the Home Journal with your own. I told her of an incident in my own life, that it was impressed so strongly that I could never forget her father. Before my husband and I were married we were taking a drive over "East hill" one day. We were going slowly along rather a lonely road, when my husband, put his arm about me and kissed me. When I looked up, inside a fence, under the shade of a tree resting his horses (I can see the picture yet) stood a colored man. I was of course very much confused, but Mr. C. consoled me by saying that Mr. Lewis knew all about it himself.—This I told to Miss Lewis, when she returned in a few days with the articles ordered, she said "I told father," he says he, "does not remember it, but if he did he would say, like Henry Ward Beecher, that he never saw two lovers together but that he wished he was one of them."—Which I thought pretty smart.—I wish to tell you that my youngest daughter Dorothy, found "Innocents Abroad," in the library, took it to her room, and for weeks kept it with her bible on her table by her bed. When I asked her why she kept it there, she replied that after reading her bible, she always read a chapter in that, it was *so interesting.* So you see it runs in the family.—I have just bought for her birthday, "Prince and Pauper," and I know she will *"love it."*—Asking pardon for intruding, and thanking you if you read it, I am in all sincerity,

Louise Davis Chubbuck.
(Mrs. Manley T.) 1427 Berryhill St.,
Harrisburg, Pa.

Internal evidence suggests this undated letter was written during the winter of 1907–1908, after the "Chapters from My Autobiography" installment discussing Susy Clemens's death appeared in the 10 November 1907 Sunday supplement of Harrisburg's *Pennsylvania Press.* Louise Davis Chubbuck (born c. 1856), was a former resident of Elmira, where the Clemens family spent most of their summers at Susan Crane's Quarry Farm during the 1870s and 1880s. Her daughter Ruth (1886–1906) died of typhoid fever in January 1906. Her youngest daughter, Dorothy, lived from 1893 to 1973 (USCR; "Died in Hospital Where She Was One of the Students," Harrisburg, Pennsylvania, *Patriot,* 20 Jan. 1906).

The "young colored woman" must have been Susie A. Lewis (born 1871), the daughter of John T. Lewis (1835–1906), a free-born African American from Maryland who had a small farm near Quarry Farm. Susie completed a commercial college course but evidently did domestic work to support herself (USCR; "Elmira Echoes," *New York Age,* 23 May 1891).

The troughs to which Chubbuck alludes were four horse-watering basins lining the road approaching Quarry Farm. Each bears the name and birth year of a Clemens child. The troughs are now used as flower planters.

183

CABLE ADDRESS: ESPERANTO NEW YORK
BUSINESS MANAGER EDITOR
STEPHEN W. TRAVIS, JR. DAVID H. DODGE
THE AMERICAN ESPERANTO JOURNAL
A MONTHLY MAGAZINE DEVOTED TO THE INTERNATIONAL
LANGUAGE
PUBLISHED BY
THE AMERICAN ESPERANTO COMPANY
211 WEST 126TH STREET
NEW YORK CITY, U.S.A.

December the Tenth 1907

Mr. SAMUEL L. CLEMENS,
New York City,

Dear Sir,

The American Esperanto Journal, which will be published during 1908 in New York (heretofore in Boston), will be a much improved and well-illustrated publication of the magazine order. One of the departments of which we expect to make a feature will be "EMINENTAJ USONANOJ" (Well-known Americans), of international reputation, since our European circulation is a pretty good one. The majority of the articles are written in Esperanto.

You are schedulaed as one of the subjects of this series, in a forthcoming issue, and while we can obtain abundant material in the way of information and pictures of you from various sources, we know nothing of whether you feel any interest in Esperanto or not. Would it be too much trouble for you, or your secretary, to drop us a line or two on this subject? If you can, at the same time, spare an autographed picture of yourself to be added to the illustrations of the article it would be much appreciated.

Yours truly,
David H Dodge.

Clemens's dictated comment: M^r. Clemens takes only that interest in Esperanto which anybody takes in a new movement which promises to be one of the world's great events; just as he would take an interest in a new religion without any idea of joining that church
Answd Dec 17 '07

Esperanto is an artificial language invented during the 1880s by a Russian subject who hoped it would become an international language that would foster world peace. Founded in Boston in 1907, the *American Esperanto Journal* merged with *American*

Esperantist in 1908. David H. Dodge was editor of the magazine and financial secretary of the New York Esperanto Society.

184

WHITEHALL BUILDING
17 BATTERY PLACE

Jan 18, 1908.

Mark Twain.
New York.

Dear Sir:—

Have just finished my first reading of "The Jumping Frog." I bought the copy at one dollar net. I consider that I beat you on the deal and enclose herewith my ck for fifty cents.

Respy
Clyde Potts.
Morristown. N.J.

Clemens's comment: Answd. Feb. 5, 08

Harper and Brothers issued *The Jumping Frog* in an illustrated one-dollar edition in 1903. Clyde Potts (1876–1950) was a prominent civil engineer who lived in Morristown, New Jersey, and had an office in New York City—apparently in the Whitehall Building. He later served twelve terms as mayor of Morristown (1923–c. 1930, 1932–1949); the town's Clyde Potts Reservoir is named after him. Clemens's reply has not been found ("Who Was Clyde Potts" [2006], www.tlc-nj.org, and Joey Stark, "Potts, Clyde" [2006], iagenweb.org/boards/jefferson/biographies, both accessed 29 Oct. 2011).

185

NUTLEY
NEW JERSEY

My dear Mr. Clemens,

Although a stranger, I give myself the privilege of writing to you to tell you of what seemed to me an altogether charming remark which our young twelve year old son made in regard to your work.

We had all been enjoying Tom Sawyer and Huckleberry Finn extremely and reading the books aloud during the winter, as well as your autobiography. The numbers of which we can hardly wait to have come out.

I had been working over a list of books for children's reading, and as I often do, had asked Weld's opinion saying "Weld, how do *you* feel about Tom and Huck. Do you think it is as good for a boy to read about them as about King Arthur and his knights." He thought a moment—and then said,

"Mother, if you *didn't* put them in, I think it would be robbing a boy of something that was pretty good"—

Believe me—with gratitude for the delight your writings have given us all.

Sincerely yours,

Gertrude Weld Arnold.

February Third.

Isabele V. Lyon's comment: Answd. Feb. 21, '08.

This incompletely dated letter was probably written in early 1908—midway through the months when Clemens's autobiography was being serialized in newspapers. Gertrude Weld Arnold (1868–1941) also alludes to working on her own book, which was published as *A Mother's List of Books for Children* in 1909. That volume includes brief entries on *The Prince and the Pauper* and *Tom Sawyer*. Gertrude was married to a noted bibliophile, William Harris Arnold (1841–1923), whose publications include *Ventures in Book Collecting* (1923). When Gertrude died, she left a bequest to Harvard University's English department that created an annual prize for the best student essays on book collecting ("William Harris Arnold and Gertrude Weld Arnold Prize," Harvard Univ. Prize Office, isites.harvard.edu/icb, accessed 30 Oct. 2011).

Gertrude's precocious son, Weld Arnold (1895–1962), had an adventurous career. After graduating from Harvard in 1918, he served in a World War I machine gun company; studied geographical surveying in London; participated in exploratory expeditions in Brazil, Sumatra, and Tonga; studied meteorology at Caltech; served in the Air Force in World War II; taught civil engineering at the University of Nevada; and spent his last years as a regent of that university. While at Caltech during the late 1930s, he made what may have been a pivotal contribution to rocket science by donating to a struggling rocket-research group one thousand dollars in small bills. The money ensured the survival of the group, whose leaders went on to found the Jet Propulsion Lab and Aerojet Corp. Where Arnold got the cash is a mystery discussed in several books about rocketry ("Resolution in Memory of Weld Arnold," Univ. of Nevada Board of Regents, minutes, 6 Oct. 1962, system.nevada.edu/Nshe, accessed 12 Dec. 2011; "Weld Arnold," trees.ancestry.com/tree, accessed 30 Oct. 2011; Iris Chang, *Thread of the Silkworm* [New York, 1995], 72–73, 82).

186

Pukoo Molokai
Feb 24 1908

Hon. Sam L. Clemens

Dear Sir—

I am a great admirer of your works one & all, and since my visit to the Hawaiian Islands your description of your sojourn here so many years ago: I have re read with a double interest—

The school teacher here at Pukoo is a Native & a very bright young woman— She and her husband were at our house a few evenings ago & my son who is the Government Physician here & myself were entertaining Mrs Julia Anahu by reading her selections from your Work describing your trip to the Islands—

While she could enjoying the Book, she did not just exactly like the "quiet fun„ you had at their expense She would laugh & laugh & then she would say 'Oh! that Mark Twain I wish he would come down here again, *I would fix him*„

Your description of the Islands & of the Natives—although written *so many* years ago—holds true today—They still live on fish & poi & still ride with those fantastic costumes of bright colored drapery & they still do not over burden themselves with clothing & they are still the same light hearted music loving childlike people you found on These wonderful Islands so long ago—Please *answer* this—if only a few lines That I may have the *honor* to possess your autograph—Of one whose writings I so much admire & enjoy

Yours sincerely Mrs Amy C Hayes
Pukoo Molokai F.W.

During his four-month stay in Hawaii in 1866, Clemens wrote travel letters to the Sacramento *Union* that he later adapted to create chapters 62–77 of *Roughing It* (1872), the book to which Hayes's letter alludes.

Amy Campbell McLeod Hayes (1858–1912) was the Canadian-born wife of Henry Sweet Hayes (born c. 1833) of San Francisco. She apparently was in Hawaii in 1906 visiting her son, Dr. Henry Homer Hayes (1881–1957), a government physician there. She wrote to Clemens again, on 8 January 1910, to express sympathy for his daughter Jean's death.

Henry Jr. first went to the islands under an assumed name, filling in for another physician whose ticket could not be changed at the last minute. Though intending only a brief visit, he decided to stay permanently. In 1914, he married his second wife, a native Hawaiian woman, Flora Allen Kaai (1893–1968), who later became a territorial legislator and acted in several films, including *Blue Hawaii* (1961) with Elvis Presley ("Pioneer Woman of Richmond Is Dead," Oakland, California, *Tribune*, 10 June 1912; USCR; G. F. Nellis, ed., *The Story of Hawaii and Its Builders* [1925]; Welcome to Hawaii, USGenWeb Archives, files.usgwarchives.net, accessed 14 Dec. 2011; Jessica Orr, personal communication, 27 July 2012).

Julia K. Anahu (1878–1940) was a school teacher and principal. In 1925, she and her husband, William Kaulukou Anahu (1879–1966), adopted three children of deceased relatives. Her adopted son, William Machado Anahu (1917–1945), later became an all-American football player at the University of Santa Clara and a posthumously decorated fighter pilot in World War II (USCR).

187

DEPARTMENT OF JUSTICE.
OFFICE OF
UNITED STATES ATTORNEY,
DISTRICT OF HAWAII,
HONOLULU.

Honolulu, T.H., May 23, 1908.

Mr. Samuel L. Clemens, Esq.,
New York, N.Y.

My dear Mr. Clemens:

For the first time in my life,—and it will be the last time,—I am requesting an autograph, and becoming thereby an autograph fiend. I do not know whether you will grant my request or not, but I tell you that your signature to the enclosed post card and a direction to your secretary to see that the same is properly deposited in the mail will not only be very much appreciated by me, but may be demanded by me and is demanded by me as a matter of right. I may state my reasons for this compulsion as follows:

First,—I have purchased three copies of your Huckleberry Finn, two copies of your Tom Sawyer, and two general De Luxe editions of all of your works.

Second,—I desire your autograph not for myself so much as for my eight year old daughter, who in person has addressed the post card enclosed.

Third,—In the United States of America you have no warmer admirer of yourself than am I, and I am sure from sizing up my daughter, she will probably discount me in this admiration.

Fourth,—on the post card enclosed you countenance sentiments which appeal to me very strongly, owing to some seven year residence in the Islands.

Fifth,—For fifteen years I resided in the West, near which some of the scenes of your "Roughing It" were located.

Sixth,—I do not believe a damn word that Senator Stewart has said about you.

Seventh,—And last, but not least, I want the autograph to give to my daughter.

Very sincerely yours,
Robt. W. Breckons

Unidentified secretary's comment: Sent

A native of Illinois, Robert W. Breckons (1866–1918) graduated from Georgetown University in 1890 and immediately began his legal career in Wyoming, where he served as a government attorney and state legislator. (Clemens's stagecoach trip across the plains in 1861, which he describes in *Roughing It,* took him through Wyoming.) In 1902, Breckons was appointed U.S. district attorney in Hawaii. An ardent Republican Party leader, he resigned in 1913, when Democratic president Woodrow Wilson took office, and launched a private law practice in Honolulu. He was a rapid reader, often seen reading books, and usually carried a pocket-size classic with him. His only child, Evelyn Allison Breckons (1899–1934) later graduated from Maryland's Goucher College and married a divorced salesman, Ray Baker Rietow (USCR; "R. W. Breckons Dies in Honolulu Home," *Wyoming State Tribune/Cheyenne State Leader,* 27 Nov. 1918; "Tribute to Robert W. Breckons from Many Hawaiian Admirers," ibid., 20 Dec. 1918; "Robert W. Breckons," ibid., 26 Dec. 1918).

Former Nevada senator William Morris Stewart (1827–1909) knew Clemens in Nevada during the early 1860s and employed him as private secretary in 1867. Stewart's 1908 book, *Reminiscences of Senator William M. Stewart,* has a chapter on Clemens filled with anecdotes about his disreputable behavior during the 1860s.

188

Boscawen N.H.

My dear Mr. Clemens:—

I have just finished reading your "Personal Recollections of Joan of Arc," for the fourth time. As Joan has always been a favorite character of mine, I am writing to tell you how much I have enjoyed it. I reread it about every year, and like it better for each reading. I want to thank you for the pleasure that it has given me.

I have also read the "Connecticut Yankee at King Arthur's Court" with very great interest. I am a senior in the Salem High School, and for a theme I told the story. The teacher gave me an A, and I learned that he had heard of the book, but had not read it. Later when we were studying the "Idylls" of Tennyson, I heard him recommending your book to a pupil for a good picture of Arthurian times.

Thanking you again for the sincere pleasure I have gotten from your books, I send my salaams to The Boss, remaining

His humble admirer,

Lina W. Berle.

July twenty-ninth. "Kinderhof."

Clemens's dictated comment: Dear Miss Lina | You are a faithful good student & "The Boss" is proud to have such an admirer. | Sincerely yours

This incompletely dated letter was probably written in 1908, before Lina Wright Berle (1893–1996) started her senior year in Massachusetts's Salem High School. According to Berle's niece, "Kinderhof" was the name of a house her family, and later she, owned in Boscawen, New Hampshire (Mary Clay Berry, personal communication, 27 June 2012). During the following academic year, she reportedly became the youngest freshman at Radcliffe College, and her even younger brother, Adolf A. Berle Jr. (1895–1971), became a freshman at Harvard. Their earlier education had been supplemented by their father, the Boston Congregationalist minister Adolf A. Berle Sr. (1866–1960), who trained his four children in foreign languages and mathematics at an early age ("Child Prodigies Attend Harvard," Duluth New-Tribune, 10 Jan. 1910; "Harvard's Quartet of Mental Prodigies," Oregonian, 27 Feb. 1910). Adolf Jr. later became the youngest graduate of Harvard Law School. He was a member of the U.S. diplomatic mission to the post–World War I peace conference in 1919 and during the 1930s was a member of President Franklin D. Roosevelt's "Brain Trust."

Lina graduated from Radcliffe in English in 1913 and earned a master's degree two years later, with a thesis comparing Thomas Hardy and George Eliot. After briefly teaching English in a girls' school in Albany, New York, she spent the remainder of her working life as the office manager of her brothers' New York City law firm, Berle & Berle (Mary Clay Berry, ibid. In an interview given when she was ninety-seven, she recalled how her father had encouraged his four children to read: "We always read everything we could get hold of. We began early. . . . If you grow up in a reading household, as I did, college education doesn't add anything" (A. S. Crosman, "Lina Berle," in Young at Heart [Bothwell, Wash., 2005], 13–20).

189

408 Albemarle Road
Brooklyn, N.Y.
Sept. 19, 1908

Mr. S. L. Clemens,
Dear Sir,

I have wanted for a long time to time to thank you for the pleasure which your books have given me, but I have hesitated for fear that even thanks ought not to intrude on the privacy of a public character. But now I am making the venture. Having known Huck Finn twenty two years, and Tom and Sid and Mary and Aunt Polly still longer, I feel as if these friends might give me an introduction, especially so since the thing that I have enjoyed most in your books is the glimpse of yourself between the lines. So I have known you, though you have not known me. I only say *how long* I have enjoyed this, for if I should say how much I have enjoyed it, you might think me extravagant or insincere. My wife, (who remembers meeting you with her sister and cousins, when she was a little girl at the house of her uncle, Mr. Cable in New Orleans) says that I read Mark Twain the way old ladies read the Bible (I am a clergy man)—a chapter before going to bed.

Those boys and girls of your novels seem to me the most remarkable thing in American literature, and for me they have proved altogether the most enjoyable thing in American literature. I do not believe that any other literature has any representations of child life which are so universal and yet so concrete. I have a boy of my own now, and I am just having the fun of introducing them to him—these children that never grew up, "whose mortal years immortal youth became—"

Once, after overworry, I staved off a breakdown by loafing around and reading your Following the Equator. I thought of Harris when I climbed up that tower on the Rigi. It is pleasant to recall your scenes and characters, just as it is pleasant to laugh over funny experiences of my own. It is like having lived twice. Becky Thatcher's wooing is, I think the purest love scene ever written. The scene in that small pox hut is the truest pathos I ever met in reading. Your speech at the dinner on your seventieth birthday gave me keen delight. Until you proved that the good do not die young, I was afraid that I should outlive all my friends— Tom's punishment when Sid broke the sugar bowl (and his reflections,) old Finn's supposed reformation, when he fell off the shed roof, his cussing of the "govment," the jumping frog, and the limburger on the coffin, and the nigger with such a tail, "why he had a hundred!" and Sandy and Hello Central—I don't know whether they are things of beauty, but they are a joy forever, and I could not resist the temptation to write and tell you so.

Very truly yours

Frederick A. Wright

This letter contains allusions to at least seven different Mark Twain works. Harris climbs the Rigi in *A Tramp Abroad* (1880), not *Following the Equator* (1897). Becky Thatcher and Sid appear in *Tom Sawyer* (1876). The smallpox hut and Sandy and Hello-Central are in *A Connecticut Yankee* (1889), and "old" Pap Finn is in *Huckleberry Finn* (1884). The jumping frog story (1865) appeared in several collections, and limburger cheese was at the center of "The Invalid's Story" (1882). The "nigger with such a tail" is a slightly misleading description of a passage in chapter 25 of *A Tramp Abroad*. The suggestion that Clemens could be glimpsed "between the lines" is a theme that Forest G. Robinson explores in *The Author-Cat: Clemens's Life in Fiction* (New York, 2007).

Frederick Amaziah Wright (1871–1950) was the rector of the Church of the Holy Apostles in Brooklyn at the time he wrote this letter. A graduate of Columbia University, he became an Episcopal priest in 1899. In 1936, he retired from the rectorship of a church in Tuckahoe, New York. His wife, Margaret Griswold Cox Wright (c. 1876–1964), was the daughter of Frances Antoinette Cable, the author George Washington Cable's sister. She would have been about six when Clemens visited Cable's home in 1882 and was probably among the children at Cable's house during the visit of Joel Chandler Harris described in chapter 47 of *Life on the Mississippi* (1883). Wright's son, Walter Boardman Wright, was born in 1899. Wright himself was active in poetry societies and published several volumes of verses (USCR; "Frederick Wright, Clergy-man, Poet," New York *Times*, 30 Oct. 1950).

190

EXECUTIVE COUNCIL OF
THE NATIONAL CIVIC FEDERATION
281 FOURTH AVENUE, NEW YORK CITY

October 31, 1908.

Dear Mr. Twain:—

I want to thank you for the keen pleasure I had in reading your "Extracts from Capt. Stormfield's Visit to Heaven." It is a little bit late to thank you for something that was published last year, but I am like the fellow who had just heard of the Crucifixion of our Saviour—a little behind hand.

Samuel Gompers and I read your article together one afternoon when we were coming from Washington on the "Congressional Limited." He roared so loudly over it several times that there was danger of his being ejected from the car. finally it got so bad that by the time we reached Jersey City we both had to get off.

Sincerely yours,

R. M. Easley

Mr. Samuel L. Clemens,
Redding, Conn.

An account of an old sea captain's eye-opening introduction to heaven, "Extract from Captain Stormfield's Visit to Heaven" gently satirizes Christian notions of af-terlife. The story first appeared in the December 1907 and January 1908 issues of *Harper's Magazine*.

Ralph Montgomery Easley (1856–1939) founded the National Civic Federation (NCF) in 1900 to combat big-business abuses and foster better relations between capital and labor. Probably the most influential figure in American labor history, Samuel Gompers (1850–1924) founded the American Federation of Labor in 1886 and was both its president and a vice president of the NCF in 1908. After Clemens died, Gompers inserted a brief eulogy to him in a published essay on the labor movement. Extolling Clemens for exploding "fallacies, frauds, and superstitions," he called him "more than a humorist . . . a profound philosopher" ("Ralph Montgomery Easley," in *Dict. American Biog.*, and "Gompers, Samuel," in *Encyc. of World Biog.*, both at ic. galegroup.com, accessed 28 Oct. 2011; Gompers, "In the Labor Movement," *American Federationist* 17, no. 6 [June 1910]: 519).

191

Saginaw, Mich.
Dec. 1, 1908.

Hon Samuel Clemens,
Redding, Conn.

Dear Sir:

Please accept hearty congratulations upon your seventy-third birthday, from your name sake, Mark Twain Davis.

I am engaged in teaching in the rural schools here, and am putting in my fourth year in my first school and am 21 years of age.

My father choose my name and I think he could not have given me a better one. I am always overly proud of it. People do not seem to forget my name when they once hear it, and I generally write it in full. My folks live here on a farm and have quite a large family, and I am striving to get a better education as my brothers are also.

I remain, Wishing many happy years to still await you.

Mark Twain Davis.
Saginaw, W.S.,
R.R. 13. Mich.

The oldest of seven children of a Michigan farming family, Mark Twain Davis (1887–1958) was the only family member with a clearly literary name. He achieved his educational ambition: by 1910, he was teaching school; by 1917, he was practicing law and helping launch an insurance company. He married in 1916 but had no children (USCR; 1917 draft registration card; "Mark Twain Davis," www.wikitree.com/wiki/Davis-1663, accessed 27 Oct. 2011).

192

INDUSTRIA ET SPE
THE MOLSON'S BANK, MONTREAL
A.D. 1855

Dear Mr Mark Twain,

I did like your books very much I did get Tom Sawyer and I did like it very well. and so I got Huckleberry Finn There were both very nice.

I did like them better than any books I ever read.

So I thought I would like to tell you how much I liked them.

I been sick along time.

I can not think of anything else to write so I will says good-bye. If you should answer my letter I would very glad.

> Your loving
> Gilbert Draper.
> 85 Mackay St
> Montreal
> Quebec

Clemens's comment: Auto.

Written in the meticulous longhand of a boy born in June 1902, this undated letter was probably composed around 1909. Gilbert Draper (1902–1935), the son of a Canadian banker, later became a prominent Montreal journalist. He also composed songs and published mystery stories in American magazines (1911 Census of Canada; "Gilbert Draper Is Dead in 34th Year," Montreal *Gazette,* 23 Apr. 1935).

193

Jan 1st 1909

Mr. Sam'l L. Clemens:
Redding

Dear Sir:—
Thought this too good a joke to pass by—therefore the enclosed sketch—

> Yours truly
> Wm Steinke
> 443 W22
> N.Y.C.

Clemens's comment per Mary Louise Howden: We think its about the best one we've got yet. **and** ans Jan 5 MLH

In late December 1908, the publisher Robert J. Collier called Clemens's Redding house and told his secretary Isabel V. Lyon he was giving a baby elephant to Clemens for Christmas and advised making preparations for it. He later sent a supply of hay and carrots to feed it and followed with an elephant trainer on loan from a circus. Lyon took Collier seriously, but the elephant turned out to be a toy and the "trainer" was Collier's butler. The story was widely reported in the national press (Paine, *Mark Twain: A Biography,* 1475–1477).

William George Steinke Jr. (1887–1958) was a newspaper cartoonist, and the figure he drew in his letter (figure 25) is a self-portrait. During the late 1920s and 1930s he achieved some fame as "Jolly Bill" on a network radio program. His daughter, Bettina Steinke Blair (1913–1999), enjoyed some renown as a portrait artist (USCR; "Guide to

FIGURE 25. Letter and sketch from William Steinke Jr. Courtesy of the Mark Twain Papers, Bancroft Library, University of California, Berkeley.

the William 'Jolly Bill' Steinke Papers," Dickinson Research Center, www.national-cowboymuseum.org, accessed 1 Nov. 2011).

194

MIDDLERREST
104 RANDOLPH AVENUE
PEORIA, ILLINOIS

JAN. 2nd, 1909.

Dear Mr. Clemmens:—

I am 11 years old to-day and have read almost all of your books written for boys of my age and have laughed and enjoyed them like everything. My Papa was reading in the evening paper about your Xmas gift of that elephant and I just thought as I had a type-writer given me for my birthday that I would write and tell you that I wish that it had been me instead of you that was given that elephant. I know that I would have just piles of fun with it. I know you like children for I have read that you did and I have often thought that I'd give a good deal to meet and talk with you. Of course I don't know enough to entertain you very well, but I'd do my very best and what I would like would be to have you tell me stories like you did Susie. I just love books and to read them and I have a pretty good start of a library of my own. Many books are given me. This Xmas and on my birthday I received "The Isle of the Lake" by WM. Goss, "Dan Monroe" by Stoddard "The Boys fortune hunting in Egypt" by Alger, and "Two little Savages" by Seton. Say, but that is an all right book I think. Then my darling friend Mrs. Frances Hodgson Burnett who calls me her man and her Knight of the Blue Flower and her Intimate friend forevermore, and whom I love best of all next to my dearest Mama and Papa and am so proud to have as a friend, sent me among other things that she picked up for me while abroad this last season a dear book called "Down Along O' We." It is written in dialect. Mrs. Burnett, you know is the authoress, and she sent me 350 views of London alone and as I am collecting post card views she has sent me cards from all of the places she visited. I 'spect that you know her for she is such a dear, splendid woman and writes the best books for boys and girls. Did you ever read her books? I tell you they are good. I love her and I was always so ill and never was able to go out and play and romp like other boys until I got acquainted with Mrs. Burnett and she made me feel encouraged and I am getting well and strong. Now, you must not think I am writing this to have you write to me, although it would be jolly nice to hear from you, for I am not. I only heard Papa read about that elephant and having read so many of your funny books I just felt as though I wanted to write and tell you how I would like just such a present and to wish that this year would bring to you all that you most need and want. Please Mr. Clemmens this is written in confidence so do not speak of getting it or please do not laugh at it for indeed I wrote it because I like you so very much and I thought that on account of your being Susie's father you would understand all about children and then you would know why I wrote. And do not think I want you to send me anything for I do not; I only want you to like me and think of me once in awhile as a boy who loves you and your books. I know that there are lots of mistakes in this letter but you will please not mind them for I have written this all by myself and you know how it is when a boy don't know very well how to put the marks in. I wish you the happiest kind of a New Years and a comfortable, healthy and prosperous one too.

Your little boy friend here in Peoria, Illinois,
EDWIN A. W. BOHL,

This letter was prompted by the same newspaper coverage of Collier's elephant joke that inspired William Steinke's letter (see letter 193). Willard Goss's *The Isle of the*

Lake: An "Outing" Story for Boys (1903), William Osborne Stoddard's *Dan Monroe: A Story of Bunker Hill* (1905), and Ernest Thompson Seton's *Two Little Savages* (1903) are boys' adventure stories. Horatio Alger wrote no books set in Egypt but did write a novel titled *A Boy's Search for Fortune: A Story of the Pacific Coast* (1882).

Edwin Bohl (1898–1915) was probably telling the truth about his relationship with Frances Hodgson Burnett (1849–1924), the English author of *Little Lord Fauntleroy* (1886), *The Secret Garden* (1911), and other children's classics. In a 24 June 1908 letter to her son, Vivian Burnett, editor of *The Children's Magazine,* Burnett mentioned sending a telegram from aboard her ship "to little Edwin Bohl. He had written me such a wonderful letter. He is a wonder child. . . . He tells me that he has been getting better & stronger ever since my first letter to him & that his Mamma & papa say that it is I who have made him well." (I am indebted to Gretchen Holbrook Gerzina, author of *Frances Hodgson Burnett* [New Brunswick, N.J., 2006], for supplying the text of Burnett's letter, which is in the Special Collections of Princeton University Library.) Clemens owned several Burnett books, including *Little Lord Fauntleroy.* In a 1908 letter, he suggested that Burnett got her idea for that book "from reading the 'Prince and Pauper'" (Clemens to Fred V. Christ, 28 Aug. 1908, Mark Twain Papers; see also Gribben, *Mark Twain's Library,* 1:114–115).

Young Edwin's eagerness to romp outdoors may have been his undoing. On 18 December 1915, he and a friend were killed when the sled they were riding in the snow collided with an automobile (USCR; "Fatal Coasting Accident," Peoria *Daily Register Gazette,* 20 Dec. 1915).

195

ENOCH HARPOLE
ATTORNEY AT LAW
ROOM 10, 92 LA SALLE ST.

CHICAGO, ILL., 21st January 1909

Samuel L Clemens

Dear Sir: Pardon me ("a stranger and a pilgrim here") for making a suggestion to you regarding your profession as a medical man. I of course am reminded of the subject I am about to come to, by your remarks as a practicing Physician. It is customary and a great honor to a physician to name some disease after him Dr Bright discovered the Kidney disease that you mentioned. Then Dr Riggs discovered Riggs disease. (I think he should not have done so, but he did) Now why not hunt up some disease and call it Twain's disease, or Twain's rash, or complaint. for instance sometimes I see double, Twain meaning two, might be a good name for that condition.

I would be glad to help hunt up something suitable. how often have I had something that doctors could not diognose. In selecting a disease I would get something nice, not one that the possessor will use profane language against the man that made the discovery.

> Pardon my apparent presumption.
> Yours Respectfully
> Enoch Harpole

On 20 January 1909, Clemens spoke at the annual dinner of a New York medical school's directors and faculty at Delmonico's Restaurant. Introduced as "Dr. Samuel L. Clemens," he told about "imaginary ailments of the imaginary patients" at his imaginary medical school in Redding. The event was widely reported in the press ("Twain Talks to Doctors," New York *Times*, 21 Jan. 1909)

A Chicago attorney, Enoch Harpole (1850–1916) was born in Ohio. A year after graduating from Iowa State University in 1873, he began practicing law and worked in Kansas before settling in Chicago (USCR; W.G. Cutler, *History of Kansas* [Chicago, 1883], www.kancoll.org/books/cutler, accessed 16 Dec. 2011).

196

> 810 W. Oregon St.
> Urbana—Ill.

Mr. Samuel Clemens,
Hartford, Conn.,

My dear Sir:

Sometime ago the cover of one of the Sunday magazines was embellished with one of your most striking pictures, the aureole of sunny hair being very noticeable. I cut it and laid it away for framing only to have it discovered by my three year old son, who like others of his age has strongly marked religious tendencies. He brought it to me and in a very awestricken manner asked "Is this God, Mama?" Seeing my illy-concealed amazement and amusement—he walked off grumbling "It looks like Him, anyway."

I write this—not out of parental conceit—but because I really doubt whether among all the comparisons odious and otherwise which have been made regarding you, any has equalled this one.

I trust you are not too busy training your elephant to glance over this and appreciate it as we did.

> Very sincerely
> Joseph Cullen Blair's Mother
> Sada V. Blair.

This undated letter was probably sent after 20 February 1909, the date when the correspondent's son, Joseph Cullen Blair Jr. (1906–1988), turned three. The picture of

Clemens to which it alludes appeared on the cover of 27 October 1907 Sunday supplements carrying Clemens's "Chapters from My Autobiography." It was probably clipped from the Chicago *Record-Herald*.

Born Sada Van Horne, Sada V. Blair (1872–1954) taught school before becoming the first female student to enter the University of Illinois law school. However, she dropped out in 1898 to marry Joseph Cullen Blair (1871–1960), an instructor of horticulture at the University of Illinois who would later became dean of the College of Agriculture. Throughout her married life, she published magazine articles on a variety of subjects (USCR; Fran Myers, "Mrs Blair Devoted to Home, Family, Author of Children's Articles," unidentified newspaper article [c. 1938], trees.ancestry.com, accessed 17 Oct. 2011).

197

DR. GEORGE S. BROWN
BIRMINGHAM, ALA.

June 7th. 1909.

Mr. Saml. L. clemens
New York.

My Dear Mr. Clemens;—When you so kindly permitted me to call on you about a year ago, merely because I happened to be a native of Hannibal, you did not allow me to thank you as I wanted to, for the great amount of good your books have given me from the time you wrote the first one. Of course you knew I would not do it well and you had already heard all the varieties. Really tho, in giving you thanks, I did want to claim the small distinction of having been a boy in Hannibal. I was a poet too (albeit a dumb one) for I remember at the age of fourteen (thirty five years ago) discoursing to the effect that your books had the power to lift me from any depth of melancholy and that they helped me to be good because they showed that to be good was to be sensible. The meaning of every sentence you have ever written is so crystal clear that my egotism suffers a little with the thought that I have little advantage over your other lovers in knowing The Cave, Soap Hollow, Hollidays Hill, The ferry Landing and that "the river road is a rocky one" and that I had an Aunt who talked like "Aunt Polly." Still never a week goes by that I do not read about Tom and Huck because they bring back to me the smell of the blue-grass woods and the tropical growth of the riverside until my heart swells and the tears start. Even though your picture of it is all so clear that your friends on the under side of the world can see it as I do, I have one small distinction yet to treausre in that it is all interwoven with the infinite tendernesses, the faces of lost childhood friends and the yearning sadness of my lost youth.

In the centuries to come Stratford-on-Avon will be visited as the grave of the only man who knew who wrote the Shakespeare plays and bought them cheap. You have immortalized Hannibal and for all it will be the Mecca of all men and women who would do homage to the one who taught the sanest morality since Christ. Dear Sir I have to thank you for about the only state of mind I have that is worth having. I am very grateful to you and—I love you more than one man *could tell* another. I tell it you as tho doing my devotions.

> Most gratefully, affectionately and respectfully
>
> Geo. S. Brown

Jean Clemens's comment: a letter worth keeping | Don't Destroy It after you Have Read It, Father!

Clemens's comment: Send copy of What Is Man

George Summers Brown (1860–1913) was born and raised in Hannibal, where his father, James Burkett Brown (1827–1915), bought a drugstore with money he made in the California gold rush and later served as mayor. Brown clerked in his father's store and later trained in allopathic medicine and became a distinguished surgeon in Birmingham, Alabama (USCR; "Deaths," *Jnl. Amer. Med. Assoc.,* 1 Nov. 1913, 1644; J. H. and Roberta Hagood, *Hannibal Yesterdays* [Marceline, Mo., 1992], 97, 108).

Brown's visit to Clemens probably occurred in New York City around May 1908. On 23 April, he married his second wife in Montgomery, Alabama. The couple then left for Europe and could well have passed through New York along their way. On 18 June, Clemens moved to Redding, Connecticut. Evidently unaware that Clemens had relocated, Brown sent his June 1909 letter to Clemens's old Manhattan address ("Brown-Bradford Wedding," Montgomery, Alabama, *Advertiser,* 23 Apr. 1908).

198

My dear Mr. Clemens,

I was distressed and shocked to read of the death of your daughter, Believe me, my heart goes out to you in sympathy in your awful bereavnt. To think, that you who have been the means of dispersing so much joy and happiness into the hearts and homes of millions of human beings, should be elected to suffer the terrible pangs of greif and misfourtune that you have endured in the past twenty years. It creates doubt in my mind about an overruling providence, who cheath those most, whom he loveth.

If there is anything in it, and you believe it, it must be a great consolation to you in your distress to know that, he must be exceedly fond of you. For you have received more than your share of dead sickening sorrow, I only regret I can't assist you to bear the very heavy load of greif; which is enough to break down a stronger man than you.

I am sending you this in the hope that it may help you a little, and to show you there are many hearts that are beatting in sympathy for you in this your time of need. It has been my misfortune, never to have seen you; but I know you from Tom Sawyer up, and you have given me so many good times I couldn't resist writing to you at this time. When you returned from Burmuda a couple of weeks ago and you declared to the reporters that you had written your last, I felt a pang of bereavement when I realized that "Mark Twain" was dead and would never speak to me again.

Yours in sympathy, a stranger in flesh but a brother in spirit.

Wm Mathers
Newport R. I.

Dec. 27th 1909.

Clemens's comment: Very good.

The day before Christmas 1909, Jean Clemens (1880–1909), Clemens's youngest daughter, died suddenly. Afflicted with epilepsy, she apparently succumbed to a heart attack during a seizure. Her death elicited hundreds of condolence notes and letters from friends and strangers.

William Mathers (born c. 1845) immigrated from England in 1863 and appears to have settled in Newport, Rhode Island. The 1880 U.S. Census listed him as a house painter; in 1900 he was listed as a musician; in 1910, the keeper of a boardinghouse.

199

GRANVILLE I. CHITTENDEN
ATTORNEY AT LAW
200 ERNEST AND CRANMER BLDG.
TELEPHONE MAIN 217

DENVER, COLORADO, Feby. 3, 1910.

Mr. Samuel L. Clemens,
Hartford, Connecticut.

Dear Sir:

I have seen with great regret in the Newspapers that you are in poor health and I take the privilege of writing you this note in the hope that it may relieve in some slight degree the tedium of sickness.

I have read your literary works with unbounded pleasure and profit. "Innocents Abroad" and "Roughing It" are among the most cherished volumes in my library.

I am only one of thousands, who, though unknown to you, have learned to love you for your kind heart which is revealed in your writings. Your affection for your friends, your love for the good and true and your hatred of all injustice and of all sham and shoddy have always appealed to me very deeply indeed. Your description of Lake Tahoe has entranced me. Some day I hope to visit that beautiful body of water.

When you took up your pen again several years ago old memories were awakened in my heart. I had read "Roughing It" in my early youth. I planned now to have a little fun of my own. I said to myself, I will read it again and, if possible, I will neither smile nor laugh. But I had scarcely read a chapter when, in spite of myself, I began to shake with laughter and I found the same pleasure and entertainment through all its pages as in the olden time.

I hope you will not feel under the slightest obligation to answer this letter. I do not want you to do so, because it would be a burden to you.

I wish you a speedy recovery from your illness and long life and happy days.

Very Sincerely
Granville I. Chittenden

In 1910, Clemens's health declined steadily. On 6 January, Colorado Springs *Gazette-Telegraph* reported that Clemens had gone to Bermuda for his health.

Granville Ingraham Chittenden (1861–1913) was a prominent Denver attorney originally from Illinois. In 1884, he graduated from Hamilton College in Clinton, New York. Two years later, he graduated from Union College of Law in Chicago and began practicing in Chicago. In 1891, he moved to Denver, where he focused on corporation mining, real estate, and probate law. From 1896 to 1898, he was sheriff's attorney for the city and county of Denver. The 3 November 1913 Denver *Post* reported that Chittenden had died a week after slashing his own throat. However, a former college friend later wrote that Chittenden had died from illness "resulting from a nervous collapse, following business worries" ("Granville Ingraham Chittenden, A.B., LL.B.," in R.L. Maynard, ed., *History of the Class of 1884: Hamilton College, 1884–1914* [New York, 1914], 173–176; USCR).

200

GEORGE B. BYRON
ATTORNEY AND COUNSELOR
SUITE 829–31
STOCK EXCHANGE BUILDING
CHICAGO

April 19—1910

Dear Mark Twain:—

Together with all other reading men and women, I deeply sympathise with you in your illness, and also together with them I rejoice at the favorable reports from your bed-side which we receive from day to day.

You have given me more delights than any other author I ever read, and if everyone whom you have charmed as you have charmed me, were to write you now and tell you about it, the post-office at Redding would be blockaded for months to come.—I believe you are better loved than any other living man, and if the heart-felt wishes of each and all of us for your speedy recovery can avail you anything, I am sure you cannot remain long sick. Dear Mark, we simply *cannot* spare you, you *must* get well.

Again expressing my very best wishes, I am

Very Truly Your Friend

Geo. B. Byron

By mid-April 1910, newspapers were publishing almost daily reports on the state of Clemens's health. On 21 April, he died in his Redding, Connecticut, home. This letter may be the last note from a stranger that he read. Its writer, George Buxton Byron (1852–1925), began his legal career in Manitowoc, Wisconsin, where he had been justice of the peace during his mid-twenties, while he studied law. After passing the bar and practicing law for several years, he moved to Chicago. (USCR; 21 Sept. 1911 membership application, Illinois Society of the Sons of the American Revolution).

Note on Sources

Ron Powers's foreword to this volume suggests readers might think my task as editor was "embarrassingly simple"—that all I had to do was breeze through the files of the Mark Twain Papers in Berkeley, request photocopies of juicy letters, arrange them chronologically, think up a clever title, and then ship the results to the press. Well, as a summary of my own original expectations, that description is not far from the truth. It is, however, very far from the reality of the work that actually awaited me. When I first conceived this book four years ago, I assumed my main challenge would be selecting letters, as finding information about Mark Twain's mostly obscure readers would be too difficult to be worth the trouble of even trying. Indeed, I could scarcely even imagine how to go about it. Consider this: If one were writing a major research piece about a correspondent such as eleven-year-old Edwin Bohl of Peoria, Illinois (letter 194), it might make sense to go to Peoria to find local records on the boy and hope he did not move elsewhere later. Who, however, could do that sort of thing for the nearly five hundred correspondents I eventually researched in the course of selecting the two hundred letters that found their way into the present volume? The answer, obviously, is no one—at least not in one lifetime.

Happily, the Internet is revolutionizing historical research methods, and this volume is a testament to its possibilities. The overwhelming bulk of primary sources I have cited in annotations were found online—on both proprietary and public websites—and many were found through email connections made on the Internet. The most important of these websites merit brief descriptions here.

Virtually all census reports, passport applications, draft registration forms, and passenger manifests and most city directories cited in this book were found on Ancestry.com, a proprietary website whose voluminous online records are continually expanding. While I was conducting my research, that site made available searchable facsimile copies of all U.S. Census records through 1930 (except those for 1890, which were lost in a fire in 1921). The site started making searchable 1940 census records available, while adding other documents, after I completed most of my research in late 2011.

The thousands of newspaper articles I examined were found on a variety of websites, such as the Library of Congress's Chronicling America pages. The vast majority, however, came from GenealogyBank.com, a proprietary site that offers millions of articles from thousands of American newspapers. Its resources—like those of Ancestry.com—continue to expand rapidly. Indeed, I have no doubt that if I were to repeat my research now, I would find many useful sources not available earlier. In fact, this proved to be true when I did follow-up research in mid-2012.

A marvelous feature of Ancestry.com, GenealogyBank.com, and some other online sites is that although they offer facsimile reproductions of documents, their texts are searchable. Because of problems in decipherability of handwritten and crudely printed documents, the sites' search engines do not always produce perfectly accurate results, but their overall accuracy is impressively high, and imaginative searching can often compensate for inaccuracies such as misspelled or mistranscribed words. As one who in the past spent countless hours scrolling through microfilm pages of old newspapers, I frequently wondered how many rolls of microfilm I would have had to search to find the articles to which online sites directed me in a matter of minutes. In fact, how would one even know in which newspapers to look? Articles on Mark Twain's correspondents frequently appeared in newspapers published in unexpected places—and at unexpected dates.

A third major online resource for this project was Google Books, the primary source for most of the early magazines, journals, trade publications, school and alumni publications, and many other published works I have cited. Most of my citations are to works published before 1923 that are in the public domain and available in full-text versions on Google Books. In fact, a large proportion of these works are available in facsimile formats one can print and even download in PDF files. Researchers can use these sources with the same confidence they would have handling the original library copies of the publications from which they were scanned.

Another valuable public website is Findagrave.com. Although I have cited it in only a handful of annotations, its pages often helped point my research in correct directions and confirmed facts found elsewhere.

In the interest of conserving space for letters and annotations, this book cites only a fraction of the sources on which I drew. Moreover, in many instances, I used highly truncated citations, such as "USCR" for all U.S. Census reports. This was necessary to avoid having the citations overwhelm the letters. As most readers will be far more interested in Mark Twain than in his correspondents, the conciseness of the citations should not matter greatly. Nonetheless, those who wish to see fuller documentation will get their chance in the near future. I have printed copies of virtually all my research correspondence and the online records I consulted and will eventually deposit all this material in the Mark Twain Papers at the University of California, Berkeley. Before doing that, however, I wish to determine whether a market exists for a volume of the choice letters I reluctantly excluded from this book.

ACKNOWLEDGMENTS

It is always a pleasure to thank the people who have assisted my work, but because of the large number involved in *Dear Mark Twain,* it is difficult to know where to begin. Logically, perhaps, I should start by thanking the late John Lauber—not the prep school victim of a presidential candidate's alleged bullying but the author of *The Inventions of Mark Twain.* When I read his book's discussion of Samuel Clemens's correspondence while flying home from Seattle in 2008, I experienced an electrifying jolt that gave me the idea for *Dear Mark Twain.* I only regret I cannot thank Professor Lauber in person, but I was fortunate to be able to convey my gratitude to members of his family through his son, Rick Lauber.

I would be remiss not to thank Samuel L. Clemens himself for having the foresight—or whatever it was that motivated him—to save so much of his correspondence and to write such striking comments on much of it. It is a pity other literary figures did not do the same, as there are not likely ever to be volumes such as *Dear Charles Dickens* or *Dear Henry James.* Speaking of such titles, I should acknowledge my debt to Barry Feinberg and Ronald Kasrils, editors of the 1969 collection of letters from members of the public titled *Dear Bertrand Russell.* That book differs greatly from *Dear Mark Twain,* partly because Lord Russell himself was involved in its publication. Nevertheless, I have shamelessly plagiarized its title because I have always enjoyed recalling Russell's comment about how much he liked its wording. I am confident Clemens—another admitted plagiarist—would be equally pleased by the phrase "Dear Mark Twain."

Next, of course, I must thank the long line of Clemens's literary executors and editors, from Albert Bigelow Paine down to Robert Hirst, who have borne the heavy responsibility of preserving and organizing Clemens's correspondence and manuscripts. I am deeply indebted to the entire staff of the Mark Twain Project at the University of California's Bancroft Library in Berkeley, both for their contributions to preserving the Mark Twain Papers and for their material assistance to me. Without their generous cooperation, this book would have been impossible. Leslie Myrick provided me with an electronic file of the Project's sixty-thousand-plus-entry database of letters that I was able to convert to my own database system and use to organize my notes. Neda Salem cheerfully endured my unceasing requests for files and other assistance and did the painstaking work of photocopying the delicate manuscripts. Victor Fisher patiently answered many questions and proofed my final letter transcriptions.

It seems slightly onerous to single out one person for special thanks, but I would be dishonest if I did not give Barbara Schmidt credit for doing a substantial part of the research behind the book's annotations. She modestly declined my offer to put her name on the title page, but she was, in effect, my research partner. For each of nearly five hundred letters, I generally began by transcribing the letter and doing some light research on its contents and its author before turning my transcription and findings over to Barbara. She then did the heavy research and sent what she found back to me. This typically started a back-and-forth correspondence, as we worked out problems and identified new leads. Thanks to the wonders of the Internet, we ultimately exchanged perhaps four thousand email messages relating to this book. Anyone who has worked with Barbara or who is familiar with her twainquotes.com website will not be surprised to hear that she frequently turned up information that had completely eluded me. She was born to do research, and this book is the better for that fact.

I am fortunate to have numerous friends who shared my enthusiasm for this project and were eager to help. Ron Powers, who had approached the press about editing a collection of letters to Mark Twain even before I did, readily conceded the field to me, encouraged my work, and later did not hesitate to accept my invitation to write this book's foreword. JoDee Benussi and Jules Hojnowski both helped with transcription work and offered useful suggestions. Holger Kersten translated German tongue twisters that I could barely decipher and helped track down German correspondents. As he has done for all my previous Mark Twain books, Kevin Bochynski provided generous research help and encouragement and read draft manuscripts. Kevin Mac Donnell provided research help, scans of illustrations and documents, and many helpful suggestions. Others who read drafts, provided encouragement, or answered occasional research and translation questions include Phil Bader, Charles F. Bahmueller, Lawrence Berkove, Mary Leah Christmas, Tim Champlin, Mark Dawidziak, Terrell Dempsey, Shelley Fisher Fishkin, Connie Ann Kirk, K. Patrick Ober, Noelle K. Penna, Fred and Margy Walzer, Martin Zehr, and Cindy Lovell and Henry Sweets III of Hannibal's Mark Twain Museum.

I am equally indebted to the new friends and contacts I have made in the course of my research. Some of these are relatives of Clemens's correspondents, some are scholars in other fields. These include Leigh Barrett, Barbara Beaulier, Ward Briggs, Michael Buerk, Gretchen Holbrook Gerzina, N. John Hall, Ron Hohenhaus, Wendy Howard, Rick Lauber, Sharon McCoy, Anita and Ian Muchall, Wallace and Darlene Muzzy, Jessica Orr, Sandy Ponchard,Bonnie Rapp, Richard T. (Dusty) Rhoads Jr., Jerry Rogers, Arthur H. Saxon, Robert Stewart, Greg W. Zacharias, and William Butcher, Arthur Evans, and other members of the Jules Verne Forum.

Even more numerous are the representatives of the many archives, museums, libraries, historical societies, and other institutions that Barbara Schmidt and I approached for research assistance on specific correspondents. My thanks go to Jean Ann Ables-Flat of the Riter C. Hulsey Public Library in Terrel, Texas; Todd Augsburger of the online Organette Music Repository; Marjorie Bardee of the Lancaster, Pennsylvania, Historical Society; James Bauer of the Genessee County, Michigan, probate court; Mary Lynn Becza of the Joint Free Public Library of Morristown & Morris Township, New Jersey; John F. Bennawit Jr. of the Lancaster County Archives; Melanie Brown, town clerk of Paden, Oklahoma; Tara C. Craig of Columbia University's Butler Library; Tom Culbertson of the Rutherford B. Hayes Presidential Center; Diane Ducharme and Diane E. Kaplan of Yale University Library; Michelle Enke of the Wichita, Kansas, public library; Dawn Eurich of the Detroit, Michigan, public library; Eileen Gilbert, of the Boscawen, New Hampshire, public library; John A. Heldt of the Lewis & Clark Library in Helena, Montana; Barbara L. Krieger of Dartmouth College's Raunder Library; Karen Ann Kurlander of the Morris County Historical Society of New Jersey; Paul E. Lewis of Ridley College in St. Catharines, Ontario; Bob Lyngos of the Alpena, Michigan, public library; Laura Markiewicz of the McGill University Archives; Christine Morin of the Salem, Massachusetts, High School library; Claire Muir of Gold Museum, Ballarat, Australia; Allan Ochs of the History Center of San Luis Obispo County, California; Alyssa Pacy of the Cambridge, Massachusetts, public library; Holly Peterson of the Friends of Historic Boonsville, Missouri; Amy Prendergast of the University of Southern Alabama University Library; Richard J. Ring of Trinity College's Watkinson Library, in Hartford, Connecticut; Connie Ritter of the Mark Twain Birthplace State Historical Site; Jacque Roethler of the University of Iowa Libraries; Isa Small of the L. E. Phillips Memorial Public Library in Eau Claire, Wisconsin; Phil Stephensen-Payne of the Galactic Central website; Zoe Ann Stoltz of the Montana Historical Society Research Center; Jonathan R. Stayer of the Pennsylvania State Archives; Jeanne Walsh of Brooks Memorial Library, in Brattlesboro, Vermont; George West of the Knoxville County Public Library in Barbourville, Kentucky; and Margaret Zoller of the Smithsonian Archives of American Art.

Some of those whom I have acknowledged above assisted with letters that did not find their way into this volume. More specific details on the contributions of others can be found in the notes following the book's introduction and in many annotations to the letters.

I have made extensive efforts to locate the legal heirs of the authors of letters still considered under copyright protection but succeeded in just under half my quests. Not surprisingly, all the heirs whom I did find were thrilled to have their ancestors' letters appear in this book. For their generous cooperation, ready consent, and, in many cases, additional information about their ancestors, I am grateful to Edward Mason Anthony IV, Gail Bannon, Mindy Beechler, Mary Clay Berry, Carol Brent, Robert Lewis De Beygrine, H. Graham Dripps, Ariela Edelman, Bob Gibson, Patricia Shine Hayes, James Kasanin, Ken Kingsbury, Elizabeth Mahoney, Gael May McKibben, John W. Philbrick, Anne Pinkey, Carol Brenholtz Puryear, Elizabeth Robertson, Gerald J. Shine, Richard Stein, Nancy Katherine Webb, and Leslie Perrin Wilson.

On a more personal note, I must express my gratitude to my late mother, Marian Bambrough Rasmussen, who put me up and put up with me in her Berkeley home during many of my visits to the Mark Twain Papers before she died in 2010. That was the home in which I grew up and in which I developed my love of Mark Twain, thanks to a "complete" set of his books with which my brother, Mervyn, and I shared our bedroom through our boyhood. I am also grateful to my sister, Janice Loshin, for extending the same hospitality to me in her Marin County home during my last several research trips to the Bay Area.

Finally, I wish to thank the editors of the University of California Press with whom I have worked. I am especially grateful to Laura Cerruti, whose enthusiastic support never wavered, even when I missed my early deadlines. Thanks also go to Mary Francis, Kim Hogeland, Claudia Smelser, Leslie Larson, Kate Warne, and Lorraine Weston, and to that excellent copyeditor and fellow former Berkeley High School *Daily Jacket* reporter, Madeleine B. Adams.

* * *

Half of the royalties earned by this book go to support the work of the Mark Twain Project at the University of California's Bancroft Library in Berkeley.

INDEX OF CORRESPONDENTS' LOCATIONS

This index lists the places from which correspondents' letters were addressed or postmarked and uses the correspondents' own forms of the place names.

U.S. STATES AND TERRITORIES

INDEX OF MARK TWAIN CHARACTERS AND WORKS

This index lists all titles that are subjects of substantive comments. Note that some works, such as "A Dog's Tale," appeared both as magazine stories and as books with the same titles.

CHARACTERS

WORKS

GENERAL SUBJECT INDEX

Boldfaced names are correspondents whose letters are in this book. See also *Index of Mark Twain Characters and Works and* Index of Correspondents' Locations